David G   uch of his
early chi   g's School,
Canterbury, and soon after joined Leicestershire. He made his
England debut in 1978 and went on to win 117 Test caps, scoring
a then-record 8231 runs, and captained the side on 32 occasions.
He also played for Hampshire, and retired from the game in 1993.
Subsequently, he has had a second highly successful career as a
broadcaster, being one of the team captains of the long-running
game show *They Think It's All Over*, and he is now the host of Sky's
Test match coverage. He lives in Hampshire.

Simon Wilde, who worked with David Gower on the writing of his
memoirs, has been the cricket correspondent of the *Sunday Times*
since 1998. He is the author of numerous books, three of which
have been shortlisted for the William Hill Sports Book of the Year
prize. His most recent title was *Ian Botham: The Power and the Glory*,
which is also published by Simon & Schuster.

AN ENDANGERED SPECIES

DAVID GOWER

with Simon Wilde

**SIMON &
SCHUSTER**

London · New York · Sydney · Toronto · New Delhi

A CBS COMPANY

First published in Great Britain by Simon & Schuster UK Ltd, 2013
This paperback edition published by Simon & Schuster UK Ltd, 2014

A CBS Company

1 3 5 7 9 10 8 6 4 2

Simon & Schuster UK Ltd
1st Floor
222 Gray's Inn Road
London WC1X 8HB

www.simonandschuster.co.uk

Simon & Schuster Australia,
Sydney

Simon & Schuster India,
New Delhi

A CIP catalogue record for this book is available from the British Library

ISBN: 978-1-47110-238-7
Ebook ISBN: 978-47110-239-4

Typeset in the UK by Hewer Text UK Ltd, Edinburgh
Printed in the UK by CPI Group (UK) Ltd, Croydon, CR0 4YY

To my wife Thorunn, and daughters Alex and Sammi,
who between them have been my inspiration
and kept my feet on the ground.

CONTENTS

I

THERE'S NO EASY ANSWER . . .

Life is good. The alternative, I have to say, is not something I am particularly looking forward to but that is not really my point. Somehow I have arrived at this point of my life, happy in middle age, to know that I have achieved things that others have not and happy that for all the ups and downs that are an integral part of life as a sportsman, I can look back with great satisfaction on two careers: one as that sportsman and one, still I hope very much extant, as a broadcaster, both of which I have hugely enjoyed and both of which have been deemed by others a success.

That last point too is vital. Nobody I have ever met in cricket, not even the most introspective, the most selfish of players – you know who you are, you don't need me to point you out! – has ever survived on personal satisfaction alone. That is not how it works. It is surely not why any of us would play the game, any game, especially a team game, just to be smugly pleased with ourselves at the end of the day because we have done well.

Far more valuable is the warm glow that comes with the pat on the back, from one's captain, from one's team-mates, from those that applaud from the stands and those that welcome you at the back of the pavilion at the end of the day. Personal pride and selfish satisfaction can get you through a day when you might have thrived while others and the team have suffered, but it is a consolation, no more than that. The greatest moments are those balcony moments, one of you with a trophy in hand, the rest jubilant in celebration of a job well done.

It is twenty years since I consigned my bats to now unused 'coffins' in the attic and folded my England sweaters for the final time before they too were laid to rest next to the water tank in one of my original official touring suitcases, adorned with the blue, red and yellow stripes, the MCC touring colours under which we still toured in my first days as an England player. In that same suitcase are the blazers, a couple with the braid and the crest, George and the Dragon, that were formal issue to all who represented England up until the Eighties, when England decided to be England all the year round and the MCC ties were dropped. And you can take 'ties' in whichever sense you see fit.

Since then I have met four kinds of people. There are those who have not a clue who I am, or was, and could not give a monkey's. There are those who remember the good times and say thank you for all the pleasure, which I will take any time and which adds to the pleasure I undoubtedly got from those good times too. Then there are those whose image of me is of the lazy left-hander with the great gift of guiding the ball with inestimable ease into the hands of second slip.

There is one other type: the man, never a woman, who wants to ask every question under the bloody sun about the current state of the game, who the best batsman is today, who was the best in your day, who was the fastest bowler you ever faced, what about Kevin Pietersen, is IPL going to kill Test cricket, who do you work for now, are you still in cricket, why did you never think to leave the ball outside off stump? – all in quick succession, and each question following on, before you have had a chance to answer the one before. He is the man for whom the 12-bore was invented.

Now I don't mind one little bit – in moderation – talking about the game that has made my life what it is. I would like to think there are other topics out there too and many other aspects of my life and others' which would be that much more interesting to explore, but I have to admit that I am still looking for some of the answers to questions posed to me, and which I have posed to myself in those rare moments of self-analysis, which maybe I should have tried more often.

This book could well have been called *There's No Easy Answer*; not much of a title, I grant you, not even much of a subtitle, but a clue nonetheless. Because there really is no easy answer to the question so often posed about me: why, during the hundreds of innings I played for Leicestershire, Hampshire and England, could I some days wield a bat with instincts nigh on perfectly attuned for every ball I faced, and on others give a passable impersonation of someone trying to play cricket while wearing a pair of diver's boots?

I came to realise that this wasn't a normal condition. To an extent, every batsman has to strive to achieve that ideal state where brain and body function in harmony with bat, but I discovered that not every player had to work quite as hard as I did to get into the right frame of mind.

Why could I sometimes do it, and sometimes not? This wasn't just a mystery to other people. It was often a mystery to me.

In the early days, when I was but a gifted amateur masquerading as a professional cricketer – if £25 a week qualifies you as a professional, which I doubt – ignorance was indeed bliss and fear of failure, fear of anything for that matter, any sense of obligation – they were all still to come. All I had, all I needed, was that schoolboyish, yes public schoolboyish, enthusiasm for playing the game and having some fun with it. When it worked it was great

3

but I got the message very quickly and very clearly from Ray Illing-worth, my first captain at Leicestershire, and all those who had vested interests in my development, that my attitude and approach would have to harden if this was to work as a career. Luckily, that message never entirely got through!

Obviously, enough of it did seep into my subconscious to allow me to succeed at the highest level but as the years rolled on, the truth is, the game seemed to get more complicated, not easier. Throughout my career, I would look for signs, search for a feeling. Was this to be a good day or a bad one? I may have looked relaxed to the distant observer, but as with the infamous duck gliding across water there was usually plenty of furious paddling going on under-neath. There were, thankfully, many days and long periods where the game did seem comparatively easy; those times when form rolls from one day to the next and when one would look forward to and anticipate each and every day. At other times the struggle often started hours before I ever got close to taking guard, often when I woke in the morning and continued through breakfast, the journey to the ground, and pre-match warm-ups (of which even I did a few). But I usually did not get any real sense of how things might go until I walked out to bat and prepared to face that first delivery.

Generally, I liked the big occasion. I could feed off the buzz of a large crowd better than most. I didn't often fail badly at Lord's in front of a full house, and a ground packed with hostile Australians could stir the soul in a wonderfully positive fashion. But it wasn't guaranteed. To me, the litmus test for a player is how he feels as he walks onto the field in front of a capacity crowd. If he feels his chest swelling with pride and feels those competitive juices flow-ing, all is well and he is in the right place. If he feels maybe cowed, frightened (anxious is okay, which counts as naturally and some-times usefully nervous) or diminished at that moment, it is, you could probably say, not a good sign.

The clearest example of that I ever saw was at the MCG in a one-day international shortened by rain. We had batted first and, thanks to Allan Lamb, posted a decent total. As we took to the field to try and defend that total, something close to 90,000 Aussies in that enormous stadium created an atmosphere that would have tested even Muhammad Ali. As Allan Border – it was apparently a day for Allans with two 'ells' – walked out to open the innings you could pretty much see him sucking in the atmosphere, swelling as he took every step, and by the time he took guard his eyes were blazing with intent. Bowling the first over for us was Norman Cowans, who to be fair to him had been having a pretty good tour in Australia, as well he might. That day he was like Samson after the haircut and what might have come out of his hand at 90mph the day before emerged at what the Aussies call 'half rat power'. I was at midwicket and found myself doing the 70 metre dash to the boundary a couple of times in that first over as the ball was smashed over my head by AB. In those moments the game slipped away from us – and it was that ferocious atmosphere that did it.

Sadly, there were days when it got to me like that too. Sometimes, rather than feeling uplifted by the atmosphere, I would be stifled by it, hobbled by nerves. You do need nerves, but the good ones, the ones that give you a positive tension, a sort of buzz that brings you sharpness and energy. The bad ones bring lethargy and doubt. On those bad days I would be overcome by a cloying tension, a tautening of the spirit that stopped me doing what I wanted to do.

Before going out to bat, I would usually prepare by trying to keep my mind as relaxed and clear as I could. I knew this was an important first step to playing well. Doing a crossword was always a handy way to calm myself down. The worst thing was to allow yourself to fret, sitting in a chair with all your kit on, waiting for your turn to bat, watching those before you. If they made it look hard it certainly was not going to help your own mental preparation, and even if they made it look easy it did not guarantee that you would be in the right frame of mind when your turn came. That way, you could be all but mentally wiped out by the time you actually came to walk out to the middle.

How I prepared depended to an extent on what position I was batting. If I was in at three, I'd have to be padded up from the start, and ready to go, and I'd probably have a little look at how the game was going for a few overs, just to see whether the ball was seaming or swinging . . . hopefully it was doing neither! But I wouldn't watch for long. I was not that good at sitting and watching. I'd have to get up and walk around. I'd usually keep half an eye on what was happening, at least to start with. And if a wicket fell early . . . well, off you went. Let's go and play.

Sometimes, having kept an eye on things as my mates above me in the order did their bit, I would opt for the horizontal in the dressing room, sleeping or at least half-sleeping with, I promise you, the brain ready to respond the moment that wicket fell.

The perfect example of that was in a match which could not have been more crucial for me, and so I treasure the memory, as one does when things go well. It was the final Test match against India in 1990, the final game of the summer at the Oval, and there was speculation as to whether I'd done enough to get on the Australia tour that winter. I needed a score and was under a fair bit of pressure. We'd had a poor first innings – *I'd* had a poor first innings – and we needed to bat around five sessions to avoid defeat.

It was the fourth afternoon, and Graham Gooch and Mike Atherton started our second innings. They got in and got going. I watched a bit to start with but by the time Gooch was out, with about 40 minutes left in the day, I'd been flat out in the dressing room for some time, not a hundred per cent asleep exactly, but in that alpha state where you are largely resting. The brain was still ticking over but not operating with the kind of feverish energy it would have been had I sat on the edge of my seat, waiting. I heard the crowd respond to the fall of a wicket and got myself up. I had no idea what had been happening . . . how Gooch had got out, who was bowling. But by the time I'd put on my gloves and looked out at the light, I was completely switched on.

I walked out to the middle with no preconceptions, and played out those last 40 minutes as though it was the simplest thing in the world. I thought, 'God, this is good.' My mind was completely uncluttered. You can watch too closely and make things difficult for yourself; how team-mates go about things is not necessarily the way *you* have to do things. That evening batting felt delicious. I came off at stumps thinking it was a shame to stop.

The next day, I am happy to report, I batted all day to secure the draw – and my place on tour.

These days you often see players sitting in the dressing room plugged into music (at least, I assume it is music). More thought is now given to how players can get into the best frame of mind to perform well, although even in my time at Leicestershire we used to have a sports psychologist who would make up tapes for those who wanted it – self-affirmation stuff designed to boost self-confidence . . . 'I'm good at this game', 'I'm the best', 'I can do this', that sort of stuff. It wasn't for me but I accept that it was right for some others. Ian Botham thinks it is a lot of mumbo-jumbo and anyone who needs such help should be in hospital. His preparation was a cup of tea (during the day only) and a game of three-card brag at the back of the dressing room, which was all he needed to relax. It's all a matter of what works for you.

To an extent, batting is a performance. Half the battle is kidding the bowler, but also yourself, that you are the dominant force. Of all the great batsmen I played against, Viv Richards showed the way best. His walk to the crease was just awesome. Every swaggering step oozed confidence and reeked of studied arrogance. Whether it was a conscious desire or not, it succeeded in portraying to his opponents and pretty much anyone within a ten-mile radius of the ground, even those listening on radio, a sense of absolute invincibility. Displaying a lack of fear, and an air of dominance, is the art of batting, especially against fast bowlers who we all know can hurt you if you make even a small misjudgement. There is nothing to be gained from visible exhibitions of self-chastisement or frustration. They only encourage the opposition. The best players are their own psychologists. What others have to learn about self-belief, they possess instinctively. In their own minds, they really are the greatest.

I think I came close to that now and again but would never put myself in the same league as Viv or our mutual great mate, Botham. Ian had – has – many a talent both on a cricket field and elsewhere, and one of his greatest assets is the ability to portray an unwavering self-belief. There were times that I saw that self-belief tested. Viv's lot, the West Indies team of which he was the superstar and which he led with proud determination to continue the winning ways set by Clive Lloyd, was about the only one capable of denting even Beefy's great self-confidence – but never for long.

I once did a Q&A session in the Nursery Pavilion at Lord's, just prior to an Ashes tour. Beefy and I were on stage, long since retired I might add, with the BBC's Pat Murphy chairing the discussion. The topic came up and I deliberately asked Ian if he had ever suffered even a moment of self-doubt. The answer, predictably, was an emphatic 'NO'.

I can tell you honestly that I did have times of self-doubt, agonisingly so, and I will tell you of those later. I lacked the swagger of a Richards or Botham, but what I did have, I think, was an ability (which could be something of a double-edged sword) for looking relaxed at the crease. Believe it or not, I did work at maintaining a casual demeanour. I wanted to send a message to the opposition that I was unfazed – and unafraid. My general air was not born of super-confidence, far from it. As a young man I was pretty shy and insecure, traits I masked with flippancy. My act worked better with some opponents than others: Dennis Lillee, who bowled at me a lot, reckoned that although I exuded confidence I was not quite so sure of myself inwardly, to which I can only say, 'Well spotted, Dennis!' But an element of anxiety tended to bring out my best and I didn't mind receiving a bouncer first up if it jolted me into action. Some days the tension would dissipate almost the moment I reached the crease, on others it could take twenty minutes to settle and sometimes the whole thing was just agony!

As an observer, as I have been for the last twenty years, it always strikes me that the greatest trap for the commentator – and for the non-professional spectator, for that matter – is the assumption, the expectation, that every player on display that day will be phys-ically and mentally at a peak, primed to do great things. I am full of admiration for those that produce consistent feats of high performance but ever mindful, I hope, that the mind is not a perfect tool, that it can let us all down at times and that learning to deal with mental challenges is probably the greatest skill of all in professional sport.

As a batsman, all those years ago, it was as simple as this: If I felt good as I walked to the crease it would be the most obvious thing to show that I felt good; a spring in the step, a confident sounding call of 'two please' to the umpire to take guard, and a breezy look around at the close fielders, maybe a cheery 'Morning' to the wicketkeeper if he was standing up to the stumps. If the inner me was having not such a good day, it had to be a conscious approach to do exactly the same thing and the hope was that only I would know it was pretence.

Either way, the same old question lurked in the semi-conscious-ness: was this going to be a good day, or a bad one? During my 117

Test matches, I usually took guard highly unsure of the answer, uncertain whether I was about to sink or soar. I scored 8,231 runs in those 117 Tests but it was an ongoing struggle – and one that, towards the end, I often felt I was losing.

Once I was batting, it usually didn't take long to get an idea about how things would go.

All being well, by the time you'd reached the crease you'd responded positively to the applause of the crowd and the sense of occasion, and felt uplifted. Hopefully, the mixture of anticipation and nerves experienced in the dressing room were slipping away and instincts were starting to take over. You would be feeling fully switched on, bright-eyed and alert. When that happened, it was a great feeling, a lovely feeling. You took guard and thought, 'Come on, let's do it.' You felt you had a real chance of controlling your destiny, of scoring the runs that were rightfully yours.

On other days, though, the tension just would not lift. It stayed in your chest, and was sometimes so pronounced you could really feel it physically. I could take guard in the normal place but my stance might feel just wrong, awkward. I could suddenly and worryingly realise that I was not watching the bowler's hand or the ball properly. I might be lunging rather than moving. Nothing was quite in sync and I'd be churning inside, thinking how do I get myself together and inject myself with the will to score runs? On the worst days it was genuinely as though I had forgotten how to bat.

Sometimes, the heavy feeling in the chest went away after a few minutes, and you would think, 'Actually, I'm all right.' But if it lasted much longer than that, it usually spelt trouble. Built like me with an instinct of, 'See ball, hit ball', you soon knew whether that instinct was in good working order or not. If it wasn't, I would have to try and make a plan, to try and leave the ball or block it

– what do you mean you don't remember ever seeing me do that?!
– and pray that the depression hanging over me would lift. Why it
was sometimes there I really do not know. Maybe it is a chemical
thing. I would defy any doctor or psychiatrist to explain it. But if
you couldn't find a way of coping, you could be in for a lot of
sitting in the corner of a dressing room moping, trying to finish a
crossword.

I didn't often make runs when an innings started badly. One
time I did was in a Test match at Sydney in 1980, when I scored 98
not out but was truly, spectacularly awful for the first 40 runs. I
had been out of touch for a while and threw bat at ball in desperate
abandon. The slips spent half the time with their arms in the air in
incredulity at my outrageous good fortune as the edges flew over
their heads. But then suddenly I found I was 'in' and actually playing rather well. The second half of that innings was a thrill. I'd
gone from lucky little bastard, to the Australians genuinely no
longer knowing where to bowl at me. It was as much of a surprise
to me as it was to them. Mike Brearley, my captain, said that I must
have played and missed thirty times.

The line between good and bad – between being labelled genius
or schoolboy – was always fine. Whenever I was batting, the difference between the ball bouncing off the advertising hoardings at
deep point or nestling in the hands of third slip was miniscule. All
it took for a particular stroke to go horribly wrong was for me to
be late by a very small fraction of a second. Such were the complex-
ities of timing.

One of the problems was that I did not have the ability of a
Geoffrey Boycott to analyse every last aspect of my technique. If
Boycs had a problem, he could adjust his elbow by two degrees, his
right toe by five degrees, and say, 'Got it!' And everything would
be all right again. But if my game was not working, I would be
going, 'Argh! I don't know what's going wrong here . . .' At times

like that you need someone at the other end, preferably someone whose opinion you value and respect, to get you back on track. In my later years at Leicester, when the mood swings could be almost bipolar in nature, I got a lot of useful albeit normally gruff advice from one of the toughest men I have seen on a cricket field – Peter Willey. Even Botham would not mess with him! He knew my game so well, could spot what was awry, and tell me straightaway if, for instance, I was a little too open in my stance or shuffling too much, as I tended subconsciously to do in an effort to get myself going. The better I was playing, the smaller my trigger movements would be – a little move back and across, a little gentle press forward. When things weren't quite right, I would start thinking about where my feet were and what my backlift was doing. When that happened, you really had to work hard just to keep afloat. It certainly wasn't much fun.

I am minded of something that Boycs used to say to me time after time (as we have noticed over the years, he is not averse to repeating himself, particularly if he thinks it a good line). His theory was that if we could put together my ability and his brains, we would have one hell of a player . . . which was true up to a point. But I'd hate to have to live life like that. I quite like my brain and the way it works most of the time, although I do concede it does not contain much in the way of northern grit! The fact is, Boycs and I are hewn from different pieces of rock. I'm sandstone, he's granite. They both have their uses.

To me, concentration was the ability to keep the inner voice quiet – an inner voice that nagged at me to do the extravagant thing, to take the big risks, play the eye-catching shot. I had some lively exchanges with this mischievous little voice, which would whisper in my ear, 'Next time the ball is anywhere near off stump, it's going for four through cover', or, 'Isn't it about time you had some fun with this guy? Over the top of extra should do it'. This

voice always talked a more exciting game than the sober professional voice I tried to summon in reply and probably sounded
something like Raymond Illingworth, that first county captain of
mine and an exiled Yorkshireman (why is it Yorkshiremen seem to
know all the answers?) who knew your wicket was something you
should never give away for free. 'Just watch the ball, lad. See what
happens. Take your time.' That, I know, is what he would have said.
Ah, Raymond, if only I could have listened to you and you alone.

When I was concentrating really well, he says, sounding rather
like Molesworth, batting could be wonderfully simple. You would
stand there, weight nicely balanced, bat held lightly yet firmly,
feeling comfortable and relaxed, watching the bowler go back to
the end of his mark, turn and come in . . . you'd follow the bowler,
follow the ball, and simply decide whether to play the ball or leave
it. There would be an absolute calmness to what I was doing, even
to the way I switched off between balls, which for me was as
important as switching on for the ball itself and absolutely key to
staying fresh enough to bat all day. I might add that in terms of my
stamina for a day at the crease or in the field I was naturally a fit
young man but never a great trainer. There is absolutely no danger
of me ever, for instance, looking at a country lane and thinking I'd
like to run down it.

It was all a question of tempering your ambition and keeping
that little inner voice quiet. Too often, the mischievous voice won.

I admit I sometimes succumbed to people's perceptions of me as
someone capable of playing in a lovely relaxed style. It was nice to
have that reputation and to an extent I traded on it. If Beefy's cricket
was all about muscular energy, so mine was supposed to be all
about timing and style. When good judges say you are one of the
best timers they'd ever seen, it is hard not to try to live up to the
reviews even if just as many people seemed to say, 'I hate to see
you get out that way', as commented, 'I love the way you do that.'

I preferred to think of the latter rather than the former. You not only give the paying spectators what they want but prove something to yourself – that you are still on top of your game, I suppose. I loved to see the ball fly to the boundary boards as much as everyone in the stands. *Hit the ball on the up through the covers? Not easy, but manage it and I must be playing well . . .Yes!*

There was a temptation to play to the image, partly because it was fun to do so and partly because it saved having to change into something that I felt, deep down, I wasn't – and never would be. I was what I was, and still am: laid-back, casual, call it what you will. It suited me to be that way. In my mind it lessened the hurt of failure; it was a way of saying, 'Well, okay, there's always tomorrow.' But it hurt all right . . . don't think there weren't times when I damaged dressing rooms after I'd got out!

I reckon that with any sport if you have to think much then you are already in trouble. I know that today when I go shooting, if I have to think about what I'm doing, it's not going to work. As soon as things work instinctively then you are in a good place. When I see a batsman rehearsing a shot out in the middle, or a bowler analysing his grip, it's not working. My ideal was to know in my own mind that things were right and I'd happily be there, leaning on my bat between balls, chatting to someone, before switching back on when I saw the bowler running in. At times like that, the world felt good.

This may sound romantically airy, but in a sense although I became professional enough to do well, I always retained a strand of amateurism in my game. On a bad day I was 80 per cent amateur and on a good day 80 per cent professional. I have to admit that. People say, you're an intelligent bloke – sort of – surely you worked out what gave you the optimum chance of producing your optimum performance? Yes, but that was not quite the animal I was, or am. I got, for want of a better word, bored, and sometimes it was a boredom I could only fight by injecting proceedings with artificial interest – such as trying to score all my runs on one side of the wicket. Well, I tried it once, and not while playing for England. That would have been a complete abrogation of responsibility although in one Test, against India at the Oval, I did take guard about a foot outside leg stump in response to Atul Wassan bowling deliberately at or wide of my leg stump. I did consider how much of a pillock I might look if I then could not reach a straight one!

Even today, when I'm working for Sky TV, I like to think that I am more professional than ever but still have fun, and there's an ethos there which allows and encourages us to do that. Yet there will still be the odd day – only the odd day, honest! – where you go, in exactly the same way as of old, 'Okay, I've got to do this, or we don't go on air, but . . .' That's me. I can't do it any other way.

For me, one of the hardest things was getting into the right frame of mind to perform well day in, day out. Playing one good innings was both very difficult and very satisfying. But to repeat it was another challenge altogether, especially because if any little self-doubt surfaced it was not difficult to use it as some sort of excuse for saying, 'Er, well, I got a hundred yesterday . . . Do I really have to do it again?' The internal battle has to take place early. Those battles seemed to get tougher as the years went by. My time at Hampshire, the last four seasons of my playing career, was a mix of pain and pleasure inextricably intermingled. I loved being a Hampshire player but found myself at times completely at odds with myself and the game. I remember one championship match against Derbyshire at Portsmouth. I was not out overnight and had batted well enough on that previous day but as I crawled out of bed and drove the 40 minutes to the United Services Ground I just wasn't looking forward to going out there at 11am to take on Ian Bishop, who was obviously going to be running in and bowling fast. It was one of those days when I hoped that the competitive, professional urges would kick in by 10.55am, but they just didn't. I didn't last too long, we lost by an innings and I ended up later looking at myself in the mirror without much liking what I saw.

I look at some players and think it very impressive to be so driven that you want to be the best every single day, or at least to be as good as you can be every day. I found that the best I could do was to be the best on certain days but human and flawed the rest of the time.

In the early days, I thought cricket was a pretty easy game. Playing at school and then setting out with Leicestershire, it seemed so beautifully uncomplicated. I hadn't yet learnt proper fear, that sense of mortality that comes after you've taken a blow or two from really fast bowlers, or a run of bad form for England. Even when I began international cricket, naïve blond-haired youth that I was, the game held no fears. I know I was lucky starting against some relatively weak bowling attacks, but it still seemed there was not much to be confused about. There was only fun to be had learning what I did not know. I scored a hundred in my second one-day game for England, hit my first ball in Test cricket for four – rank long-hop though it was – and scored three Test centuries by the age of 22. I was quickly dubbed the 'Golden Boy' of English cricket.

Sadly, life did not continue to run so smooth, and once the genie of self-doubt was out of the bottle it was not always easy getting it back in again. I soon realised I had not quite nailed the game as I thought I had.

These battles came to a head during the last few years of my career. Things began to go wrong on a tour of Australia in 1990–91 under the captaincy of Graham Gooch – perhaps you've heard about me piloting a Tiger Moth plane in a prank that failed to amuse the team management – and never quite recovered.

By then my 'dilettante' approach was falling out of favour with the new regime running England cricket, one that put store by perspiration rather than inspiration. My second spell as England captain had recently ended in a heavy Ashes defeat – a bitter reversal of the glory of 1985 – and my way of doing things was out of fashion. They didn't want people who could contemplate going to the theatre after a day's cricket (you might have heard about that too) or indeed people who had any sort of hinterland beyond sport.

What I think really irked them was that I didn't particularly buy into the concept of being seen to try for the sake of being seen to try, while that is exactly what they thrived on – very visible displays of effort. There is a fine line between doing only what one feels one needs do to be ready for a Test match and a rebellion, but it seems that they thought I was a bad influence on younger players who might prefer my methods to theirs. But I had been around long enough, and led my country enough times, to hold my own views about how things should be done. And to my mind running a team of sportsmen as a humourless dictatorship was not the best way to go.

My relationship with Gooch was fraught even before the Tiger Moth incident. In a Test at Sydney that we'd needed to win to keep alive our chances of regaining the Ashes, we'd got off to a bad start, Australia batting for virtually two days for 518. Gooch made a speech about us having had two poor days and it being time for us to pull our socks up. It was true but it struck me as being such a negative way of looking at things and sent my blood boiling. I wanted to focus on the crucial task that lay ahead now that we were about to bat, not what had gone wrong beforehand. I just burst out, 'Skipper, we need to be a lot more positive about this . . . I don't want to hear that we've had two bad days. I just spent all night thinking about batting, my mind's on batting, as far as I'm concerned we can do something about this game. I don't want to hear that we're crap.' I stormed out and headed for the refuge of the nets, a strange place for me to find solace, where I later bumped into a couple of the boys including Gladstone Small and they said, 'We agree with that.' I was absolutely boiling.

That I scored a hundred was partly down to me rather needing to after such a public tirade. It was one of those times when I certainly did not lack for motivation – the determination to prove Gooch was talking rubbish, and the desire to put on a show against Australia, helped things click into place, although I played shots in that innings which were far from risk-free. It was a hell of a mental effort but I simply felt I had to score runs and my reaction on reaching that hundred was unusually forceful. As I hit the ball, I actually said to myself, 'Yes! You little ripper!' It was a very Aussie expression but it was exactly what I felt. It was just such an important thing to me after the argument I'd had with Gooch.

That was also what made the later Tiger Moth episode so infuriating. In my view what John Morris and I did in taking a short flight from a neighbouring airfield that was literally minutes from the ground at Carrara, on the Queensland Gold Coast, was no more than a harmless bit of fun. John and I had both batted – he had scored a century, for heaven's sake, and I had made an entertaining and crucial 13! Throughout the match there had been a fair bit of interest among the players at the frequent comings and goings at the airfield. There had even been a couple of low-level visits from two Tiger Moths, which was what got me thinking whether we couldn't kill a bit of time while our innings continued by popping across the road to hitch a ride. We had to wait a little while but kept in touch with the ground by phone and knew that Allan Lamb and Robin Smith were still batting.

Of course I couldn't resist asking the pilot, whose name, believe it or not, was Bruce, to fly low over the ground and we came through between the floodlights at 150 feet. Lamb and Smith, guessing our identity as Lamb had been privy to my musings on the possible escapade at lunchtime, pretended to shoot us down with their bats. I spoke to Bruce via the kitchen funnel and plastic tubing which was our comms equipment and asked him to do another run over the ground before instructing him that we now wanted to head for the beaches to check out the gorgeous blondes in their bikinis and so get full value for our $75. Ideally, the management would never have known but word got out and questions from the press at close of play alerted them to the fact it was us up in those planes earlier in the day. But good grief . . . no one was hurt and no one died. It was no more than a warm-up match and for a change England were on top. We might even have been about to win a match for a change (as indeed we did the next day, although for me the celebrations were rather dampened by other events).

The management simply didn't see it like that and Gooch and Micky Stewart, the manager, hauled me in for a chat the next morning at the hotel. This quickly turned from an inquisition about the prank to my general enthusiasm and motivation. *My motivation?* Christ, I had got a hundred at Sydney – having practised privately with Hampshire team-mate Cardigan Connor because I'd got fed up of Stewart breathing down my neck – and in the Test before that got another one at Melbourne. I'd top-scored in both innings of the first game at Brisbane. We were losing the series 2–0 and they were worried about *my* motivation? I asked them whether they'd had a look at how some of the others in the team were performing. They weren't impressed, saying that I had set a bad example to the younger players.

For the next few days telexes and pigeons were exchanged with the Test and County Cricket Board in London as they worked out what to do about this grievous lack of discipline. Lambie, who, as

19

vice-captain had sat in on the original inquisition in Carrara, largely giggling quietly to himself, told me that they wanted to put us both back in a plane – but a rather bigger one with BA written on the fuselage – and send us home in disgrace. Luckily, I think, the final pigeon returned with the message that the maximum penalty according to the tour contract was a £1,000 fine.

On the eve of the fourth Test in Adelaide I was called in by Peter Lush, the tour manager, a decent, reasonable man, who I must say by now had the look of a man who would have preferred not to have been involved in all this and just wanted to draw a line. He delivered the news. A £1,000 fine it was. It seemed a lot for a 20-minute flight and steep compared to the lighter punishments meted out on the tour for issues such as dissent on the field. Phil Tufnell, bless him, was allowed more leeway having been caught coming in, decidedly the worse for wear, after an all-nighter in the casino, as we were all heading to the ground on the first day of that Adelaide Test. He admittedly had not been named in the XII for the match but there is a rule that even if that is the case every man is to be fit and available on the morning of the game in case of a genuine, not self-inflicted, illness.

Anyway, just when Lush thought that was that and we could all get on with the rest of our lives, I asked him, 'How do I pay the fine?'

'It will be taken at source from your tour fee.'

'Is that before or after tax?'

'After.'

'Do you mind if I pay cash?' You could see his face drop. Looking suitably pained, he said that, yes, I could pay in cash and I handed over the $2,500 AUD that I had just earned from a little freelance writing. Now we could move on.

What was really irksome was that from then on my form collapsed. It would be facile to blame the heavy-handed treatment I felt I had just suffered but, whatever the reason, for the rest of the tour everything went out of kilter and I could not buy a run. Little more than two weeks after being in the most sublime touch, and hitting the ball at my instinctive best, I was back in one of those patches where I barely knew what was going on. It didn't help that I was under pressure to justify myself, having just told Gooch and Stewart how good I was. On the third morning of the match I walked out to bat with the score 137 for three and smiled as the man in charge of the PA system at the Adelaide Oval played 'Those Magnificent Men in Their Flying Machines', proving that Aussies do indeed have a proper sense of humour. Certainly more so than our management!

Sadly, that was the last thing I had to smile about for a while. As fate had it, we were in a bit of trouble and Gooch was still batting when I reached the middle. All that was in my mind was surviving the rest of the morning session, but things didn't feel quite right and I had already shifted my guard to outside leg stump when to the last ball before lunch I got this leg-side ball from Craig McDermott that I could just about reach. It was too tempting to let go but the moment I hit it I knew I had got it wrong. It sailed straight to Merv Hughes at backward square leg, one of two men posted deep for just the pick-up shot I had played. I spent much of the lunch break sat in a corner of the dressing room asking myself over and over, 'Why the hell did I do that?' Gooch sat in another corner smouldering at my stupidity.

To make matters worse, when I was out cheaply caught at second slip chasing an off stump ball in the second innings of the last Test in Perth, Gooch had the temerity to accuse me of not trying. He could not have been more wrong. I was trying all right. It was just that nothing was working any longer – and for that I felt he and Stewart were largely to blame. My response was unprintable. Fortunately, no blunt instruments were within reach – well, there must have been a bat or two nearby but in current form I would only have played and missed or at best just nicked him – otherwise I might have been guilty of more than violent language.

My struggle lasted well beyond that tour – in fact, I soon entered the worst slump of my career, so bad that I genuinely feared whether I would ever recover. We played a few games in New Zealand at the end of the tour and Gooch had several moans there. Words were exchanged one day at practice in Christchurch and there was a restaurant conversation in Wellington in which we agreed to disagree about pretty much everything, although I assured him I still wanted to play for England. I knew I was heading for a spell in the wilderness with England and feared I might never return. By the middle of the 1991 season, that was looking like a racing certainty.

Gooch felt my enthusiasm was on the wane and wanted evidence that I was still committed. 'Go away and get some runs,' he had originally said. 'Show me how keen you are.' But early on in that summer he had said other things that suggested to me that whatever I did I hadn't much chance of playing for England. I was still keen but our disagreements had got into my head. I was starting to think that maybe the Gooch-like steeliness that insisted every innings must be made to count was indeed the way to go. I *was* trying. But the harder I tried the worse things got. As I have said, I found achieving that ultra-professional approach the hardest thing in the game. I admit now that I failed.

People say that I didn't practise enough, but I practised hard that year. The trouble was, the harder I practised the worse things got. So black was my despair that I could hardly see the ball. I began to question everything. I managed one fifty in the first two months of the season. It got to the stage where I had to ask Mark Nicholas to bowl me some gentle trundlers in the nets at Southampton simply to get used to hitting the ball in the middle of the bat again. I'd lost it completely and was in a blind funk. What made it all the more frightening was that I'd entered territory I'd not been in before. 'Surely I know how to play this game?' I'd say to myself. 'I've done it for long enough.' But I really wasn't sure that I did know how to do it any more. Basically I had to rebuild my game from scratch.

Looking back now, it was plainly a confidence issue. I'd gone through bouts of self-doubt before of course, but never anything this bad and it had created a great big tear in my instincts. Until the tear was repaired my game was useless. In the end, Bob Woolmer, who was coaching at Warwickshire, put me onto a chap called Brian Mason, who was a psychologist of sorts and a keen cricket fan. Bob brought him down to see me during a match at Portsmouth and Brian and I met several times. I tried to pretend, I think, that this was not really my sort of thing, classic self-denial. But Brian's commitment to helping me out of my near terminal slump was total and it dawned on me that if he was prepared to put such immense effort into getting me back on track, then I should certainly match his effort and take on board everything he could tell me. There was a lot of stuff about how the brain works but the main spur was that here was someone, who had no particular need to, who seemed to care more about me than I did myself. Brian's interest was what I needed to draw me out of my trough of self-pity and despair. Ultimately only I could heal myself but it sometimes takes a while to be honest enough to accept this. I needed someone who was otherwise uninvolved to help me find a way out of the darkness. Goodness knows what my Hampshire team-mates thought of me that year.

England recalled me the following summer during a difficult series against Pakistan. Wasim Akram and Waqar Younis were causing all sorts of problems with their fast swing bowling and after two matches Pakistan were 1–0 up. This was a spicy enough challenge in itself on my return to the side after eighteen months away but an added dimension to the game at Old Trafford was that I needed 34 runs to overtake Boycott as England's leading run-scorer. I wasn't big on records but this had been one motivation for getting back in the side (as was the fact that I needed one more cap to go past Colin Cowdrey's England record) and my proximity to Boycott's 8,114 runs had been a big talking point in the media for some time. I was a bit nervous starting, and had a couple of slices of luck edging through the slips and being put down at first slip, but this was one of those occasions when I overcame an uncertain start to play well. I went past Boycott with a cover-drive to the boundary – a proud moment even if my turbulent relationship with the management meant that it was as much a relief as anything to finally get there. I should have scored more than 73: a century was there for the taking and we were in a battle to save the follow on. But I failed to play myself in again for the afternoon session and fell to a flash outside off stump, as if to prove that you don't always learn the lesson you think you've learnt. It was a wasted opportunity.

One evening during that game, I took a taxi ride with Gooch. I can't remember all the details about the evening but I'm pretty sure we hadn't just shared a candlelit dinner for two. Somehow, though, we ended up in the back of the same taxi on our way back to the hotel.

For all our differences, I was well aware of the enormous efforts Graham had gone through to turn himself into a highly successful cricketer. I envied him his discipline and determination, and as I say I had tried to learn something from his approach even though it was alien to me.

At one point I just said to him, 'Well, how *do* you do it?' The subtext to which was, *I've tried to maximise my ability, but am damned if I can do it.*

And he just said: 'Well, either you want to do it, or you don't . . .'

I knew then it had been a mistake to ask. The element of portraying to the world, and in this case your captain, your own determination to succeed is a better trick than going, 'Well, how *do* you do it?' If you are 20 years old and just coming into the side, 'How do you do it?' is a perfectly reasonable question. But when you are 35 and have played more Tests than anyone else for England – as I had at that time – it sounds too much like an admission of weakness.

I don't know if Graham remembered that conversation or not, but I was to play for England only twice more.

When I look back I sometimes wonder: if I could have jettisoned my amateur instincts, could I actually have turned myself from Cavalier to Roundhead? The answer is still no. All I could do was come to terms with the fact and console myself with the thought that there was still a lot of good in my career. And there were some amazing highs. After all, not many people have captained England to victory in the Ashes and in a Test series in India. I averaged almost as much as leader as I did when playing in the ranks, so I was able to cope with the burdens of leadership. I averaged almost 50 at No. 3, one of the toughest positions in which to bat. And I converted almost half my 18 Test centuries into scores of more than 150.

Could I have done better? Yes. Should I have done better? Well, maybe.

When I retired, I think I realised that there were things, many things, that I could have done better, or at least differently. However, I firmly believe that time spent pondering one's regrets is time wasted and I certainly felt that I'd done enough to feel more than satisfied.

2

AFRICAN ADVENTURES

I possess a couple of photographs of me as a small boy wearing shorts but no shirt. It is the attire of a child attuned to outdoor life. The hair is trademark blond, bleached by the sun. I'm around five or six years old and in both pictures I am holding a cricket bat. One shows me facing the bowling of my father at the Gymkhana club in Dar es Salaam; the other is taken outside the modest cottage I later lived in with my parents in Goudhurst, Kent. These were the two places we called home, the places around which my early life revolved.

The Gymkhana was where my father, like many colonial officers, spent a lot of his time. Richard, or Dickie as he was known, had gone out to Tanganyika – now Tanzania – in the early days of the Second World War and spent the bulk of his working life there. He had been barred from military service thanks to poor eyesight – fortunately not a shortcoming that proved hereditary, or I might have wafted at even more deliveries than I did outside off stump – so after leaving Pembroke College, Cambridge he opted for a career in the colonial service as the next best option.

This was an extraordinary time in East Africa, with the British ruling over a triumvirate of colonies in Kenya, Uganda and

Tanganyika, and it was men like my father who ran the place from local government up to central government level. The first thing he had to do was learn Swahili, which was a first step to becoming what amounted to a tribal elder, and thus armed he had for many years charge of several thousand square miles across the Ukutu region in northern Tanganyika, with all sorts of people under his command. The locals would go to him with their problems and he would effectively act as judge.

One of my regrets is that because he died when I was so young we never really spoke about all that he did in a big way, but I believe he gained a reputation as a fair-minded, authoritative figure. He didn't need to be sergeant-majorly but he did need a sense of fairness and an ability to adjudicate on right from wrong. In this, he was probably helped by his own father having been a judge in the African colonial service.

Dickie was the youngest of three boys and both his brothers served in the war. Derek, the middle son, was killed in the D-Day landings and John, the eldest, had a distinguished role commanding destroyers.

It was a long time before I discovered the full story of what happened to Derek and John. Derek was a lawyer but had signed up at the outbreak of war as a private, was assigned to the Royal Artillery and before long was identified as officer material and sent to Officer Training Camp. He spent virtually the entire war in training exercises in preparation for D-Day. He was to be a Forward Observation Officer, or 'FOO', arguably the most vulnerable role in the entire war. In the days before drones, the Allies had to send out observation tanks to work out where the enemy was and direct their own side's shells accordingly. Each FOO had with him a driver and radio operator, and the tank they shared had a dummy gun on the front and a cleared-out turret in which the FOO sat with his maps and slide-rules. These were the men who put the fool in foolhardy, one might say, but someone had to do it.

Derek survived the mayhem of the Sword beach landing at Hermanville on 6 June 1944, and on the following day his regiment pushed into the Normandy countryside. Outside the town, there was a gentle slope up to a ridge where it transpired the Germans had a second line of defence consisting of 88mm guns, the most effective guns of the war, bedded in and looking down over the town, perfectly positioned as Derek's tank emerged into the open fields. An 88mm shell went straight through the turret, killing Derek and his driver instantly, although amazingly the radio man, though terribly wounded, survived. He was 28 years old.

While this was happening, John was only a few miles away on *HMS Swift* off the coast of Ouistreham, the port for Caen. His ship had been among the initial wave of navy vessels to come in for D-Day, his first task to bombard targets on Sword beach. He had already had an eventful war, taking part in the Dunkirk evacuation, escorting convoys through the Arctic Sea and towing to safety a stricken submarine off Norway. The previous day he had, in typical Gower fashion, against orders, rescued 80 men from a torpedoed Norwegian destroyer, the *Svenner*.

Two weeks later the *Swift* went over a mine, literally blowing it up, and blowing John off his feet. But he had been taught as a notable athlete how to flex his knees and avoided injury while many others suffered broken limbs. Not that he said as much when he subsequently filed his report to navy command, saying simply, 'I was blown off my feet but luckily landed back on the bridge and was able to command the evacuation.' The boat quickly sank but only a handful of crew were lost. The contrast between John's fortunes and those of Derek could not have been starker. One was amazingly lucky, the other not. Awarded the Distinguished Service Cross, Uncle John lived to the ripe old age of 95.

When I eventually visited the war cemetery at Bayeux, where Derek's name is engraved on a vast memorial, I found it unavoidably emotional. The cemetery itself is heartbreaking in its sheer size and beauty – thousands of pristine graves, laid among perfectly mown lawns and beautifully tended flowers. There is no grave for Derek though. In his case, thanks to that 88mm shell, there were no remains to bury so he is one of many who suffered a similar fate, all remembered by name alone on that memorial beside the cemetery. The simplicity of the entry is hard to bear, listed among so many others of the fallen in a section for the Royal Artillery, a section of five Captains who would almost certainly have all been FOOs, and the more poignant for him sharing the same initials as me. And there was a Remembrance Day card left by John: 'To my brother Derek, still miss you terribly.'

From the photographs I've seen of Derek in captain's uniform, he just looks like a nice, gentle man, doing the right thing by his country. People used to comment on my sangfroid at the crease and I remember Pat Pocock once saying of me, 'Confront him with a firing squad and he'd decline the blindfold.' Well, maybe. There again, maybe not! In reality, I've no idea how I would have coped had I been asked to go off to war at the age of 21 rather than make my debut in a Test match. Our generation just can't comprehend what our fathers went through. Keith Miller's comment about pressure has been much repeated, but it seems particularly apposite in the case of my family. 'Pressure? Pressure is a Messerschmitt up your arse.' Any pressure I experienced was a pin-prick compared to what my uncles went through.

There was actually something of a seafaring tradition in the family, as a late eighteenth century ancestor, one Erasmus Gower, circumnavigated the globe before becoming governor of Newfoundland and returning to England to live and die in the cricketing cradle of Hambledon. Given this adventuring pedigree, it is somewhat unfortunate that I should be remembered for some ill-timed exploits sailing a boat in the Caribbean Sea while my team were losing to the Windward Islands, and flying a plane over the heads of team-mates during a match in Australia. My genes really should have known better.

Many of my memories of my father relate to sport, either me watching him play or him showing me the basics of some game or other. I suppose sport was the main bond between us. When we moved to England he put up a cricket net in our garden and took me to watch all sorts of professional sport around the Midlands, of which there was plenty: rugby at Leicester Tigers, football at Nottingham Forest and Leicester City, and cricket at Grace Road and Trent Bridge. I saw both Graeme Pollock and Gary Sobers bat, experiences which must have provided some sort of inspiration. I was eight years old when I saw Pollock score a Test century. He was, of course, a left-hander, an absolutely awesome player to watch and always one of my favourites.

My father was a good sportsman, certainly a better all-rounder than I ever was. He got a hockey blue at Cambridge but not cricket because unlike me he was committed to building a professional career and focused on exams in the summer months. He was also very capable at golf and tennis. As far as I was concerned, his job after he finished work was to bowl at me, kick a football with me, or show me how to use a golf club (not that I was ever much good at that!). These were all activities I could happily mess around with by myself for hours on end if there was no one else I could rope in. In fact, all I really recall from my childhood is mucking around with balls. Thus at a crucially early stage I learnt something about sporting mechanics.

It should be pointed out that my father started me out as a right-handed batsman, even though it was my inclination to pick up a bat the other way round. It was my mother, Sylvia, who eventually persuaded him to let me stay as a left-hander, which was absolutely the right thing to do. This may not have happened without something of a struggle, as the photograph of me facing my father's bowling at the Gymkhana club – when I must have been about five years old – shows me doing so right-handed. (Incidentally, Graeme Pollock's mother tried to get *him* to switch to being a right-hander when he was a small boy, without success.)

Of course, I naturally spent a lot of time with my mother when my father was at work, so clearly there was scope for her to bring her influence to bear in coaching terms, and her bowling duties in the garden should not be forgotten. She had played cricket at school and her side of the family was very sporty, with her father, Percival Ford, playing second XI county cricket. Indeed, various branches of our family have displayed talent for a variety of sports, including athletics, rowing and croquet.

I am a right-sided person in pretty much every respect, though I could describe myself as semi-ambidextrous as there are a few things I do naturally with my left hand, including dealing cards. Tagged as a left-hander with bat in hand, people always seem surprised if I sign an autograph with my right hand but I would steadfastly – and pointlessly, I suspect – argue that even in this regard being a 'left-hander' allows my right side to dominate, as it is my right eye and, more importantly, right hand that 'lead'. I have long maintained that left-handed batsmen are misnamed. They, or rather we, should be called right-handers and everyone else should be described as left-handers. But I accept that isn't an argument I'm going to win.

Home life in Dar es Salaam was pretty idyllic. Initially we lived in a house out by the beach but later moved to a big house nearer the golf course and Gymkhana. It was a typical colonial upbringing. We had a cook, gardener and maid, or *ayah* – a local woman who acted as friend, confidante and babysitter – and they all lived with their families in half a dozen huts at the back of our house. My playmates were their children and I remember having one friend in particular – his name now lost in the mists of time – with whom I would charge around the garden looking out for the snakes and hornets that so often lurked under our house which was built on stilts partly to keep out such unwelcome creatures. If we found a snake, the garden boy would beat it to death with a rake, much to our excitement. I would go to their house to drink strong, very sweet tea. Those memories are far stronger than anything I ever got up to at the international school I attended. Up to the age of six, when I came back to the UK, I would have been bilingual. I spoke Swahili to my father and English with my mother.

My parents got married relatively late. Their courtship started when my father was back in the UK on leave, and it must have been tricky given the enforced separations, but my mother was herself born to parents who travelled to Africa, so the idea of starting a new life overseas would not have been strange. Her father Percy had been a railway engineer in Kenya and she had been born in Mombasa, returning to England with her sister Elizabeth for their schooling. Their families had in fact known each other in Nairobi before falling out of touch and then renewing contact back in Kent. Unbeknown to the family for many years, my mother had worked for MI5 either side of the war in an office in London, so service to king and country spread wide across the family.

My parents were married in the village church in Goudhurst in 1954 and I came along three years later. My father was then 40 and my mother 38, so perhaps they knew there would probably be no more little Gowers on the way after me. I like to imagine that as their only child they both doted on me!

For some reason it was deemed a better idea that I should be born back in Kent (which is a shame really as Tanzania has yet to produce an England Test cricketer), so my heavily pregnant mother returned to deliver me into the world at Pembury Nursing Home in Tunbridge Wells. Apparently I was due on 31 March but clung on grimly to make April Fool's Day 1957 – due punishment for my tardy timekeeping.

My middle name of Ivon was, and still is, something of a family name. My paternal grandfather – the one who was a judge in Kenya and who sadly died before I was born – was called Ivon Llewellyn Owen Gower, and my cousin, Christopher, Derek's son, also named his son Ivon. Ivon is more of an Anglo-Welsh name than a purely Welsh one, but however diluted there was clearly some Welsh blood in my lineage. There was reckoned to be land in the family in Pembrokeshire two or three generations earlier, which an errant ancestor had gambled away in a moment of boredom, and a connection with a place called Castell Malgwyn, now a country house hotel, in Cardigan.

I certainly regarded myself as Welsh enough to claim allegiance at school to the Wales rugby team (largely because they happened to be quite good at the time). For even vaguer reasons I supported Leeds United at football (and they too happened to be top of the tree back then). This would not have concerned my mother one iota except that when I insisted on possessing a replica Leeds kit she was none too happy to discover that it consisted of white shirt, white shorts and white socks, all of which could have been easily purchased at any sports shop, plus a measly little LUFC badge which she was required to sew on herself.

As soon as my mother was fit to travel, back we both went to Dar es Salaam by plane on a journey that in those pre-jet days required several stops en route. We might have lived there happily for many years but Independence changed everything. This was a period when Britain was divesting itself of its remaining colonies and Tanganyika was granted hers in 1961, becoming a Republic in

December 1962, soon followed by Uganda and Kenya. Everyone in the British colonial service in Dar es Salaam had the choice of leaving straightaway or staying on through an interim handover period until Julius Nyerere took control as president. My father had the option to stay longer to advise the Nyerere administration through its early years but decided in effect to leave the new rulers to their own devices and we went back to Kent.

What I remember most vividly was the road trip we took across Tanganyika before leaving. Out of Dar es Salaam we headed in our Cambridge blue, state-of-the-art Ford Anglia, along lots of dirt tracks, bound for the Serengeti with a couple of suitcases perched precariously on the roof rack. One vision I have is of my father swearing furiously as the roof rack slid off, dumping those suitcases unceremoniously onto the road in a cloud of dust. We saw lions sleeping in the branches of trees at Lake Manyara and got chased by an elephant in the Ngorongoro crater – the excitement of the moment heightened when the driver momentarily stalled the Land Rover! We saw rhino, leopard and buffalo, all at close quarters. It was magical stuff.

I went back to Ngorongoro many years later, soon after the new millennium, and the change was dramatic. Back in the early Sixties, there was one lodge and a few log cabins on the crater rim, with a handful of vehicles taking people into the park. You could drive around in solitude in near pristine conditions. When I returned, it had become something of a racetrack with vehicles jostling for best position, and countless lodges on the rim. I'd love to be able to visit now, with that part of the world as it was back then, wilder and uninhabited and as it should be.

After all that, we put our car on the boat out of Dar es Salaam down to Beira in Mozambique, and then drove into South Africa, through the Drakensbergs to Cape Town, where we boarded the *Union Castle* and sailed for home, my parents observing the old ritual of dunking me in the swimming pool when we crossed the Equator. We must have returned home pretty much on my sixth birthday.

That road trip was my first serious exposure to wildlife and, little though I then knew it, triggered a lifelong love affair with Africa. Perhaps the memories grew all the more golden because we never had another family trip quite like it. There was once a skiing trip to Davos (the start of what was to prove a shaky relationship with the Swiss Alps) but many of our subsequent holidays were taken in Scotland with Uncle John, who rather bizarrely retired from the Navy to run a Butlins camp.

I returned to safari in Africa many times and became involved in various conservation charities. The next time I went was no less glorious. I was in my mid-twenties and busy with cricket, but managed to find time to sign up for a ten-day safari in Kenya with my then girlfriend Vicki (my interest had been rekindled by a tiger-spotting trip to the Kanha Reserve during my first tour of India with, of all people, Graham Gooch). By anyone's standards it was pretty luxurious. There were the two of us with our guide, Tor Allan, in a Range Rover, with a second truck for the staff, consisting of two or three chefs, a house boy and riggers who set up camp. There was a tent for us, a tent for Tor plus a mess tent that included a kerosene fridge full of champagne (my one showbiz request was for a case of Bollinger to be on hand for our arrival, which sounds precious when I look back on it now but never mind . . . I'll get over it). Each day we'd return to camp with hot water ready in a canvas shower tank, cold drinks and delicious dinners cooked on hot coals in what was in effect a suitcase in the ground. The only downside was that every sound carried for miles across the savannah; if a lion roared it sounded like it was two feet outside the tent and Tor's assurances that it was actually two or three miles away didn't make it any easier to sleep.

The whole thing was an extraordinary experience. I also made a useful acquaintance. On our way from Meru, in the north-east, to the Masai Mara in the south-west we stopped at the Ark lodge in the Aberdares. There we met an Indian tiger conservationist called Fateh Singh Rathore, whose big personality was matched by a large moustache and safari hat, and who had gone to Kenya to see how wildlife was managed there. Fateh Singh had said that the next time I was in India I should look him up at his Ranthambore reserve, which I duly did and had some great sightings of tigers. I returned in 2011 through some work I did for the World Land Trust, one of my charities. The place was much changed with new hotels but still fabulous.

The conservation work came later. I had befriended an English businessman called Nicholas Duncan while playing grade cricket in Perth and he was passionate about supporting wildlife parks in Zimbabwe. Over the years he was to involve me in fundraising events whenever I visited Australia. The challenges for the Save African Rhino Foundation have grown over the years as the political situation in Zimbabwe has deteriorated. Originally, to put it bluntly, whites were in charge of the national parks and the head rangers were white, and you could give money to them knowing it would go to the right places. They'd purchase the vehicles and equipment needed to manage the parks effectively and prevent poaching, but these people got sidelined by an increasingly Mugabe-dominated black government that put deadbeat ministers in charge who barely knew what an elephant looked like.

Nicholas, a charming and totally driven man, was undeterred. Continuing to raise funds, he bypassed the heads of the parks and went straight to the men on the ground. I did three or four trips with him to Zimbabwe, to play fundraising matches in Harare and Bulawayo. We invited all sorts of people to come and play and made a point of involving the South Africans as well as the

Zimbabwe national team. It meant that the likes of Mike Procter and my great hero, Graeme Pollock, came to play and they were absolute stars. My wife Thorunn and I also helped to host a safari through Zimbabwe, Zambia and Botswana, with half the guests from Australia and half from the UK, which involved some 'Ashes' cricket matches between the Poms and Aussies on the trip. One particularly memorable encounter took place in Botswana on an airstrip in the Okavango Delta in which anyone fielding in the scrub either side of the runway was in serious danger of falling into bat-eared fox holes!

There are thousands of issues in the field of wildlife conservation but the most stunning disappointment has been the dramatic rise of rhino poaching in South Africa, which of all the African nations ought to be best placed to deal with this problem in that it is less impoverished than many. Unfortunately, the Kruger National Park is vast and difficult to police and 180 rhinos were killed there in 2012 alone; in the country as a whole, 650 were lost in the year, a huge increase that shows much work remains to be done.

My main conservation charity is the David Shepherd Wildlife Foundation. The first time I saw David's art I loved it because it was so evocative of my early experiences on safari. The great thing, apart from the portrayal of the animals themselves, is the way he captures the shimmering heat and the sparseness of the vegetation. I bought my first Shepherd painting, Rhino in the Kaokoveld, at the Halcyon Gallery in Birmingham, and the gallery owner, Paul Green, asked if I'd like to meet David. I said I'd love to. David must be the world's most enthusiastic conservationist (and conversationalist!) who has been championing the cause for 40 years since coming across a pile of dead zebra alongside a poisoned waterhole in Kenya. He has a lovely family who have all followed his lead: one daughter Melanie has been in charge of what is now the David Shepherd Wildlife Foundation for the last 15 years, though she has just relinquished those reins, and another daughter, Mandy, is the finest of painters in her own right. The next generation is represented by Emily, Mel's daughter, who is following in her grandfather's footsteps as an artist but with her own distinct and wonderfully ephemeral style. When they asked me to get involved with the Foundation, it wasn't a hardship; it was something I naturally wanted to do.

South Africa has become a regular port of call in more recent times. For various reasons, dinners and suchlike, after the readmission of South Africa as a Test-playing nation, I found myself travelling to Johannesburg regularly. Every time I went I would make a point of spending time in the parks and was recommended by Allan Lamb to go to Londolozi in the Sabi Sands region adjacent to the Kruger. Londolozi was set up from scratch by Dave and John Varty, Dave the one with the business head and John a film-maker who pioneered a docu-drama style of wildlife film. As a regular visitor one thing led to another. We had enormous fun with their rangers on night drives and by the time I had finished they allowed me to borrow a Land Rover and a tracker and go off by myself. That was bliss as I was no longer bound by any constraints or the wishes of other guests and it meant that if I wanted to spend two hours watching one leopard – and leopards are what Londolozi does best – then I could. I didn't have to move on because a bunch of Americans in my vehicle were saying, 'Okay, can we go and find one of those stripy horses now?' It is a wonderful place of sanctuary and one of the times I went there was to find peace after the traumas of the 1989 Ashes debacle.

I have also managed to steer my good friend and colleague, Sir Ian Botham, towards the game parks. Beefy is a man of many interests, with golf and golfers probably vying with wines of the world at the top of the list. A 'wild life' has been pretty much up there through most of his career but one would not have expected 'wildlife' to feature heavily, and indeed it did not until one of Sky's early tours to South Africa. One of the benefits of touring as a commentator is the opportunity to take time in between matches to pursue those other interests and in South Africa the game parks are a great draw, beautiful places to spend a few days away from the cities. I love it and I think I can take some of the credit for getting the big man involved too, to the extent that he has now definitely been bitten by the bug – but fortunately not by the Anopheles mosquito. Having said that, there is a school of thought which suggests that if any malaria-bearing mozzie did try it on with Sir Ian, it would be the mozzie who would come off second best, with severe alcoholic poisoning. Originally riding around in a Land Rover before breakfast in search of animals would have been the last thing on Beefy's mind but nowadays any trip to South Africa or India is a guaranteed safari trip. Once Beefy takes something up, he does it big time. I helped him buy his first relatively proper camera, a compact Olympus with a more than decent zoom on it, in the shops in Sandton City in Johannesburg. He took that first camera to Leopard Hills and took some remarkably fine photos with it. Nowadays he has sponsorship from Olympus and carries the full kit around with him without necessarily doing more than pretend to know what it all does. He does get some amazing shots.

Also responsible for his adopted love of wildlife was a man called Jack Brotherton, who just happens to co-own Leopard Hills, an absolutely stunning property in the Sabi Sands. God only knows where they met but Ian does have this happy knack of becoming best mates with all sorts of very good and very useful people, Jack being very much in both categories. Jack not only owns the lodge but flies his own plane and helicopter so when Ian was invited to the camp for the first time, getting there was hardly a problem. When the ODIs kicked in on that tour, Ian and I had the most fantastic time, with Jack flying us first to Leopard Hills for a couple of days, then back to Johannesburg for the match, up to their sister property in the north, Madikwe Hills, and then on to Bloemfontein for the next match. Sadly, after that Jack felt he had to go home and do some work so left us to scheduled flights only! When at Leopard Hills Beefy fires off a thousand shots on every drive (camera only) safe in the knowledge that when he gets back to camp he just hands the camera to the head ranger, Marius, whose job is then to edit them down.

I can't mention Leopard Hills without referring to the Beefy birthday cake story. One time we were there during his birthday, so naturally and inevitably in the evening we had a big party in the Boma – big barbecue, big fire, dancers and singers from the villages singing 'Happy Birthday, Dear Beefy' . . . the full works. Then late on, when Beefy had drunk himself into a semi-stupor, out came the birthday cake we'd prepared. It was pretty dark and the lighting was not good, which was of course crucial to the whole enterprise. With a big candle on the top, it was presented to him with a flourish. 'Beefy, you must now cut the cake . . .' Then, 'Go on, you first, take the first slice and eat it . . .' Which he did and was just into the first mouthful when he realised something had gone horribly wrong on the catering front . . . Or deliciously right if you were us. He was still spitting it out as we informed him he had just eaten a prime cut of fresh elephant dung, albeit covered in some delicious icing. It was beautifully done, and it took another whole bottle of red for him to wash away the taste.

However much he drinks though, he always seems able to recover with astonishing rapidity. Wherever he goes, he'll take on anyone in drink, even if he's been up since the early hours. One of the trickiest things I've ever had to do – ever – was get Beefy back to his room along a metre-wide walkway, with some very solid boulders on one side, after a long day on safari and a long evening on the red.

I've had to share rooms with him on safari and while I would make my excuses and head for bed, thinking of the 5am wake-up call, he'd come in several hours later, only to still bound straight out of bed, head into the shower and off for a cup of strong black coffee, while I grabbed a few more minutes of peace. That is how he lives his life – full on. He has an appetite for life and an incredible thirst for fine wine, so much so that when we first heard about his knighthood in 2007 the first reaction from within the commentary box was that it must have been for services to the wine industry rather than cricket or charity work – or maybe for recycling, though I would hate to be the man who has to do Beefy's run to the bottle bank!

So, one way and another, Africa has been a constant theme in my life. I've been lucky enough to travel widely but you never lose the emotional ties with the places of your childhood, and to me southern Africa remains one of the most magical places on Earth.

Life back in England meant big changes for us. It was not long before I was sent away to prep school and then on to King's, Canterbury, which was where my father had gone. After a few tearful days, I realised that school was actually quite good fun. There was lots of sport and I loved that. It was something that came naturally to me. It brought me out of myself and built my confidence. But it was to be a long time before I saw it as anything more than just fun. I liked the academic side of things too, learning things quickly and well, at least until my last two terms at King's when I lost the will to study. If my shortlived career at University College London could ever be described as having got off the ground – and I would doubt it – then it certainly crashed and burned shortly after take-off.

Initially, as mentioned, we moved back to Kent, which was where my only surviving grandparent, Jessie, my mother's mother, lived by herself in a beautiful big house outside Goudhurst. She had returned to England shortly before the war while her first husband went off to India and then Brazil. She remarried into the Bowring family, who were prominent in insurance, and, her husband having long since died, she lived by herself except for Vivienne, her cook, who was officially the sweetest woman you could ever meet. Vivienne continued to send me Christmas cards long after we'd left. It was a stunning place, set in hop fields and apple orchards. We moved into one of the workers' cottages. It was pretty small but served well as our temporary home and we would be invited for tea in the big house, when Vivienne would bake the most delicious coffee cakes. It was perhaps a half-hour walk up the hill to the village primary school, which I attended for the next couple of years.

Ideal though this situation seemed, it contained a problem. Having opted to come home, my father had been reassigned to the Foreign Office and was commuting daily to Victoria to sit behind a desk somewhere in Whitehall. For someone who had spent 25 years in East Africa, such a mind-numbing existence must have been intolerable and he soon started looking for another job. Eventually he took one as registrar at the College of Further Education at Loughborough (now integrated fully as part of Loughborough University). Then, as now, the college had a huge reputation for sport. Over the years it has produced an extraordinary number of top sportspeople, including Sebastian Coe, Clive Woodward, Keith Fielding, Steve Backley, goalkeepers Bob Wilson and Mark Wallington, and England cricketers Chris Read and Monty Panesar.

We therefore moved to Leicestershire but my parents, probably imagining that they would be staying in Africa, had long since put me down for private school in Kent, and to school in Kent is where I still went. After a short spell at Quorn primary school and more walking across fields to get there (nice in the summer, not so nice in winter), I was dispatched to Marlborough House prep in Hawkhurst. This meant a train journey from Loughborough to St Pancras, a cab across London to Charing Cross and another train down to Etchingham, where a school bus picked you up. In later years, the journeys to King's, Canterbury would be no better. They were all-day treks even if my parents took me by car, as they sometimes did. Plans are plans, I know, but when I think back I do wonder, 'Christ, could there not have been another plan?' I think what actually clinched the decision to stick with King's was that, believe it or not, I secured an academic scholarship to go there.

Every now and again my parents would come down and see me if there was an exeat weekend, but given the distances involved I didn't see much of them in term-time. My grandmother was too old for much but fortunately my mother's sister Elizabeth, a lovely elegant woman, lived in Tunbridge Wells and would occasionally pick me up and take me off for the weekend.

Whatever the disadvantages of boarding school – and I know some parents think it barbaric to send children away for months at a time – it does teach you independence and an ability to survive your own company. As teenagers, we were acutely aware of what we saw as the main drawback, which was the lack of contact with the opposite sex. This was largely confined to the occasional 'dance' arranged with either Benenden or Ashford schools. However, given our trepidation in such matters, these felt not so much like dances *with* the local girls' school as dances *against* them. The girls arrived on a bus like a sports team and we weighed them up from a distance for clues as to their potential (lest this sound like we were assessing them for their potential ransom value or even their future prospects, let me assure you our interests were solely concerned with what might or might not happen in the next four hours before they were all counted back onto the buses and taken back to have their chastity belts examined. Chance would have been a fine thing!) We would be allowed two halves of bitter in the Junior Common Room and then stood around wondering what to do next. Soon enough a bell would ring and off the girls would troop, back to the bus. The whistle had blown for full-time and if you hadn't scored by then, whatever that meant, tough!

As the years went by, you devised ways of increasing your experience of the real world beyond. King's was a school with the most gorgeous architecture. The snag was that it was entirely enclosed by its ancient walls and its gates would be shut at 9pm every evening. For anyone wanting to sample the delights of Canterbury's history and, perhaps more particularly its numerous public houses, this was something of a handicap. I became familiar with a couple of escape routes. One was via a gate, about 10ft high with spikes on top, which you had to approach from the wall alongside, which, as it happened was in fact the wall around the headmaster's house. It was all a matter of behaving like a well-trained spy, making sure no one spotted you going through. In this regard, I became very much my mother's son. The other route involved the little postern gate set into the great gates that were the cathedral's main access point, and for which I managed to acquire a copy of the key from the headmaster's son, Andrew Newell, who was a good friend of mine. I was once caught by a master with this key in my back pocket. Rightly suspicious, he took it away but was unable to find the door to which it belonged. In fact, it didn't fit very well and you had to jiggle it around in the lock to make it work. Thus, armed with £5 and a furtive look, an evening on the town could be yours.

I was 16 when my father died. He had been ill for a while, forcing him to retire from work. On the death certificate, it would have said that he died of Hodgkin's lymphoma and motor neurone disease, but I had no idea about the Hodgkin's at the time. Naturally, being away at school, I wasn't exposed to his illness all the time but it is a horrible thing to watch someone suffering from MND, especially someone like my father who had been so active. Basically his body slowly but surely shut down. When the house stairs became an insurmountable obstacle, his bed was moved into one of the living rooms, but the worst thing was the way his speech dried up and he was left communicating through short notes, written with painstaking effort as he clutched a pen in a very ungainly grip. He had not been particularly into music before, but in that last year of his life classical music became his salvation. He would listen to gramophone records all day long. He also read a lot. The tragedy was that while his body became increasingly useless, his mind remained absolutely intact. For such a proud, intelligent man to be unable to communicate properly must have been awful.

I can't imagine how my mother coped with caring for him for so long, which she did until very near the end when he became so frail he simply had to go into hospital. But to make matters worse, she herself — who had been so very fit in her youth too — had developed asthma and was being treated with steroids. My father had only been in hospital a few days when she told me one morning — and I can distinctly remember what a bright sunny day it was — that he had died.

It is hard to say precisely what effect such an event has on you when you are the age I was then. I guess I became pretty wrapped up in my own thoughts, but there wasn't much I could do. I had to go back to school and return to the things I had been doing. Looking back, the only thing I might have done differently was pay more attention to the needs of my poor mother.

My last year at King's was pretty fundamental to what happened later. By the end of my fourth year I'd sat three A-levels and got an

A1 in History, a C in French and a D in Combined Economic History and Politics. The fact that I never quite got to grips with French may have owed something to my missing every other lesson to play sport, so if you had looked at my notes on Jean Anouilh's *Antigone* there would have been regular blanks, and they were blanks I wasn't especially conscientious about filling in. I've no idea why I was so bad at EcPol (I knew the abbreviation if nothing else). Extraordinarily, these grades were good enough to get me the offer of a place to read Law at University College London the following year. Maybe History was enough almost on its own to convince them there was something to work with.

In the Christmas term of 1974, I sat the Oxbridge exam with the aim of getting into St Edmund Hall, Oxford, which had a great sporting reputation at the time and was still willing to accept sporting ability as a valid part of your application, although the climate was changing on this issue and I had apparently chosen just the year that they felt they should be stocking up on academics. Thinking I had no chance getting into Oxford to read Jurisprudence (Oxford's spelling of Law!) I applied to read History. I probably wrote one decent answer out of three in each of my papers but just made up the rest – including an utter load of tosh on King Alfred, about whom I knew nothing apart from some rumour about some cakes. I was still given an interview but failed to revise the stuff I had known and so made a prat of myself when all my newly acquired knowledge on Alfred was not required. I was probably a bit intimidated but I didn't really feel I was a proper Oxbridge candidate anyway so got back into that Cambridge Blue Ford Anglia that we had brought back from Tanganyika without even attempting the interview that Keble College had offered and was perhaps happy enough, deep down, to take the place at UCL.

King's came up with the idea of my staying on for the last two terms to study a couple more A-levels but my heart wasn't in it. I barely went to a lesson. The Easter term turned into a hockey and pub term. I just couldn't see the point of me taking any more A-levels and I could never get rid of the little voice at my shoulder saying, 'Come on, this is boring.' Not for the last time, the little voice won.

If it hadn't been for the hockey I would have been a wreck because I was sneaking off to nearby pubs on a regular basis. I made sure I chose the grottiest ones to reduce the chances of bumping into any masters, but things came to a crunch during an exeat weekend when I took a train from Canterbury to Ashford to go to the cinema with a girl I knew. Sent packing back to Canterbury by a posse that had tracked us down, I fell asleep on the last train, missed my stop and ended up in a siding outside Ramsgate. I eventually hitched a lift back to Canterbury, and climbed over the wall and into my bed, but I was supposed to have been back by 6pm, and was in big trouble.

I was summoned to various meetings with masters, housemasters and even the headmaster about my future. They were broadly sympathetic – after all, it had been their idea for me to take more A-levels – and were still keen for me to stay, but I went to the headmaster with a well-rehearsed argument. I knew I was lacking in motivation and told him that if I stayed things would only go wrong again. He just looked at me and said, 'Well, if you really don't want to do it, we'd better let you go.' I mainly felt sorry for my mother, because I'm sure she would have been hoping for me to finish my schooling on a more positive note.

I'm afraid I was soon to be a further disappointment to her. Even though she expected me to get a degree as my father had done, my attitude towards work did not improve. I had just no desire to be an academic any more. It is hard to say what part my father's death played in this change of outlook, but he would possibly have demanded loftier ambitions from me than sport. I went to London very naïve, and just didn't get involved in study, wasting my time totally. Apparently, you need to read a lot if you are to study law but I've still no idea where the law library is. From memory, I spent a lot of time in pubs and kebab houses and the only thing I did well apart from drinking and socialising was play hockey.

At least I didn't get into many brushes with the law, although I was once apprehended by the police late one night carrying empty beer kegs down a road not far from Gower Street (where else?) with a couple of mates. Lagging behind as ever, I watched from a doorway as the police stopped them first and asked what they thought they were doing. In fact, we weren't stealing the kegs but putting them back: we'd nicked them a couple of days earlier from outside a pub in the hope they'd help in the brewing of our own beer, only to find that they were missing the relevant connectors and therefore useless. Unsure how else to dispose of them we finally decided to return them from whence they came, only to be caught in the act. For a moment I thought I'd escaped detection until the officers sidled over and said, 'You coming too, then?' Eventually our persuasive charms overcame their suspiciousness, and they let us go without charge.

My most permanent reminder of that unsatisfactory time is the absence of two of my front right teeth, which I severely damaged after slipping on a beery floor during a university dance in some darkened room somewhere. Falling face-first, I was out cold for a minute or so, but when I came round it was to feelings of excruciating pain. Fortunately, University College Hospital was not too far away, though they refused to treat me until the next morning on the grounds that I was too inebriated. For a while I wandered around with a gap in my smile before returning to UCH dental department, where they took great care to rebuild those teeth with posts and crowns. In that at least I was very fortunate to have had access to that hospital as my NHS dentist at home was all for whipping out the stumps and getting me dentures. Those posts and crowns have done sterling service ever since but now and again one of the posts tends to come loose and I once lost one of those new teeth as I was introduced to the hostess of an eve of rest day drinks party during a Test in Birmingham. We looked on the floor for ten minutes before she found the missing item in the pocket in the front of her smock dress. My dentist in Leicester cemented it back in the following morning.

The best thing that happened was that I had stayed in touch with a guy called Chris Kilbee, who had been a year ahead of me at King's and had captained the cricket team in the year before I did. He was a really good friend and was now working in London but he and his elder brother John played for St Lawrence & Highland Court just outside Canterbury and persuaded me to join them. For the first couple of months of that long hot summer of '76, I spent virtually every Friday afternoon driving down to Kent to play a weekend of cricket before returning to spend the rest of the week in idleness. The standard of cricket was good – there were some former and current county players involved – and we had a fantastic, sociable time.

I physically sat law exams at the end of that first year but to no great effect, not for the last time achieving a score in the low twenties when theoretically 100 was a possibility. It was then that I got a call from Mike Turner, the secretary at Leicestershire, asking if I was free to play for the county in a Benson & Hedges Cup quarter-final at Worcester. I thought for a nanosecond before saying, 'Yes . . . I think I can do that.'

I literally packed my cricket bag at Gower Street, left for Worcester, and never went – nor looked – back.

* * *

It must be obvious that by this time my cricket had become something of substance, though I would maintain that I was still only playing for the challenge and for fun. The talent I had for sport was self-driving. I did not find myself having to bust a gut to get into the school first XI for cricket, the first and second teams at rugby, or the hockey first XI. Certainly with cricket it felt like a virtuous circle – the more I played the better I got, the better I got the more I enjoyed it, the more I enjoyed it the more I wanted to play.

King's was pretty keen on producing good academics and musicians – that was definitely the impression from the magnificent medieval backdrop of the school itself and the cathedral, and 600 boys walking around wearing wing collars, black ties, pin stripes and boaters – but sport was big too. Plenty of international hockey players, rugby players and rowers rank among its alumni, so there was kudos to be gained from sporting talent.

Though I have no recollection of this, Uncle John said I astonished the family with my batting in the garden at the age of six. By the time I played my first organised match in my first year at Marlborough House, I already seemed to have a lead on most people. I scored my first hundred for them, and was even doing a bit of bowling in those days, or at least what counted for bowling at school. The master in charge of cricket was Derek Whittome, who provided all the right encouragement and guidance I needed at that age, and I have always been very grateful to him and Colin Fairservice, the former Kent player, who looked after cricket at King's. Both wisely allowed natural ability to flourish while recognising that it was sometimes important to learn a little technique.

Colin was such an avuncular man. He had been around at King's a long time and in fact retired the year after I left. I can see now, even more than I did then, how vital it was to have someone like him keeping a fatherly eye on me. He was a gentle but firm guide. I first played for the first XI in the final match of my first year against OKS, the old boys' team captained by Charles Rowe, soon to be of Kent. After that, I was in the side for the rest of my school years. Our fixture list consisted of perhaps six schools and eight or nine club sides such as MCC, Band of Brothers and Stragglers of Asia. One of the pleasurable spin-offs of facing the club sides was that if the opposing captain invited us to join them for a drink at the local Beverley pub we were allowed to go (rather than wait for an invitation, we often just begged one!). As a consequence, the pub became something of a favourite, even if not always at authorised times. In my last year I sneaked off there with a mate, and had just got two pints nicely poured, when in walked Colin and Alan Dyer, who was to take over from him as cricket master. Caught red-handed! Colin just said, 'Okay boys, we'll have those . . . now off you go.' And we were reported and gated. So, yes, Colin could be firm as well as kindly.

Colin said some nice things about the elegance and timing evident in my game when I arrived at King's, but together we put in a lot of work in the school indoor shed. I may have become rather averse to net practice in later life but in those days I was keen to learn all I could, though the best advice Colin ever gave me was simply and paradoxically to not listen to too much advice. Subsequently when I returned to play at Canterbury with Leicestershire, Colin would always come and watch. He was how a coach should be and I have a lot of affection for him, even if I did exasperate him at times with episodes like the one with the Tiger Moth – which, ever the schoolmaster, he saw as evidence that I'd never really grown up.

Although my development as a sportsman was rapid and completely natural, the one thing I lacked was the instinct to win at all costs. I remember a game of squash – just a house match or something of that ilk – which I was winning with ridiculous ease but somehow managed to lose after feeling sorry for an opponent

I was in danger of humiliating. I eased up and before I knew it I'd lost control of the game – and, soon enough, myself. I hated the feeling of not being in control, which is the main reason why I don't play golf. Surely if I can hit a moving ball in 0.4 seconds, given 20 seconds I ought to be able to hit a stationary one in the right direction. Not so. For some reason cricket didn't present these problems. With cricket I felt in control. Golf, of course, is sheer torture. I did give it a go a few times a year, benefit days for others mostly, and now and again on tour but, while acknowledging that I have never ever been moved to really learn how to play the game, the key is that I know I just cannot play it as well as I should and not even the odd birdie or long par 4 at St Enodoc will ever convince me that golf is fun. When they invented it they spelt it wrong – it should be 'flog'.

With rugby, I worked my way into the second team before falling out with the coach, Ian Gallop. Brassed off at being required to spend an entire training session against the first XV in which we had to play the role of defenders while the first XV honed their moves, I demanded to know when it might be our turn to touch the ball. 'You do as you're told,' was the reply. 'If you don't like it, on your bike . . .' And within 30 seconds, I was.

I did eventually get a call-up to the first team as fly-half but was never that dedicated and was eventually bumped back down again. I was pretty good handling the ball and as a goal-kicker but not quite as enthusiastic as Mr Gallop would have liked in the defensive arts, tackling my opposite number, that sort of thing.

During what proved to be my last summer at King's, I played my first matches for Leicestershire's second XI. I had turned out occasionally for Loughborough Town the previous summer, and the Central Midlands League in which they played contained a few old pros with Leicestershire connections. Don Munden, Loughborough's opening batsman, was a good man to learn from and had strong links with the county; he was one of three brothers who had appeared for Leicestershire back in the Fifties and Sixties.

Leicestershire also heard from people who had seen me scoring hundreds for King's. The reports had gone to them rather than to Kent because, put simply, that was where my home was. Kent were also a strong county who were winning trophies on an annual basis and not really on the lookout for talent. They had a team of established players and had already identified Chris Tavare as the next promising young batsman. Tav had scored mountains of runs at Sevenoaks and was now at Oxford. Leicestershire were not a bad side themselves and actually won the championship for the first time in 1975 under the shrewd leadership of Ray Illingworth, but they were not as star-studded an outfit as Kent and had to compete for players with a host of other Midlands counties.

I played a fair bit of second XI cricket in 1974 and really enjoyed it. I did okay, too. Mick Norman and Terry Spencer, both of whom I'd watched play at Grace Road, now ran the seconds between them. Terry was a lovely guy while Mick was charming, a typical schoolmaster batsman who lived two worlds, teaching at a prep school in term time but with enough talent to play county cricket in the holidays. The rest of the side was largely young lads trying to make their way. Mick noted my high backlift and how I didn't move as I waited for the ball to be delivered, and reported back to Mike Turner in glowing terms after we shared a century partnership against Warwickshire at Lutterworth. On the back of that, I was offered a summer contract for the following year – basically an invitation to join the staff for the period between leaving King's and going to university.

My attitude was very naïve. I'd really no idea what it all meant or what I wanted out of it. I know I was meant to have said some things around this time about how I was going to play for England – captain them even – but they were the words of a schoolboy and shouldn't be taken seriously. It was just a nice idea. When Leicestershire said they were going to pay me £25 per week, I was delighted and surprised. I'd have done it for nothing, to be honest. Because I had been born in Kent, Leicestershire wrote to Kent asking permission to register me and Les Ames, their secretary, wrote back to say, in effect, go ahead if you want to. I doubt if he knew much about me. Why would he?

As it happened, because I dropped out of my last term at King's, we were able to phone Leicestershire and ask if I could join them for the start of the 1975 season. Would that be okay? Of course it would. And so on 1 April – my eighteenth birthday – I jumped into the family's trusty Ford Anglia, navigated myself to the gym at Leicester Polytechnic and – thinking I'd better be smart for my first day of duty – presented myself to the rest of the playing squad smartly dressed in a suit. I've never been much of a tracksuit person but perhaps a suit was not the best choice of attire. That I could even contemplate going dressed like that shows how little I knew. Needless to say, my appearance caused a fair amount of mirth. I promptly advised my mother that evening that the suit would not be accompanying me the next day.

I scored steadily for the seconds during 1975. There were a couple of bowlers I came up against who were quicker than I was used to – you rarely got ultra-quick bowling at school – but that was okay. I coped. Then, in the second half of the season, I made my first XI entrance in the Sunday league, summoned for my first game after John Steele was injured. We'd got off to a mediocre start in the competition and weren't competing for prize-money, and I stayed in the side for the rest of the season. I scored a maiden half-century against Essex and after a stint as twelfth man played three championship games without doing anything extraordinary. It was a fascinating transition going from watching on the boundary edge as a youthful spectator to actually being out there on the field. There was a delightful buzz just from taking part. It was as simple and beautiful as that. There was no apprehension. How could there be? I was 18 years old and having a great time.

In early September, I set off for London with the good wishes of Mike Turner ringing in my ears. He said Leicestershire were really pleased with how I had done but, aware of my mother's wishes, was keen that I should go and get my degree on the grounds that it would be a good thing to have if all else failed. If I only played in the holidays, that was fine by them. There were plenty of contemporaries who did just that — Chris Tavare at Kent, Alastair Hignell at Gloucestershire, Vic Marks and Peter Roebuck at Somerset.

But unlike them I was unable to get through university. I was growing up fast and my outlook was changing fast. When Mike contacted me the following summer I did not hesitate. I played at Worcester and, although we lost, I scored 35 as opener and then played first-team cricket until I went on a Young England tour of the Caribbean. For better or worse, for richer or poorer, in sickness and in health, till selectors do us part, I had begun my life as a full-time cricketer.

3

A WEST INDIES BAPTISM

Life in the Leicestershire dressing room was a real eye-opener. To a cosseted youth, the sheer variety of characters, backgrounds and upbringings, the language and the humour, was mind-boggling. That there were other ways of doing things from how I'd done them at school and university was in itself a revelation. And as for the conversation . . . well, it rarely touched on the juvenile things we talked about at King's and when it did – in respect of women – the things these blokes seemed to have done left me open-mouthed. 'How does that work?' I wondered as I listened to lurid tales of their nocturnal conquests.

From a cricketing point of view, the best thing that could have happened was to be exposed to all that the game could throw at me at an early age. I wanted to learn as fast as I could; I was very naïve and innocent in many ways but that only added to the fascination. To me, this was not only a different world but the real one, and I wanted as much of it as I could get.

It didn't take long to realise that my enthusiasm wasn't entirely shared by more seasoned team-mates, among whom was a certain disenchantment at their lot. While I was simply happy to be there, let alone be paid a couple of thousand pounds a season for the privilege, they were less enamoured with wages which would have struggled to reach five figures and which turned out to compare poorly with those at other clubs. With Leicestershire starting to do well on the field, the sense of grievance had sharpened, to the point where the team conducted an unofficial survey among other clubs to find out exactly how they were being paid and what their expense allowances amounted to.

This was not an era when players moved freely between counties and, although they did occasionally switch, most were discouraged from doing so by a benefit system that locked them into staying ten years. Ken Higgs had joined us from Lancashire only after he'd had his benefit at Old Trafford. Ray Illingworth came from Yorkshire a few years after taking a benefit there. And Barry Dudleston left us for Gloucestershire the year after receiving his benefit at Grace Road. When my star rose I did not have an agent demanding I be paid more, but Mike Turner seemed to me to be very good about raising my pay. I guess in hindsight I could have afforded to be more demanding. Wages weren't universally high and the difference was perhaps only a few grand in any case, but given that so much of my energies were put into the England team I was content to be paid around Leicestershire's norm.

All sorts of things at Grace Road made opposition teams either chuckle or wince. Most counties would offer the opposition a choice of drinks at the end of the day. If they wanted a pint of bitter or a gin and tonic, they got it. But we didn't do that. All we had was a milk crate containing some Everards beers and a few bottles of lemonade for those who wanted to make shandy. And that was it. The lack of choice embarrassed us and irked them. Hot water in the dressing rooms was also in short supply. There were two baths and three showers behind the home and away dressing rooms and it was first come first served - or at least it would have been except Ken Higgs reckoned he had chief claim as senior fast bowler and if he required a bath after a long day in the field he was going to have one. So to prevent the opposition snaffling all the hot water he took off the taps and kept them to himself. At Grace Road the money was rationed, the beer was rationed and the hot water was rationed. Oh, and the opposition dressing room was half the size of the home one, so we rationed the space as well. No wonder someone dubbed it Graceless Road.

Even though money was in generally short supply, some clubs managed things better than others. The contrast between Leicestershire and a club like Essex was particularly stark. Their players were much less gnarled, ready for a joke at any time and generous with their hospitality. When we went to play at Chelmsford, or one of their festival grounds such as Southend, there were several sponsors' tents to choose from at the end of the day. There would not only be drinks on offer but food as well, which was always handy as it spared us dipping into our daily meal allowance (£2.50 as I recall). In the end I decided we had to reciprocate so one year, when Mike Turner happened to be away, I brought along a one-man ridge tent and pitched it next to the boundary rope. After play, we solicitously invited over the Essex boys, and ushered them into our splendid new hospitality area – one at a time, as any more than that would have been impractical – where we had on display an array of beverages (actually, the same old crate of Everards beer). They appreciated the joke.

When we had an away match, the senior pros did the driving because they'd get mileage money and I was bunged in a back seat, grateful for the ride. As captain Ray Illingworth was perhaps the only person given a car by the club and I waited until my England days for my first sponsored car. Many of the hotels we stayed in were barely functional. Once when we played Kent at Tunbridge Wells – the town of my birth – we were about to head off to bed after a nightcap at the bar when the hotel manager asked which of us would like tea or coffee in the morning, before adding that only six of us would be getting either as they only possessed six cups! Team hierarchy naturally meant that the morning cuppa went to the captain and five senior pros.

Years later, on another away trip to Kent we stayed at a guest house on the outskirts of Canterbury owned by an ex-merchant seaman who ran his establishment like a ship. I thought I recognised the place when we first arrived. It had actually been my first junior boarding house at King's and where there had been dormitories full of 13-year-old boys there were now partitions and a different clientele, albeit one still behaving largely like 13-year-old boys . . . This former seafarer kept the place spick and span, with meals served at precise times and doors locked at 11pm sharp. I managed to get round this last rule after an evening out with Chris Cowdrey by putting a ladder to the upstairs window, but Nick Cook was not so fortunate when he came down for breakfast on the Sunday only half-dressed. The manager said he would not serve him until he had put something on his feet. Doubting he was serious, Nick just sat there, but in the end realised he wasn't going to get his morning eggs until he did as he was told. We never stayed there again.

Mike Turner and Ray Illingworth ran Leicestershire between them. Mike, who had taken a teaching diploma at Loughborough, had switched from wannabe player to management at a young age. Illy was armed with extraordinary knowledge – an Ashes winning captain, disaffected with Yorkshire, and ripe to use. Mike ran the club, Illy ran the cricket, and it was a hell of a trick they pulled off because their aspirations far outstripped the club's resources. In fact, their aspirations must have bordered on the delusional when the two teamed up on Illy's arrival in 1969. Illy would tell Mike what he wanted and Mike would tell him whether they could afford it. But by the time I joined, the club was already winning trophies. They had lifted the Benson & Hedges Cup in 1972 and John Player League in 1974, and added the B&H Cup and championship in 1975. I well remember going to Lord's as a lowly second-team player to watch that B&H Cup win over Middlesex in 1975, perched on the grass in front of the Tavern, savouring the atmosphere of a full house with the other young players, dreaming of the day when it might be our chance to be heroes.

I had a good relationship with Illy and I owe him a lot. We were hardly peas out of the same pod but he had watched me bat and decided he liked what he saw. It would have been his decision to bring me into the first team, and to be backed by Illy was as good a start as you could ask for. He wasn't going to risk you on a whim. He did more than anyone to turn a feckless ex-public schoolboy into a professional cricketer. He was forever on at me about my casual dress sense, and after a string of rollockings I responded by coming down to breakfast one morning in Taunton wearing a dinner jacket and bow tie. 'Is this all right, captain?' I asked.

Illy spluttered: 'Bloody hell, Gower, have you just come in?'

He could be dour and yet inadvertently funny. The doctrine of infallibility applied to him as it seems to do with so many Yorkshire cricketers. Grace Road pitches were pretty flat and if he didn't make any runs . . . well, the ball must have hit the only piece of plantain in sight. It could not possibly have anything to do with the shot he had played. Nor did he ever play a game in which he did not try his damnedest. Years later I went with him on some jolly to Barbados where we played a local XI and he gave us the most fearful dressing-down after he had suspected we were not all giving 110 per cent. It was the same after he had left to go back to Yorkshire and I faced him in a Sunday league match on a low slow pitch at Scarborough. I tried to knock him out of the ground over mid on, didn't quite get hold of it, and was duly caught by that same mid on. It absolutely made his day. It was that competitiveness that kept him going for so long.

Of all the guys at Leicestershire, perhaps the one I formed the closest bond with was Brian Davison. Maybe it was because he also had an African background. He was an extraordinary character. He had served in the Rhodesian army and been fully involved in fighting the early insurgents. He told some amazing stories about his time out in the bush, dangling people out of helicopters to extract information from them, and was seemingly built of steel. He smoked a lot of Gunston cigarettes, and if there was a tip on them would take them off, and he drank too. He was not a man to cross and if there was someone he didn't rate he'd let them know. He had a slightly awkward batting technique but was utterly fearless. Faced with a quick bowler, he'd take them on without thinking twice. He could hit a cricket ball horribly hard, was a great fielder, and was a key component in our one-day successes of that era.

Davo was a very good mentor for me and became a very good and long-lasting friend. His wife Caroline was a lovely cook and it turned out he had hidden depths as an expert in antiques. He worked really hard at the game but only netted as much as he felt necessary. He wasn't like Boycott, who could never have too much practice. He looked at me and saw the fallibilities and casualness but had a knack of cajoling me into getting serious. I think he saw looking after me as a bit of fun. Like Illy, he acknowledged that I was what I was – laid-back, casual, call it what you will – but could do with a jolt now and again. He taught me a bit of responsibility and made me, if not tough, then tougher.

It was no coincidence that Davo was batting with me when I scored my maiden hundred against Middlesex at Lord's in 1976. The two of us had had a big night out the evening before and I'd ended up in a car behind the Clarendon Court Hotel with a girl on the wrong side of midnight (I was learning on several fronts by this stage, as you can tell) so I was not in the best shape the next morning, as was perfectly apparent in the early stages of my innings. I can't confirm how many balls I made contact with during the first half-hour but it couldn't have been many (a habit I had trouble shaking off). But there at the other end was Davo, and at the end of the over he'd come down and have a chat, a glint in his eye, asking if I was okay, chiding me and encouraging me to keep going. Somehow we battled through and things got easier. It wasn't an innings of absolute beauty and I was nervous approaching my hundred – I was in unchartered territory, as I had been the night before – but I got there and we later bowled out Middlesex to win the game.

With the likes of Illy and Davo so obviously not wanting me to waste my talent, I would have been a fool not to have striven to get better.

One thing you don't come across before entering first-class cricket is high-quality spin. The difference between a good spinner and a very good one is almost indefinable, but you know it when you see it. It is that mesmerising loop through the air, those Graeme Swann-style extra revs and drift. And when you face one of the best for the first time, it comes as a very rude awakening.

It happened to me in my second championship match when Leicestershire travelled to neighbouring Northampton. There in the opposition line-up was Bishan Singh Bedi, one of the great left-arm spinners of all time. He had a simple, graceful, fluid action with, as I was to discover, any number of subtle variations. I faced him for the first time late on the first day. We had bowled out Northamptonshire in a couple of sessions but were in trouble ourselves at 40-odd for five. Illingworth was already batting and all I wanted to do was get through to stumps alongside my skipper. What experience I had taught me that I should get well forward – and being quite tall I was usually able to do this well enough – but with Bedi the ball rarely landed where I expected it to. It would dip and drop a yard and a half in front of me, or bounce more than expected. Every ball he sent down seemed to vary fractionally in pace from the one before. This was a sophistication I just had not encountered before.

Unsurprisingly I was very soon caught at short leg off the glove without scoring. Off I trooped, tail firmly between legs, back to the dressing room to offer profuse apologies to my seniors – some of whom had already fared little or no better than me.

There are all sorts of aspects to dealing with spin but as I discovered with Bedi one of the most important is judging the length, and one other easy mistake to make is to try thrusting your front leg down the pitch without paying attention to the line and then having to, at best, play round your own pad. So, best to avoid that lunge and adopt whatever version you like of what is now referred to as the 'forward press', in the way that is now *de rigueur* in the modern game, or hold back and give yourself that split-second longer to make your move. You must learn the importance of using the space either side of the crease, going back far enough to give yourself more of a chance to see the ball off the pitch, or forward enough to get to the pitch of the ball. These are things we talk about a lot now as commentators but the basics of the game are as relevant now as they were to me then and have been throughout the history of the game. What is still interesting is how modern coaches are striving to keep those basics intact while always striving to find new and productive tricks. Either way, as a young player you just have to pay attention when your seniors are offering advice and learn to put these techniques quickly into practice before someone decides you are not as good as you thought you were.

So, Illy was soon taking me to one side for some urgent remedial work. Fortunately, we had a lot of spinners at Leicester who could help. Apart from Illy himself, there was Jack Birkenshaw, another off-spinner of recent England vintage, as well as John Steele, Chris Balderstone and Barry Dudleston, all left-arm spinners of varying degrees of proficiency. Steele's bowling was low and slow and he could land the ball on a sixpence. Balderstone was slow and flighty and you could use your feet to him. Dudleston was a handy part-timer. So, on practice days I would have dedicated nets against an array of four or five guys twirling away as I worked on developing a method that might get me through match situations. One of the things Illy tried to teach was blanking out the personalities involved, focusing only on the ball and playing accordingly.

I learnt pretty quickly. Less than a year later, when I was scoring that first century for Leicestershire at Lord's, among the Middle-sex bowlers that day was Fred Titmus, one of the very finest of off-spinners and a hugely experienced operator. He bowled some of the most outrageous arm-balls imaginable, big swinging deliveries that started well outside off stump only to veer down leg. Again, this was something I'd not seen before. That learning process is a vital part of any player's development and never stops; each and every time you come up against a new bowler you have to find out what his USP is, what his variations are, and log them in your mind for the next time.

Bit by bit, I filled in the holes in my education. Shortly after that, I went on a Young England tour of the Caribbean. The side was captained confidently and capably by Chris Cowdrey, who was to become a very good friend and, eventually, my best man. He was – and is – very amusing company and from the outset we seemed to agree on what was funny. We shared a sense of lunacy and that came before the shared love of sport. I'd first got to know him on a schools tour of South Africa a couple of winters earlier, on a team known as the Crocodiles (I have no idea why) and, as he was at school at Tonbridge, we'd also met on the playing fields before but at rugby not cricket. Sadly, due to one of those disputes that schools get themselves into now and again, King's had long since ceased to play Tonbridge at cricket, but in our one crucial clash on the rugby field the result of the match hinged on one incident between the two of us. The ball had been kicked over my head and was coming to rest over our try line and I was the defending fly-half scampering back to touch down the ball with Chris in hot pursuit. Obviously I had the better turn of speed, got there easily and fell on the ball to touch it down. As the ball squeezed out, Chris, having finally arrived on the scene, optimistically picked it up and touched it down too with added dramatic emphasis, attempting to claim the try but knowing full well that the referee should be blowing for the 22-yard dropout. As we now know all too well, referees and umpires, much though they fully deserve our respect, can have blind and deaf moments and this was one of them. Tonbridge were awarded the try, Cowdrey kicked the conversion and returned to the halfway line sniggering! It has been a point of banter ever since, with Chris claiming to this day that the try was perfectly legitimate.

Before the team left for the West Indies, we had a bit of a net session together in London, and I found myself facing David Munden, son of Don and a handy leg-spinner. I had not faced much leg-spin before – there were not many leg-spinners around in English cricket – and was still learning to pick the googly. Chris had no such difficulties. As the son of Colin, he had obviously been steeped in the game from the start and probably knew from an early age he was going to play professional cricket (he had few academic aspirations and had not gone to university). He was pretty surprised. 'How can you not pick a googly?' he asked. 'It's obvious.' I'm not sure how many googlies, if any, I'd faced to that point. It showed how far he was ahead of me in some respects, although he did later say that he thought me a complete 'natural' at 17. Well, maybe.

A lot of my early encounters against wrist spin came overseas. My season of grade cricket in Perth pitted me against a host of wrist spinners on a weekly basis, and on my first England tours, which also happened to be to Australia, there were yet more opportunities to learn about the dark arts of wrist-spin, with Jim Higgs the man chosen by the Aussies on that 1978–79 tour to test our understanding of leg-spin. As before, it was a question of look and learn – and learn I did. Until you've had a good look at someone, you are vulnerable and it's a case of searching for clues, and adding information, as fast as you can. I was bowled in a state match in Tasmania with a chinaman for the simple reason that I just did not pick it.

The best players of wrist-spin will read it from the hand. I remember Greg Chappell, when I was first working with Channel 9 in Australia, picking leg-spinners and googlies consistently, whether watching the bowler from 100 yards away or off the television monitor. I could never claim to be quite as competent, although I would say I became a pretty good reader of the ball from the hand over the years, but would keep open the option to try also to read the ball in the air and, if that still left me guessing, then you had one option left, to watch it off the pitch, in which case the trick was not to commit to any big shot and defend, plain and simple.

The best I ever played against was Pakistan's Abdul Qadir, who did keep me guessing some of the time. It was actually a matter of great pride to him to be able to disguise at least one of his two googlies enough for it to remain undetected. He was the best before Shane Warne, with almost as many varieties, including a great flipper, but without the same talent for inventing new names for all those varieties. I would read him from the hand most of the time and then read the seam in the air the rest. When I failed to read it, I just hoped it would miss the outside edge and, judging by my scores in Pakistan, I must have either got it right often enough or used up a lot of luck in playing and missing. The privilege of the left-hander!

Illy said he was amazed at how quickly I improved against spin. Bedi got me out again when we faced each other in the championship in 1977 – his last year at Northampton – but I felt comfortable against him when India toured England two years later. He did not play in the first Test in which I scored a double-century but took part in the second where I hit 82 at Lord's before being bowled leaving one alone from Karsan Ghavri that confusingly came back up the slope. By then I was confident enough to use my feet to get down the pitch and hit the great man over midwicket. That's how far along the learning curve I felt I'd moved.

If spin bowling presented me with a subtle test of skill, raw pace posed a rather more brutal examination of nerve. Generally speaking, I reckoned I was pretty good against the fast men but walking out to face them always raised the question: *How am I going to do this?* It's a battle that is never won because even when you think you have got the hang of a particular opponent, you are only one mistake away from a very painful lesson in hubris.

The waiting to bat against the quick bowlers is hard and when you are young the apprehension can be acute, although I think it is not until you have taken a blow or two that you become truly aware of your vulnerability.

I had made five first-class appearances for Leicestershire when in June 1976 we were due to play a three-day game against the touring West Indians. They were not yet quite at their peak but not far off. They were routinely making mincemeat of county sides and it was becoming clear what a potentially great group of players they were as Clive Lloyd starting teaming up Michael Holding and Andy Roberts with the new ball. Holding was rested for the game at Grace Road but Roberts was down to play and thanks to the mayhem he had wreaked during his time at Hampshire there was no more feared bowler in the game. He took ten wickets in the Lord's Test, had sat out a match at Northampton, and was ready for a workout.

A young Wayne Daniel was down to share the new ball with him. I'd already come across 'Diamond' in one of my early second XI games at Lutterworth, where he'd raised our eyebrows by starting his run-up from the edge of the field. As Daniel steamed in, even the more experienced guys in our team like Mick Norman were muttering, 'Oh, my god . . .' as they realised they were going to be required to set an example to us youngsters in the art of dealing with a fast-moving and very hard object. I vividly recall Daniel bowling me a waist-high beamer which my batting partner David Humphries – a handy wicketkeeper-batsman who could give the ball a biff – denounced with a string of oaths. I might have only been in the game five minutes but even I knew it was not a good idea provoking a big West Indian with a ball in his hand.

My anxiety ahead of the West Indies game can be gauged from the fact I thought it necessary to pop into The Cricketers pub adjacent to the ground for a little shot of whisky first thing in the morning. This was not, I hasten to point out, my usual means of preparation, even in the days when Botham was at his most persuasive. It was highly unusual but seemed like a good idea at the time. Grace Road was a good place to bat in those days but this was a time before helmets. Dutch courage was required. Looking back now, what made me as nervous as anything was the aura of a formidable team, the aura of Roberts, and the fear of the unknown.

That I scored 89 not out in a game dominated by batsmen doesn't mean the concern was not warranted. I was absolutely right to admit to nerves. I played and missed at Roberts and Daniel a few times and ducked under a few bouncers but when you are young bravado can carry you a long way. I played some fine shots of which I was mighty proud and Illy was very complimentary afterwards about the way I played. Some people thought he should have delayed his declaration to let me get a hundred but I was not unhappy. We needed to make a game of it – and did. The skipper set the touring side what seemed like a reasonable target against the clock but they knocked them off with ease. Perhaps it was from him I acquired my generosity in declaring against West Indies!

Another test awaited me in my very next championship match and the results were not quite so encouraging. With Barry Dudleston breaking his finger against the West Indians, I was promoted to open against Lancashire, whose sharpest bowler, Peter Lever, had been missing when I'd made my first-class debut against them at Blackpool the previous year. Lever's pace – to be precise his ability to swing the ball into me as a left-hander at pace – proved too much for me. With stumps rearranged behind me, it was another lesson learned.

Given my age and inexperience, and the lack of insurance that protective headgear would have provided, I reckon I was good with pace in the early days. I was particularly pleased with the potential I showed on that Young England tour of the Caribbean where the up and-coming fast bowlers I had to deal with included Hartley Alleyne and Malcolm Marshall, a man with whom I would enjoy – I use the word 'enjoy' in its more general sense – many duels before we became close team-mates at Hampshire nearly 15 years later. Marshall later said that when it came to flair and improvisational skills I was streets ahead of my contemporaries on that tour. Kind words, indeed. My memories of him were rather more specific. Even at the age of 18 his pace was sharp but on a hard and quick pitch at Barbados I took him on, executing what I considered was a good hook shot only to see the ball travel low and flat in the region of deep square leg. The next thing I saw was a big wide smile belonging to Hartley Alleyne as he shouted, 'It's mine!' I'd got 40-odd and had been going like a train. I think Malcolm and I both remembered those early encounters with a lot of affection.

The first time I got badly hit was during a Sunday league match on a wet pitch at Luton – yes we did somehow have to play in Luton – in 1977, my first full season of county cricket. It was a game reduced to a ten-over slog by rain and I took my chances against Sarfraz Nawaz, an established Pakistan international and a fine bowler, and Alan Hodgson, a big tall Geordie. I had a hook at one from Hodgson which I only succeeded in top-edging into my left eyebrow. I took no further part in the game and left the ground with two great big panda-eyes. It was a few days before my view of the world returned to normal but I soon realised that although it hurt, it didn't hurt for long.

We were due to play Northants again the following week at Grace Road. The physical marks were still there with my blackened eyes; the perfectly reasonable question was whether I would be quite so confident with the hook shot. As it happened I didn't really have much time to think about it all, did face the same man without much to worry about, but not for long – we collapsed to 45 for nine before Illingworth and Higgs put on a record 228 for the last wicket with Ken falling short of what would have been the most improbable hundred by just two. You had to feel for him – he was never going to have a chance to get that close again. Anyway, for me things were all back in good order soon enough – in the next Sunday league match I was back in the runs with an unbeaten 135 against Warwickshire.

In fact, the type of bowling that could cause me as much trouble as anything was medium-pace swing of the type practised by countless English cricketers. Here again playing away to Northamptonshire provided the scene of some of my worst indignities. I hated playing at the County Ground, Northampton because it meant having to face on a slow, low pudding of a pitch the bowling of the Honourable T M Lamb, innocuous to many but never to me.

Seemingly every time I played at Northampton it was the same old story: D I Gower lbw b T M Lamb o (or not many more). In 1980, this was precisely how I was out in each innings, lbw for nought – my first pair in first-class cricket. Just for good measure he got me for another duck in a Benson & Hedges Cup match a few days later. It might have been in one of those ever so short innings that he put into action the old sledge 'I could bowl you out with an orange,' and actually bowled an orange at me first ball. Well, there would have been no point in saving the joke for later! It wouldn't have bounced much, would certainly have hit me on the pad and I would definitely have been given out – if it was not, as an orange, an illegal delivery. The joke, I have to say, went down exceptionally well with the Northants lads and I suspect I had little option but to join in the laughter.

When I moved to Hampshire I pleaded with Mark Nicholas, my new captain, not to pick me for an away trip to Northants because I knew no good would come of it. 'I'll be miserable and useless,' I told him. 'I won't get any runs and if you are a clever captain you will leave me out on compassionate grounds.' To which the response was always the same: 'You're playing.' Except for once, that is, when I genuinely had a suitably well-developed case of 'man flu' and convinced him I should not play. Feeling not only grotty but guilty, I watched us have an awful game. Talk about not feeling like playing some days: whenever I went to Northampton and Lamb was on the menu, I *never* felt like playing. It was my biggest phobia in cricket. Give me Holding, Roberts, Lillee, Thompson or Bedi any time, just not him. All I can say in mitigation is that when I faced him on proper pitches, like the ones at Grace Road, I invariably got runs.

The moral of the Tim Lamb story is that you do not always have to be a big spinner of the ball, or bowl at 100mph, to be effective.

I did not start wearing a helmet until my first England tour. They were just starting to develop protective headgear in Australia, where they had been much in demand during World Series Cricket. The early ones looked pretty much like motorcycle helmets because that is exactly what they were. They did a job for the World Series players but they were not designed for the job. For one thing, hearing was a problem and because it was rather like wearing a pair of ear-muffs there had been a few problems with calling and running. But when we arrived we were met by guys marketing something called the C&D helmet, which was made of fibreglass and much lighter and more practical than the earlier versions. We were all offered them. I wore one with no chin-strap and just the small side-pieces to protect the temples. I tried using the Perspex visor in the nets but it was horrible: my hands used to go through quite a long way when I played my strokes and my bottom hand clanked into the visor.

I was to be selective when I wore helmets but it made perfect sense in Australia. Any doubts were erased by taking guard over a patch of blood left by an injured Clive Radley during our first warm-up match in Adelaide. Rodney Hogg, the bowler who had pinned Clive, was mighty quick and one ball from him hit me on the side of the neck during the second Test in Perth. Although a helmet did not help me in that instance, it was clearly a near miss and thus a wise precaution.

I certainly wore one when we played against the West Indies. It would have been lunacy not to, although I did once – it must have been the 1981 tour of the Caribbean – get slightly cocky in the last Test in Antigua, where I was feeling good with some runs on the board and thought about taking it off at tea on the final day. Thankfully I didn't as Colin Croft clanged me on the side of the helmet in the first over after the resumption, the ball flying off to long leg for four leg byes. Several years later, I was rash enough to remove the helmet against Richard Hadlee, again after a tea break and feeling well set on the way to a hundred at the Oval. It seems he did not take this insult to his masculinity well, bombarding me with three bouncers in a row. I got out of the way of the first two easily enough but the third hit me a glancing blow on the side of the head. It didn't hurt much and the umpire signalled runs, much to Hadlee's disgust.

Generally, I found helmets claustrophobic and restrictive, and felt much happier batting without one provided the bowling was not of express pace and there were no obvious risks attached. As you get older and your reactions slow, you acknowledge those risks more readily and are less tempted to gamble.

It won't surprise you to hear that Beefy was quite bullish in this regard. He scored a famous century at Brisbane in 1986 wearing a floppy white hat for at least half the time. It was a brilliant display of attacking batting, laced with bravado and thrilling to watch. It also turned the match. You can ask Merv Hughes how he felt about that! But in time even Beefy was obliged to wear a visor after being hit on the cheek aiming a hook at Baz Barwick of Glamorgan. Baz was hardly a tearaway but had enough pace to inflict a depressed cheekbone and the doctors told Beefy that if he was hit in the same place again it could be serious.

These days, the Health & Safety generation wear a helmet even against a spinner on a non-turning surface. They are in the mindset that if they take it off something will happen that will make them regret it. They also play in a way that would simply be impossible were they not wearing a visor or helmet. Even the great Sachin Tendulkar wears a helmet as a matter of course.

I tell you one modern great who might have had to rethink his method if helmets were not around – Ricky Ponting. Now here is a man with exceptional talent and I have no doubts about his bravery and toughness, having seen him, despite helmets, literally

spitting blood and getting on with the job of either batting or fielding in close at silly point. However, I suspect that he would have
found it harder to hone a technique which was very front-footed
yet seldom stopped him going for the hook shot off that same front
foot if he had not had the protection and reassurance that the
helmet gave him.

If joining the Leicestershire dressing room was great fun for a
young lad, going on tour was another class of adventure altogether.
I had been on short schools tours abroad before but that trip to the
West Indies in the summer of '76 gave me a real taste of what life
on the road could be like, and I loved it. You learned as much about
life as you did about cricket but that was all part of the crack.
Frankly, if you don't like touring, you aren't going to survive, let
alone thrive, at the top level.

The Caribbean is of course a good place to start. We flew
straight to Barbados and stayed at a simple place on Accra Beach
where there was an honesty bar consisting of a five-litre flagon of
rum, a couple of mixers, and piece of paper where you logged
how much you'd drunk (if indeed you could remember). There
was a lot of partying and fun but we were a group of young 'profes-
sionals' (I must use the word loosely, I suppose) in competition to
make our mark so there was a thread of seriousness to what we
were doing. We'd been given a great opportunity to learn about
playing cricket in different conditions from home against some
good opposition, and we did well, going unbeaten and winning the
only 'Test match' in Trinidad. I did okay. It was, in the words of
Sellars and Yeatman in *1066 And All That*, 'a good thing'.

I was to play a lot of cricket in future with some of those in that
team. Mike Gatting and 'Gunner' Gould were both capped by
Middlesex the following year, as I was at Leicestershire. Chris
Cowdrey, the captain, and Paul Downton were very soon regulars

at Kent, likewise Bill Athey at Yorkshire. Paul Allott would also play international cricket.

Quite a few of us soon got picked for more development tours. Along with Cowdrey, Athey, Downton and Gould, I found myself heading off a few weeks later on a short tour of Canada organised by the sports promoter Derrick Robins. The squad was a real mixture of up-and-coming youngsters such as ourselves and senior pros, with Mike Denness, an England Test captain of recent vintage, at the helm.

Derrick, who acted as tour manager as well as sponsor, was a real character. He had originally made his money in the Midlands and was a big sports fan. He had built squash courts, chaired Coventry City Football Club and loved his cricket. He owned a fair bit of property in South Africa and had funded several tours there. One of his chief motives, undoubtedly, was to give opportunities to the second tier of English players, and some of his early tours resembled what we would describe today as England A sides. That had changed slightly by the time I became involved, but his priority was still to give invaluable experience to youngsters like myself. We were always looked after very well, and had a great time, but he expected us to behave like a proper team and if there was any outrageous behaviour off the field he'd speak to us about it. But he was a benign dictator rather than a despot. In fact, dressings-down were rarely needed. The senior players taught us how to tour and what was, and was not, acceptable, as well as what was fun.

With the sports boycott of apartheid South Africa at its height, these tours were inevitably seen in some quarters as supportive of that regime. In fact, I would say that Derrick was not pro-apartheid at all, but a sports lover who wanted to maintain links with South African sport. It was a view held by many but such nuances were lost on some and when we got to places such as Edmonton and Montreal we found his reputation had preceded him. Our games there were interrupted by protesters who lay on the matting pitches during the lunch breaks until someone cleared them off. Threatening them with the heavy roller worked as well as anything but it meant for the odd long lunch as we waited for the police to pitch up and get rid of them.

This was not my first taste of the politics of apartheid. I had been to South Africa on a schools tour two Christmases earlier along with Chris Cowdrey, representing that team, The Crocodiles. The tour was organised by St Andrew's College, Grahamstown, who had played against King's, Tonbridge and a few more public schools a year or two before and were now repaying the favour. I make no apology for saying that what we saw of South Africa we tended to think was wonderful. The underlying truth – in other words what we didn't see – was that cricket in South Africa, as with society, was entirely segregated. You can perhaps criticise a bunch of well-educated young men for not being more curious but there again it wasn't as though our hosts were that keen to explain the iniquities of apartheid to us either.

So when we got to Canada, we found that some were less enamoured that our party was apparently tainted by these rather tenuous links to the South African regime and Cowdrey's name and mine ended up on a Caribbean blacklist. This meant that the Young England team had been unable to play in Jamaica and Guyana (whose government would object to Robin Jackman on the same grounds when the full England team toured in 1981). In Canada, the demonstrators were objecting more to Derrick Robins as a supposed 'collaborator' with apartheid South Africa than us.

As a teenager, I had yet to form a view on the apartheid issue, greatly though it exercised many people. We did not try to ignore politics on our schools tour but nor were we involved in it in any way. Did we see the iniquities of apartheid? Of course not. We were looked after magnificently by the white community – no surprise there – and spent a lot of time with Anglo whites and Dutch whites, and again not surprisingly from what we saw South Africa looked an awesome and beautiful place. We were spoilt rotten. One time we stayed in a beautiful house among the orange groves near Port Elizabeth, spent Christmas Day on the beach and Boxing Day at St George's Park, where I saw Graeme Pollock score the most scintillating hundred. As a 17-year-old this made an even bigger impression on me than watching him as a small boy at Trent Bridge nine years earlier. We played matches in Stellenbosch and at the famous Wanderers club across the road from the main stadium in Johannesburg. What was my impression of South Africa in 1974? Well, fantastic. What else would I say? But of cricket and apartheid, more anon.

In the winter of 1977, I went on a second Derrick Robins tour to the Far East and Sri Lanka, where I was able to measure my progress in dealing with spin. Although inconsistent in the championship, I'd had a good season with Leicestershire in one-day cricket and had been in with an outside chance of a place on England's full tour of Pakistan and New Zealand. In the end, Mike Gatting got the nod instead, not something that greatly distressed me either at the time or later, when I heard tales about how the likes of Mike Hendrick and Ian Botham had suffered from amoebic dysentery. A lucky escape! I also spent the second half of that winter playing club cricket in Perth after a vacancy came up at Claremont-Cottesloe cricket club following Brian Rose's selection for the England tour. Garth McKenzie, Leicestershire's long-serving Australian fast bowler, recommended me as a replacement and it turned out to be a fantastic experience that teed me up perfectly for international selection at home in 1978.

I would describe my time in Perth as an eye-opener were it not that my eyes had been already well and truly opened by then. Singapore was one of our first ports of call on the Robins tour and of course as soon as we arrived one of the senior players (those who were supposed to know what was, and was not, acceptable on tour) volunteered to take the youngsters to Bugis Street. 'What's that then?' we asked naively. 'We'll show you . . .' And off we went in a rickshaw, visiting a couple of sex shows en route where girls did amazing things with ping-pong balls that had not been on the syllabus at King's Canterbury. Bugis Street doesn't get going until late so we'd had a few beers by the time we took our seats in a bar populated by what I thought were some strikingly beautiful women. In the end, of course, the more experienced of my team-mates stopped smirking and let slip that these girls were not quite what they seemed and had bits attached that you would not want to play with.

One person whom I won't name failed to heed all warnings and was taken back to a room by one of these 'ladies', only to end up retreating from it backwards, protecting himself with an outstretched chair rather like a lion-tamer.

Apart from Singapore, we visited Malaysia, Hong Kong and Sri Lanka – a truly fabulous experience for a 20-year-old – but I barely had time to get home and say hello to mum before I was back on a plane to Australia for what proved a challenge of a different sort altogether. As a member of a tour party, you had the reassurance of knowing you were among friends and contemporaries. But as a solitary English fish in a sea of Australians, life could be altogether harsher. There were other Englishmen in Perth at the time – Chris Tavare was playing for University for instance – but I don't recall seeing an awful lot of them. I wouldn't have known them well at that stage in any case. In essence you were on your own and facing lessons in life, and the first lesson was that you had to play well to gain acceptance from hosts inclined to be sceptical of your abilities.

For a while, you would be known only as 'The Pom', and 'Testing Out the Pom' was definitely the favourite game. Fortunately, after a hesitant start, I convinced the locals that I could play. Once that happened, things were brilliant because there are few more sociable types than Aussies, and few more eager to be your mates.

After spending a couple of nights staying with the 'Claremont-Cott' chairman, Robin Farmer, whose sons played for the club, I was introduced to the rest of the players, who took one glance at my long blond hair and exclaimed, 'Jeez, what have they sent us this time?!'

I did coaching sessions with the youngsters, trained on Tuesday and Thursday nights, and played matches at the weekend, but there was still plenty of time to live a fine if slightly low-budget life of hedonism. Initially, I was given a small room at a pub called The Albion on Stirling Highway run by a guy who used to be an Aussie Rules player who was a friend of the chairman. When the temperature rose into the high 30s and above, as it tended to often enough in WA, I had the option of opening the window to let in some air and being eaten alive by several hundred mosquitoes, or keeping the window closed and dying of asphyxiation. The good news was that I was granted a free lunch of steak and chips every day and a succession of cars from a used car lot run by yet another friend of the club. He gave me the use of a string of jalopies, some of which looked like they'd been in the hands of circus clowns . . . one tap in the right place and they'd collapse. Oil seemed to be an optional extra and, in one case, air in any of the tyres too but eventually he relented and provided me with a nice big Holden that guzzled gas but at least left me feeling safe.

This was the time of Kerry Packer's World Series Cricket and some of the usual stars such as Dennis Lillee were not around to make their customary occasional appearances for grade sides. That said, the standard of cricket was still mighty good and it was all very competitive. The Packer matches were pretty big news on TV but my chief memory was going to the WACA to sample an official

Test match between India and an Australia side stripped of most of the big names and led by an ageing Bob Simpson.

I started to get among the runs for Claremont before Christmas and by the end of the season felt I was smashing the bowling to all parts. I believe they still talk fondly of my hundred against Midland-Guildford in 40-degree heat! Things also looked up when Nicholas Duncan, one of the Englishmen in Perth I did befriend, offered me the use of his luxurious flat while he returned home for Christmas, and my arrival into the bosom of the club's family was confirmed when I moved in with a team-mate called Jock Cameron who had a nice house on the river.

I was pretty sad to go by the time it came to leave although the guys stuffed me completely at a farewell party designed almost exclusively to get me as drunk as possible. 'Aw, respect, mate. It's been good . . . But look here, The Pom's not pissed enough . . .' So we moved on from schooners of Swan Lager to ones with added oomph, depth-charged with Ouzo. 'Skull it mate, skull it!' The bottom line was they wanted to see The Pom destroyed – and The Pom was destroyed, completely. When the lights went dim I was dragged to a car and transported unconscious to the Stirling Highway, the main road between Perth and Fremantle. There I was tied by the wrist to a random lamppost and abandoned. Oh yes – I forgot to mention the naked bit – or should that be bits! The only saving grace, I am unreliably informed, was that the lady in the house opposite peeked through her curtains to see all this, was not best pleased at what she saw – and you can take that in whichever way you please – and persuaded my tormentors to cut me loose and take me home. I duly woke up in Jock's house two days later.

If one of the things I picked up from my time in Perth was a stupendous hangover, what I had also acquired by this time through one of my earlier tours was a girlfriend.

I first met Vicki Stewart in the West Indies during the Young England tour. In the absence of some of the other islands wanting us, we had visited Grenada, where we were billeted with various local families. One night they took us all to the Red Crab restaurant and there was this gorgeous girl whose parents Ian and Dawn helped organise the evening. Unfortunately, while I was thinking, 'God, I'd love to be with her,' she was falling for Chris Cowdrey. But then he was the captain, so obviously pulled rank!

I wrote a mental note to myself: *Next time I come back to the Caribbean I have to be captain.* For all the wrong reasons.

There were a lot of fond farewells as we moved on to Trinidad, but Vicki had obviously really fallen for Chris because she soon hitched a ride on a cargo boat and made her way over to Trinidad to join us (or more specifically, Chris), an adventurous step, to say the least, for a teenage girl. Chris had a smile as wide as Niagara Falls, while I mooched around thinking, *Lucky bastard.*

When we got home, I happened to speak to Chris and learnt that Vicki was off the scene. He had a girlfriend back in Kent and that was that. I then found out that Vicki's family were themselves back in the UK and, with dogged determination, set off in whatever piece of automotive history I was now driving and headed for their house between Reading and Henley The truth is that she didn't really want to know at first but eventually, either impressed by my persistence or feeling sorry for me, she relented. This was in the summer of 1977. We ended up spending the next ten years of our lives together.

4

PROMISING BEGINNINGS

It is odd how a seemingly small, innocuous event can take on a significance you would never have imagined possible. Little did I know when I faced my first ball in Test cricket that it would become so firmly attached to my CV. It remains one of the best things known about me. *David Gower? Didn't he hit his first ball in Test cricket for four?* Obviously if I'd never scored another run, that ball would not have achieved such importance, but as the runs flowed in my first twelve months as an England cricketer and beyond, that one shot — what *Wisden* described as 'a nonchalant pull' — encapsulated for many people the supposedly instinctual nature of my talent.

Perhaps because of my early success in an England shirt, and perhaps because the game was in need of some new heroes following the defections to Kerry Packer's breakaway 'circus', I was quickly dubbed the 'Golden Boy of English cricket'. For a while I could do no wrong in the eyes of the world and that first ball helped burnish the image. You can't do much better than hit your first ball in Test cricket for four.

That one shot became shorthand for 'effortless', though I would have to dispute that. It certainly did not feel like it at the time. On the contrary, my thoughts before that first ball were focused on the need to be wary. A few weeks before this Test match at Edgbaston, I had played against the Pakistanis for Leicestershire at Grace Road and Liaqat Ali – the man who sent down that first ball – had bowled me with a delivery that swung deceptively through the air. Now, he has not exactly joined the pantheon of the world's greatest bowlers but in that unremarkable innings of mine of 16 he had beaten my bat a number of times, so I knew what he was capable of. I knew he could swing the ball and if he landed it in the right place could be dangerous. So when I walked out for my first Test innings for England on 2 June 1978, I was conscious that, while things could go well, equally they might go horribly wrong.

The magnitude of the occasion was starting to sink in. The night before the game, I had been as nervous as anyone would be on the eve of their first Test. Sensing this, Graham Roope had offered me a quick beer after the then traditional jacket-and-tie team dinner at which our captain Mike Brearley outlined tactics, and after a bit of a chat with Graham, or more of a listen in my case, it was time for some sleep.

The following day, when my time to bat approached, not for the last time I made my way out to the middle probably looking rather more composed than I felt. That first shot was merely the result of my instincts doing what they had been trained to do.

The truth is that it was not a good ball. In fact, it was a shocker . . . a long hop at no more than 80mph on a flat, easy-paced pitch. If you want a present for your first ball in Test cricket, it would be hard to think of something more generously gift-wrapped. Had a ball of that length been bowled on that same pitch, only with a few more mph, by Andy Roberts or Michael Holding, I certainly would not have been so ready to pounce on it. But it wasn't and that was and is my good fortune.

Still, it was my first ball in Test cricket and I did sometimes wonder if I should have played the shot I did. Was it maybe a little extravagant and impulsive? The answer is of course, no. If it's there to be hit, bloody well hit it! Just because Test cricket was not then played as it is today, when players like Virender Sehwag routinely get their eye in by lashing the ball to the cover boundary, does not mean you ignore a juicy long hop, first ball or not.

There was more to the image than one swivel-pull. There was also the way I looked. I've watched the film of that innings again and there's no denying that I gave off an air of nonchalance before the ball was bowled. I strolled out to the wicket chewing gum in a way that appalled my mother at the time and still appals me now. Then there was my hair, which was long even by the standards of the day (at least among professional cricketers, if not their foot-balling counterparts), and strikingly blond and curly. The whole ensemble – unruly hair, gum, the way I batted – seemed to mark me out as someone, something, different, not that I would have even thought about it in any such way at the time.

If I was lucky with that first ball, I was lucky too to be making my debut against a Pakistan attack that was far weaker than it might have been. Imran Khan had joined the Packer camp. Sarfraz Nawaz, a very fine bowler, played in the game but delivered only six overs because of a rib strain, leaving Liaqat at the coal-face with Mudassar Nazar, a handy part-time swing bowler who would cause England problems in future, Iqbal Qasim, a respectable spinner, and Sikander Bakht, who was lively but largely unknown. In terms of difficulty, this was well down on what Australia or West Indies might have mustered, even accounting for Packer's intervention. As it happened, I was badly dropped by my patron saint Liaqat when I had scored only 15. Despite giving him a 100-minute start, I had just overhauled Clive Radley's score when I fell for 58.

There was no doubting this was a promising beginning, but I would have preferred it had people not jumped to quite so many conclusions at such an early stage. Even so, just as this bright start encouraged others, so it encouraged me, and my confidence grew exponentially. If you perform well, you quickly become accepted in any dressing room and by the end of that summer I was a slightly noisier animal than I had been at the outset.

The speed with which I had risen from the county arena to the international stage also helped gild the Gower image. I had previously played only one full season in English cricket and it had been sufficient to get my name onto some people's list of England 'possibles'. Mike Gatting might have toured with England ahead of me, possibly through his connection with Brearley at Middlesex, but my winter had not been wasted. I came back from Perth a more mature, confident and self-sufficient person, and was ready to leapfrog Gatting in the estimation of the selectors. It wasn't that I scored a huge number of runs – in fact my career average in first-class cricket was around 27 when I played my first Test – but I had excited some good judges about what I might do.

My selection for an MCC side to play the Pakistanis at Lord's in what amounted to a trial match for England hopefuls had still come as a surprise. Some new faces had been brought into the Test side following the loss of half a dozen frontline players to Kerry Packer the previous year but there were still places up for grabs. Batting at No.4, one place ahead of Gatting, I scored 27 and 71 in a low-scoring match and in the words of chairman of selectors Alec Bedser 'oozed class'.

It was on the back of this performance that I had been chosen to play my first games for England in two one-day internationals against Pakistan that preceded the Tests. There was a different feel to such contests in those days. The ODI was still evolving as a format – this was only seven years after the very first one was played in Melbourne – but they now had a fixed place in the calendar and were clearly a route into the Test side. And when you are 21 it is very exciting to be picked for your country in any kind of game. I still received a little card officially notifying me of my selection. I would still be playing in front of a big crowd. There would be an atmosphere, a special feeling.

To cap it, I scored a hundred in the second game at the Oval, an unbeaten 114 that ensured a match-winning total. I accelerated nicely towards the end but scored pretty briskly throughout, and walked off to a standing ovation from a crowd of 17,500. If that was a new experience, so too was the reaction of the media. The *Daily Mirror* ran a piece under the heading, 'Greatness? Perfection? Genius?' ('not yet,' it concluded helpfully), while Sir Leonard Hutton thought me the best young batsman he had seen since Colin Cowdrey. Another correspondent praised my 'impressive absence of emotion' – a trait that in the not-too-distant future would translate to 'laid-back'.

Of course, I would have read all these reports happily enough. I had no fear of the press then, or what they might be capable of. It all seemed good news, even if it was obvious from only a short period of reflection that such reactions, and those that followed my debut Test at Edgbaston a week later, served mainly to ratchet up expectations to near-impossible levels.

And the truth was that at Edgbaston a score of 58, while very acceptable for a first Test innings, should really have been converted into a century. I fell to a catch at square leg off a miscued clip which *Wisden* described as an 'uncharacteristic wild swing'. I don't think it was anything too outlandish but would concede it was a little careless. If only I had shown more nous. Such a dismissal suggested that, whatever the public perception, I still had plenty to learn.

Surprised and grateful simply to be given such an early opportunity to play Test cricket, I spent much of my first year as an England player in a state of serene pleasure. I was conscious that people expected special things of me after those early games against Pakistan but it didn't worry me. I was just glad to be there. The excitement of seeing your name on the team-sheet was so tangible that it masked any lurking anxieties. I scored enough runs to justify my presence, and England kept winning. In a nutshell, everything went swimmingly.

When I look back on what was written about me during that period, it is rather amazing I wasn't seriously affected by it all. Take this from the 1979 *Wisden*, which named me one of its five Cricketers of the Year: 'The sun scarcely graced the English cricket scene with its presence in 1978, but when it did it seemed to adorn the blond head of David Gower. The young Leicestershire left-hander could do little wrong. He typified a new, precocious breed of stroke-players, imperious and exciting, who added colour and glamour to an otherwise bedraggled English summer . . . the mantle of cricket's 'golden boy' slips easily over Gower's lithe shoulders.' Elsewhere, having described me as 'one of the most publicised cricketers in the country', the good book suggested that my 'launching to the limelight of the Test arena smacked of a story from the *Boy's Own* magazine . . . there are few more rousing sights than Gower hooking or punching drives square and through the covers.'

Bill O'Reilly, the great Australian leg-spinner turned newspaper sage, wrote that I was a batsman to 'change the whole face of English Test batting', while around the time I reached 1,000 runs in Test cricket shortly after entering my fourteenth month as an England cricketer my captain Mike Brearley said something about me being 'a minor genius who may one day become a major one'. How wise he was, as ever, not to get carried away. I might not have fulfilled that promise entirely but I don't think I disappointed them completely.

Brearley was a key figure during these early days. It takes me time to summon the courage to say something to people I don't know well and to start with I would have been very quiet and shy in the England dressing room he ran, but he soon made me feel at ease. Brearley would probably argue with the idea that I was too shy to speak up; being the eagle-eyed observer he was, he once noted that I was usually at my noisiest when nervous.

I responded well to him, as most people did. When he spoke at those eve-of-match dinners, he was always very precise and concise about what he had to say about the strengths and weaknesses of the opposition. As for his own players, he had the amazing capacity to empathise with you and intuitively sense whether it was an occasion for the carrot or the stick. He would have a quiet chat with you about your technique, or simply engage in a general conversation about nothing in particular, the subtext to which was simply, 'I'm watching, I'm on your side.' There were times when he wanted me to display my feelings more obviously, show more anger perhaps, but I think we were actually rather alike. Our demeanour was generally calm, punctuated by occasional explosions of temper (this is still the case with me, as immediate members of my family will testify).

My relationship with Brearley was not dissimilar to the one I had with Ray Illingworth. I was cheekier and more playful with Illy but it was still a relationship based on respect, from the youngster for the man who had done it all and the old timer for the precocious talent that was (in his eyes) obviously going to do well. They gave off a sense of paternalism which you could play off. Brearley studied the science of leadership more thoroughly, talked less about himself and consulted more, but they both knew how to get through to people and make them play for them. They both had a fantastic mental record of every opponent and were very quick to work out those they'd not seen before.

When you are as young as I was then, you naturally trust your captains. It is a trust that is implicit and unwavering. They know the job and you do what they say. Over the years, as you learn more about the game, you realise there's no such thing as 100 per cent correct captaincy, and your belief that the likes of Illy and

In front of our little cottage in Goudhurst on my grandmother's farm after the family's return from Tanganyika, proudly wearing my father's Twiga cap from Dar es Salaam.

Early promise? Tennis is my sport now in middle age but that backhand still needs work!

My first visit to Buckingham Palace, to see my father receive his OBE.

Where did that hair come from and where has it gone? King's School, Canterbury v OKS, 1974. Even then they had the leg slip in.

My first tour, with 'The Crocodiles' in South Africa, 1974–75.

Ray Illingworth, my captain and mentor at Leicestershire, presents me with my county cap in 1977.

The shot that launched my Test career. My first ball, from Liaqat Ali at Edgbaston in 1978, goes sweetly to the square leg boundary and I am up and running. Well, obviously I didn't have to run for that one but . . .

85 not out, facing Stephen Boock against New Zealand at The Oval in 1978. This landed a couple of feet inside the rope and I then played a risky sweep to a straight ball for the single that gave me my first Test hundred, in my fourth Test.

Plenty of space but few mod cons in the dressing rooms in Pakistan in 1984. The man with the camera is Graham Morris, who has been doing all this as long as I have and even managed to find time in between tours to take my wedding photos.

If you don't get a hundred, it's behind the pavilion and time for the blindfold!

Winning a Test series in India is always special. This trophy took more lifting than the Ashes some months later but marked the end of four months' hard work on one of the most eventful tours of all time, 1984–85.

My 157 at The Oval on the first day of the final Ashes Test in 1985 was one of my top three most satisfying innings. It helped set us up to win the game by an innings and 94 to take the series 3–1.

A pivotal moment at Edgbaston in 1985. Wayne Phillips had been keeping us at bay as we chased victory and only this freak catch stopped him. The ball bounced up off Allan Lamb's boot – he's still hopping here as he appeals – and I did the rest. It was a genuine catch but Allan Border, Australia's captain, has never been able to accept it as such!

There is no hiding when Beefy wants to help you celebrate. This was just the start as the Bollinger flowed following the Ashes success of 1985. I didn't mind the XXXX being poured over me so long as we kept the Bollie for drinking.

Three of the genuine greats of Australian cricket doing their best and for a moment succeeding in keeping me down. Dennis Lillee, Rod Marsh and Greg Chappell.

Well, it seemed a good idea at the time! The T-shirt which I had printed for myself before the Lord's Test in 1986 is ceremoniously passed on to the man who took over as captain immediately after our defeat by India, Mike Gatting.

I'M IN CHARGE..

Another 'it seemed a good idea at the time'. In full flying kit alongside John Morris for the Tiger Moth escapade over Queensland in January 1991. The £1,000 fine was worth it

In among the carnage of another 'blackwash' I did make runs as captain in the Caribbean in 1986 but very few of them would have been like this.

The late Chris Lander was not averse to a little exaggeration in his copy for the *Mirror*. The gist of the story was true, all too true, but the details on this page are somewhat at odds with reality. Still, 'never let the facts spoil a good story' and all that.

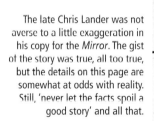

We did make a lovely couple. With Vicki, with whom I shared ten very special years. I've even let her borrow one of my sweaters!

On the ice on the Cresta Run at full-ish speed. Or should that be foolish?

Bollinger on the beach. Peter Doyle always looked after us with huge style at Doyle's at Watson's Bay, Sydney. Rob Hirst supplied the Bollinger for a charity day on the beach there. In attendance here are Philippe and Frances Edmonds and Peter's father, Jack, who founded the eponymous restaurant.

Thorunn and I are poised to celebrate after the 1991 NatWest final, for which I had stood in for Mark Nicholas as captain and thankfully Hampshire had beaten Surrey by four wickets.

Brears, undoubtedly excellent though they both were, did everything right was probably naïve. Rather than simply accept the
decisions of your captain, you are willing to question or even challenge them. I was sometimes accused of captaining by committee,
but when I captained sides I wanted people to come up with ideas,
not just be paid servants or lackeys awaiting instructions. That was
my philosophy then, and I would maintain it is the philosophy of
the England side today.

Botham's view of Brearley was similar. He had been in the side a
year longer than me and was far more self-confident. He was brash
and bullish and very capable of making decisions for himself, but in
Brearley's hands he was malleable. He occasionally needed restrain-
ing and guiding and Brearley did that. Beefy would have had as
much respect for Brearley as he did for anyone save his mentor at
Somerset, Brian Close – an extraordinary character who taught
him one thing above all others, that pain meant nothing. Like me,
Beefy's own thoughts on captaincy, and the idea that there might be
other ways of doing things, were only formulated later.

Brearley was involved in very few clashes. He once had to virtually wheel Geoff Boycott onto the field at Sydney when the pitch
was wet, and had an ongoing battle with Phil Edmonds during my
first tour of Australia, the battlelines for which were drawn by the
skipper administering Phil with a ferocious dressing-down when
Phil showed a reluctance for twelfth man duty in Perth. Phil felt he
should have been playing and was intent on winding up Brearley
– as he liked to wind up most people (today he's doing it to African
governments) – but the real clash was one of intellect, as they
were both high-powered Cambridge graduates. As a mere UCL
dropout, I didn't present the same kind of challenge to Phil and we
got on well, happily sharing rooms on tour. When I became captain
and backed him as our best left-arm spinner for a tour of India, he
did me and England proud. Occasionally he needed sending off to

the boundary to cool down after a frustrating spell, but he would come back in a better frame of mind and do his job. He was no challenge to my authority, and no problem.

The most important advice Brearley gave me during that first year came after I had been bowled by Iqbal Qasim for 56 during my second Test match at Lord's. I'd tried to smear a straight ball on off stump to square leg and missed. It was an appalling shot, made all the more criminal by how well I had played up to that point. Botham later made a century but it was a hundred I should have made. As it happened we won easily but Brearley had some firm but polite words. He didn't expect me to play like Boycott, but he did want me to bat longer and set my sights higher. It had taken him all of two Test matches to identify what would remain, to an extent, my Achilles heel.

Not that I didn't then act on his words with haste. Two games later I scored my first Test century against New Zealand at the Oval, a ground I always loved (and at which I had already made a hundred for England in the one-dayer). It was not a flawless innings but not many maiden centuries are. Like Pakistan, New Zealand were a decent rather than an outstanding side, and to make life easier Richard Hadlee, their best bowler, went off injured after bowling eight overs. I moved to 99 with a straight hit down the ground off Stephen Boock, a slow left-arm spinner with nice flight and drift, then paddle-swept him rather riskily – what would Brearley have said if I'd perished at that point?! – to bring up my hundred.

I soon learned another lesson from Brearley in Australia the next winter, which was that even when you have reached a hundred your job is not necessarily done. He had paid a visit to my room in the build-up to the Test series, reminding me to rein in my shot-making until I'd gauged the conditions and to think in terms of long innings. Again, I took his words on board, making an unbeaten 101 on the opening day of the second Test in Perth in the face of some spicy bowling from Rodney Hogg. It was then that I made my mistake, opting to spend the evening in the Sheraton Hotel bar rather than joining a general excursion to the cinema, which would have proved the more sensible option. What had been intended as one quiet drink turned into several, with locals queuing up to buy me a drink and say, 'Aw, well played, mate.' The suspicion that I might have overdone things slightly was confirmed when I bumped into our physiotherapist Bernard Thomas in the lift and struggled to bid him a coherent good night.

After battling for half an hour the next morning, Hogg had his revenge, coming round the wicket and producing what I will always say was one mighty fine delivery, aimed at middle stump and ending up doing enough off the pitch to hit the off stump. With pace too. As I maintained at the time, and have done ever since, Hogg bowled so well that morning that I wouldn't have fared any better had I gone to bed at 7.30pm with a good book and a cup of Ovaltine. But, unless you are Ian Botham, it is hard to hide it when you've had a few drinks and Brearley duly had a quiet word after I'd returned to the dressing room, suggesting that in future I should take it easy when I was due to bat the next day. I cannot fault that advice and did my best to remember it in most – but I'm afraid to say not in all – instances.

The next time I made a hundred for England, I made it a big one – a double in fact. Funnily enough, I'd recently had a conversation with Chris Old about making really big scores and he'd assured me I'd make one soon. 'Don't worry, you'll get a double one day,' he'd predicted. I was doubtful, saying that I'd never batted the sort of time necessary for such a score. 'You will,' he'd insisted. It happened sooner than perhaps even 'Chilly' (C Old – get it?) anticipated, in the first Test of the series against India following that Australia tour. Edgbaston was always a good batting pitch even in 1981, when no one managed fifty in a freakish game, it remained a good track – and although India's attack looked good on paper, it held little menace in such conditions. Kapil Dev and the left-armer Karsan Ghavri could swing the ball and would cause me problems later in the series; Chandrasekhar and Venkataraghavan were very dangerous bowlers on the dust-bowls of India but on a low, slow featherbed in Birmingham were not so frightening, and between them took none for 220 off 60 overs. My old friend Bishan Bedi was not playing.

While I'd concede not an epoch-making event, I also acquired around this time courtesy of Bob Willis the nickname of 'Lubo'. It actually started out as 'Lulu' after Lulu Sutcliffe, the daughter of Billy Sutcliffe, the Yorkshire captain of the 1950s, and granddaughter of the legendary Herbert. I met Lulu during my first Test match in Leeds and she was gorgeous. I took her out to the casino next door to the Dragonara Hotel where we stayed (and was duly spotted by team-mates) and given the combination of my long blond hair and her being blonde as well, Willis decided that I should be known thereafter as Lulu.

For the Golden Boy of English cricket to be known as Lulu was not quite the manly sobriquet I was looking for, but fortunately it soon underwent a subtle transformation to 'Lubo'. Lubo's Charcoal Grill was a restaurant (actually more of a spit-and-sawdust diner) in Adelaide's notorious Hindley Street, which I and various colleagues from that tour liked to frequent. It served massive steaks covered in garlic, washed down with some South Australian red. You didn't have to worry about choosing from the wine list, there wasn't one. You just drank what they had. As ordinary as Lulu was beautiful, it was at least cheap, cheerful and plentiful, and perfectly suited to our modest daily allowance. On each Australia tour subsequently we would make the pilgrimage to Lubo's, and each time we went the ambience had gone up a notch, with the sawdust giving way to proper flooring, the walls acquiring pictures, tablecloths and a real wine list. Eventually, four or five tours later Lubo's was no longer there. They must have sold up and moved to the hills. Even more sadly, the romance with the lovely Lulu lasted not much longer than my average innings at Northampton.

The other thing I was doing well during my first year in the England side was fielding, creating a hell of a partnership with Derek Randall, one of us patrolling the covers, the other midwicket, switching sides of the wicket depending on whether a right or left-hander was on strike. We loved trying to outdo each other. Randall's style was brilliant. He would start so deep, half-way to the boundary, but come in at such pace that by the time the ball was bowled he'd only be 20 yards from the bat. If someone tried to drop a quick single, he was on it in an instant. I too liked to come in close to cut down the angle.

Botham, Brearley and Graham Roope were great in the slips but as outfielders Randall and I were the best in the team and, even if I say so myself, there would be few to equal us today. I ran out Robert Anderson of New Zealand at Trent Bridge with an under-arm throw from mid off with only one stump to aim at and in the first over of the Ashes in Brisbane performed a similar manoeuvre from cover to run out Gary Cosier. There were lapses too, and I put down the occasional catch at mid on, but some of the catches I took on my first tour of Australia were among the best of my career, including one at Adelaide off Bruce Yardley taken at cover, airborne, horizontal and at full stretch. When catches like that stick, there are few better feelings.

Looking back now, it was inevitable, I suppose, that the wheels would come off at some point. Perhaps I had fallen into the trap of believing I was bullet-proof. Perhaps I was affected by the Golden Boy image without realising it. Maybe all those lazy assumptions people held that batting was effortless and easy for me were bound to affect my thinking at some stage. Nor could the game remain uncomplicated in my mind forever, and when the doubts crept in I had to deal with them on a public stage, which was never going to be easy.

Various factors were at work. With the Packer split at an end, the authorities were keen for full-strength England and Australia sides to rejoin battle, a fair enough sentiment, and it meant us touring Down Under for the second time in a year, which, on the face of it, sounded like a great opportunity and the perfect excuse to get straight back to Oz. There would be the challenge of playing against the best of the Aussies, the Chappells, Lillee, Marsh and we were keen to show that we could beat them as we had beaten the so-called second string the previous winter. There was also a one-off Test in India, the Jubilee Test, tagged onto the return trip home. Unfortunately, it was to prove easily the worst of my five tours of Australia, with only one innings of any note to my name, that 98 not out in the Sydney Test, but even that innings had needed several warehouses worth of good fortune for me to get through the first 40 runs or so.

While it hardly compared with the crisis that would afflict me in England in 1991, it was a sufficiently serious situation that I walked out to the middle in a Boxing Day ODI in Sydney utterly convinced I was wasting my time. So sure was I that I wouldn't score runs it occurred to me that I might as well head back to the pavilion there and then and save everyone the bother. My instincts were not wrong: I was caught behind off Rodney Hogg for two off the twelfth ball I faced. I had lost track of what my feet were doing, where my hands were going, what my bat was doing.

Things went so badly that I would have happily taken advice from any quarter and when Geoff Boycott, the master technician himself, appeared ready to put me right on that tour I would have been mad not to listen. Unfortunately he decided against sharing what he knew. I'd popped into his room to get him to sign some autograph sheets during the Test in India, when he looked up at me and said, 'I can tell thee what tha's doing wrong, tha knows . . . But I'm not going to.'

It was the first time things had really gone wrong and when I was eventually dropped by England – after the first Test against West Indies at home in 1980 – things did not at first get any easier. Even though I was assured by Alec Bedser, the chairman of selectors, that the demotion would only be temporary, my confidence took a knock. The rejection hurt and it was self-evident that I wasn't going to get back into the side until I'd put right what was wrong, but I was simply not in the right frame of mind to do so.

By leaving the Test stage for the county arena, your world changes dramatically – you are no longer on the stage of the Old Vic, but in Rep in Weston-super-Mare, and it takes time to adjust. Ultimately, you have no choice but to face down your demons and get some runs, but until you do your mood remains pretty low. I sat out all of the remaining four Tests of that series. It was a pretty depressing time.

The first question to address was: what was it I needed to do? This is what everyone who finds themselves in such a situation asks, and it happens to even the best at some stage or other – even Denis Compton averaged 7.5 on an Ashes tour, and Greg Chappell once collected seven ducks in 15 innings for Australia.

I knew my game had got out of sync but I was reluctant to make radical changes. There were plenty of critics reckoning I should cut out certain strokes that were getting me into trouble, but I knew these same shots brought plenty of runs, and I was not going to give them up in a misguided attempt to become the kind of grafter that was utterly alien to my nature. Boycott never tried to acquire my shots and I wasn't keen on mimicking his mindset. I simply didn't think it would work.

That things came right again in the end without me undertaking massive changes to the way I played was crucial. It convinced me in later times when runs were hard to come by not to act hastily but trust my game and my instincts, however much the armchair critics might have been shaking their heads asking, 'Why, oh why, will this blighter Gower never learn?' To my mind, I had learned, and what I'd learned was what worked best for me.

There has been a similar debate in recent times about Kevin Pietersen, who seems to share a talent for getting out in ways that infuriate the pundits. I'm sure he would say – indeed, he *has* said – that the shots which get him out also bring him hundreds of runs. He's a risk-taker but a bloody good one. Often the gambles work, sometimes they don't. He appears to reckon, as I did, that this is a fair trade-off.

I had from the outset had problems going back to Leicestershire between England games and performing satisfactorily, so perhaps it was unsurprising that it took a little time to put matters right when I had what turned into an extended run back in county cricket. As early as my first season as an England player in 1978, *Wisden* had commented on my relative lack of success during return visits to my county, stating: 'Many rued the variable form of Gower . . . much of [his best] was saved for England . . . His return to the bread and butter part of the game probably was as difficult for him as the transition from county to international level . . . too many expected too much too soon and he tried too hard to oblige.'

This was an issue that ran throughout my career. As England players employed first and foremost by our counties, we were expected to rejoin our counties as a matter of course the day after a Test finished, sometimes for a championship match but occasionally for an even more tiring 60-overs-a-side Gillette Cup or, in its next incarnation, NatWest Trophy game. There was little recovery time and this made the schedule during a home season even more demanding than being on tour. Generally, there was a rhythm to a tour which I liked, with a decent balance between matches and days off, which is exactly what today's centrally contracted players enjoy during home seasons now, even if modern tours would appear to be more intense, if shorter. I generally found touring interesting and fun, and even the two long tours of India, which involved some pretty average cricket against local sides in some less than salubrious venues and hotels, provided some extraordinary experiences which I treasure. For what they're worth, the figures support the view that I fared better in a touring environment, as I averaged 46.1 in Tests overseas and 42.8 at home.

For this reason, I would have killed to have played under the central contracts system we have today. I wouldn't have wanted to duck out of county cricket completely but having the odd game off between Tests would have been a massive boost. It's hard to explain to people at large, but if you have just gone through the emotional demands of a Test match, and must then drag yourself onto the field the following morning having driven halfway across the country, you just feel very weary. It's as simple as that. It's damn hard to leap out of bed crying, 'Oh joy, another day . . .' I could have escaped the county versus touring team fixtures that used to be so important to the coffers of the county clubs but were such an ordeal if you were an England player desperate for down-time.

Whenever a visit to Grace Road by a touring team was imminent, Mike Turner used to say to me, 'Don't even think about it . . . you're playing.' Having an England player turn out was a key part of his marketing strategy for games that still had the capacity in those days to bring in money. The same three-line whip operated when I moved to Hampshire. Named to play against the Sri Lankans but unenthused to do so, I tried to conjure some enthusiasm from thin air as I walked to the crease to face an off-spinner of whom I had never heard of then and will never hear of again. Rather than play myself in, as per the MCC coaching manual, I opted to attack the first ball from down the pitch and succeeded only in presenting the unknown off-spinner with a caught and bowled. He was happy enough but the man in the box in the old grandstand, who had paid to entertain his friends with the chance to see me bat for a while with my reputed skill was decidedly unhappy. He launched into a tirade along the lines of, 'I didn't pay all this money to watch that kind of s***.' To which I replied, 'You come down here and tell me that.' And he did. We actually had a fair and frank exchange of views and parted friends and, after all, he had a point, and it is the same point that Mike Turner would have made to me at Leicester, which is that we are all in the entertainment business. The fact is I could forget that at times like this and although it is not an easy thing to explain to anyone, let alone yourself, why you as a professional sportsman would not be ready and willing to entertain each and every day you are out there, the other fact is that for most of us it does happen that way. It is the human element.

It was long obvious to me that England players played a little too much and when I sat on the committee that produced the Acfield Report in 1996 we recommended that the England team should be more the primary focus of English cricket, and that the vested interests of the counties should be discarded, views that Ian MacLaurin took on board when he became chairman of the ECB the following year.

While I would have loved working in a system which made play-ing for England so much more special, I'm not naïve enough to think this would have made me a different animal. If it is in your genetic make-up not to get up for every match, then that trait won't go away just because you only play for England; it will just manifest itself in the midst of Test matches or one-day internation-als, as perhaps Kevin Pietersen again best demonstrates. He got to the stage where he struggled to raise himself for ODIs, eventually telling the ECB he could not bear to carry on playing them (I know how he felt). Alastair Cook doesn't have the aura of a superstar but he has the figures of one and that is in part down to his tenacity: he *is* able to get himself up for every game. Graham Gooch, as Cook's principal batting coach and mentor, may have had something to do with that but I would maintain that essentially it is something that must come from within.

Although my loss of form in 1979–80 marked new territory, I had gone through a lean patch in the first half of the 1979 season, around the time of my first anniversary as an England player. Then, my frustration had surfaced while playing for Leicestershire against the Indians in precisely the kind of contest I found so hard to get enthusiastic about later in my career. I cannot claim that this was an issue so early in my career, as I should and would have been keen to play and keen to learn against anyone. This was more a case of not being sure why things were going wrong and how to sort it out. It was a simple but confusing loss of form that I had to deal with. No more than that. The frustration showed when after failing in the first innings I smashed down the stumps with my bat, a most uncharacteristic response for me. I immediately knew my actions were wrong, and I can't say for sure whether I felt any better for this show of petulance or if I felt any release with the fuse pinging in that way. In fact Jon Holmes, my agent, was pleased that I had reacted in this way as he said it showed I cared, not something that was always apparent from my demeanour. Jon always reckoned my insouciant air was a way of hiding disappointments, and he had a point, but if so it failed on this occasion.

Dennis Lillee got me out six times during the Australia tour but he wasn't the root cause of my problems. I just felt generally out of nick in the way I described in that Boxing Day game. In the next Test I moved down to number six, as low a position as I'd occupied for England up to that point, and was bowled by Greg Chappell of all people. It was not a bad ball but I made it look a lot better with the expansive shot I attempted. It was in the second innings of that game – when I actually batted at No.7 because we used a nightwatchman – that I scored my sow's-ear-to-silk-purse 98 not out. It was the only time I was to get anywhere near a hundred on the tour.

Getting out to Lillee so often was more of a statistic than a problem, although he did work away at me on off stump, which was an area bowlers had identified as a possible area of weakness. It's hardly surprising – you could say the same about virtually all left-handers who have ever played the game! It may have been a chink in my armour but I scored plenty of runs through point and backward point and that was why there was no question in my mind of radical change. I just needed to acquire more discretion, especially in Australia where the bouncier pitches meant I was liable to give the bowlers more of a chance. During that innings of 98 at Sydney, I smacked Lillee to the cover boundary a few times, but in the early stages it was back foot, whoosh, miss . . . back foot, nick, over the slips, four. When I got my shot just right, I'd carve the ball for four and it would be bouncing off the boundary boards in a flash, but when I didn't life could be bloody interesting. Mind you, I always felt that the fielders would have to be sharp to catch it. I would get some awful looks from Dennis, who was never anything but nakedly aggressive, but I would just shrug my shoulders and proffer a sheepish apology.

He also tested me with the short ball after I was out to him hooking during the state match against Western Australia at the WACA at the start of the tour, caught on the boundary having made good contact – although whether you miscue it straight up or smash it straight down long leg's throat it is still the same thing in the book: caught and out.

Lillee was a wonderful sight with his long hair, long run-up, and a great action that propelled him well down the pitch (hence the opportunity if not necessity to say, 'Well bowled, Dennis' when he beat you all ends up). He was stimulating to bat against, one of the game's great characters, and definitely among the top three fast bowlers I ever faced. As I've said before, you have to earn the high opinion of Australians, but I think Dennis and I came to regard each other with mutual respect. It was interesting, I think, that he was of the opinion that had I tried to play a more cautious game I would not have fared any better. He was a good friend and a great rival.

Back in England, my luck was out. On the eve of facing the West Indies, I collected a pair against Tim Lamb at Northampton (no surprise, there), and in the Test at Trent Bridge which triggered my dropping I not only didn't get many runs but also put down a crucial catch in a game lost by only two wickets. Beefy has reminded me ever since that we might have won that series had I caught Andy Roberts when West Indies still needed 13 to win (this was the only Test in the series to produce a positive result), not least because he was England captain and would probably have lasted longer in the job had the result been different! Perhaps if I'd been playing better with the bat I would have taken the catch, although I too have kept reminding Beefy how tricky it was – I had to run back and try to take it as it came over my shoulder – and not many in that England side would have been quick enough to even get a hand on it. But I was mortified because I'd already taken a couple of similar catches that season. Nor did it help that Nottinghamshire's favourite son, Derek Randall, who had recently been dropped from the England side himself, was such a brilliant fielder. The Trent Bridge faithful, who loved to hate me as the southern dilettante (well Leicester is technically south of Nottingham) keeping the local hero out of the side, didn't fail to let me know that Randall would have caught it. When I went back to Nottingham for a championship match later that year, I was booed relentlessly for three days by a small but highly vocal section in the Fox Road Stand.

As I say, I found being out of the England side pretty disheartening. Friends urged me to keep going and not lose faith, but it

101

proved hard going. Jon Holmes gave me a pep talk over dinner one night and I responded with a hundred the next day against Derbyshire, but my form did not really pick up until mid-August, setting up a recall for the Centenary Test against Australia. An important step in my rehabilitation came from a surprising source when Fred Rumsey, the former Somerset and England bowler and a man who took a paternal interest in my progress, arranged for me to have dinner with Greg Chappell, the Australia captain, a few days before that Lord's showpiece. Greg's advice was not to listen to the critics because I'd proved I could score runs at the highest level, but focus on batting time because if I stayed in the runs would come. He also made it clear that basically no one could really help me except myself. One interestingly technical revelation was that he always started an innings deliberately trying to play with the inside half of the bat, thereby covering any slight away-swing. It's not a theory I'd heard before, let alone thought of, nor did I try and adopt it in practice, sticking to my innate belief that the middle of the bat was always there somewhere and I might as well try and find it. However, they were sound words, generously given.

I understood why I had been dropped and if I had been my captain, I'd have dropped myself. I needed to go away and rebuild confidence, learn to be tougher and more realistic in my approach. It certainly didn't do me any harm in the long run. Indeed, what pleased me was that when I next visited Australia three years later, I had one of my best tours, scoring 441 runs in the Tests. To me, that showed I'd improved.

5

THE SUMMER OF '81

It was on what I viewed as my comeback tour of the West Indies in 1981 that I played one of my most satisfying innings to save a Test in Jamaica. It was a personal breakthrough of sorts, not only because it was my first hundred for almost two years, but because in a situation in which we needed to bat a long time against a strong attack to secure the draw, I was the one who got my head down and saw to it that the job was done. I was at the crease for almost eight hours for an unbeaten 154 – a most un-Gowerlike display I know, but that only made me cherish it all the more.

It certainly revived me after my troubles of the previous year and, I believe, set me up for the future. A few months later, I was dropped for one Test at the end of the Ashes series but fortunately that proved only a temporary blip. I was still taken on the next winter tour and from then on stayed in the side for five years without a break. So that game in Jamaica was a big turning point. To my mind, it paved the way for the good days that followed.

It was a tough tour for many reasons. The death of Ken Barrington, our assistant manager, who died of a heart attack in Barbados, was a terrible tragedy and a big blow in particular to Ian Botham, our new captain, who regarded Ken as something of a father figure. Beefy himself unsurprisingly found it difficult to maintain his amazing form against such a powerful side as West Indies. We also had political shenanigans surrounding what was meant to be the second Test in Guyana, resulting in its cancellation. In the light of subsequent events – over the next three series the scoreline was to read England 0, West Indies 14 – we did well to save two of the four games that were played, even if rain did help our cause a little.

Having faced the mighty West Indies pace attack in only one previous Test, on an early season pitch at Trent Bridge, the whole series represented a big challenge for me, as well as a huge adrenaline rush. Many good judges argue – as I would – that there has been no better bowling line-up in modern times than this one, unless it is other West Indies ones of similar vintage. The only challengers would be the next generation of Australians with Glenn McGrath and Shane Warne at their peak. Many have said to me that the West Indies did not have a Warne to round off and balance their attack but my response is always the same; they simply did not need one. Unrelenting pace, and quality pace at that, might seem repetitive from the stands but it is the toughest to bat against.

I'd gone to the Caribbean with a new bat and a new attitude and generally things went well. But up until the last match of the series in Jamaica I'd played well and got some good starts without making a big score. It was very frustrating. In Trinidad, I'd batted three and a half hours in the first innings for 48 and two hours in the second before I was caught down the leg side off Andy Roberts – always an irritating way to get out. In Barbados, on a pitch with more pace and bounce, I'd shared an attacking partnership of 120 with Graham Gooch before getting out to Viv Richards's off-spin – which was an even more irritating way to end (especially when Geoff Boycott greeted me with a cheery, 'I knew tha' was going to do that'). That was an innings I really enjoyed because it felt we were meeting the challenge head on: it was one of the few passages of play that felt like a real contest and it was everything I'd wanted it to be – apart from a hundred.

By the time we got to Jamaica, there had been some criticism of my failure to kick on – I think Clive Lloyd, the West Indies captain, had alluded to it – but I didn't need anyone telling me. I wouldn't exactly say that I'd let the side down but it could have been better.

Of course, facing the West Indies quick men en masse was a very different proposition from dealing with any other attack. Save for the occasional intervention from someone like Viv, there were four nasty fast bowlers bearing down on you all day, a discernibly tougher proposition than facing them as individuals in a county attack. It was not insolubly quick bowling but you had to get through it all to realise you could in fact cope. Until you had done it, you couldn't help wondering whether it was going to lead to a broken rib or a cracked head.

Colin Croft, who took 24 wickets in that series, was very awkward. He had an extraordinary, open-chested action, and most sightscreens in the Caribbean weren't high enough (or more often, wide enough) for his arm, so getting a sight of the ball was doubly difficult. He could be very sharp when he wanted to be. But I had it relatively easy: his angled-in leg-cutters were most lethal to right-handers.

Michael Holding was consistently the quickest. He would bowl balls that you thought you could defend in front of your chest only to find they were still climbing as they reached you, and they would end up taking the shoulder of the bat and flying over third slip. There are only a small number of balls in my career that I reckon I've not yet seen and a Holding bouncer at Trinidad in that series was one of them. Even though it was a slow pitch, Mikey, patience well and truly lost, unleashed a bouncer that he had to bang in down his end of the pitch to get it up around head height. It was so short I never picked it up. Sensing it rather than seeing it,

I staggered back and evaded it by a distance, though I nearly trod on my stumps in the process.

Andy Roberts of course I'd known about for a long time through county cricket. When as a youngster you see seasoned pros looking anxious you know that here is someone out of the ordinary. A lot has been said over the years about his tricks of the trade – the cross-seam grip, the fast bouncer, the slow bouncer – which I did not appreciate at the time, but what I did know was what an impressive individual he was when he joined us at Leicestershire later that year. He was so sharp. The really good bowlers are intelligent and clever and know how to set people up, and Andy was definitely one of those.

Malcolm Marshall, who I've already talked about from our duels as youngsters, wasn't in the side at the start of that series. He was still making his way but when fully fledged was quite brilliant. He swung the ball and knew how and when to adjust to different pitch conditions, when to pitch it up and when to bounce it, all skills he honed during his upbringing at Hampshire. He was a complete bowler as well as a great bloke – and possibly the best of all. I faced him in the opening game of that tour and scored a hundred, but I'd admit I was the beneficiary of several chances.

As for Joel Garner . . . how the hell did you play Joel? Six feet eight inches in his stockinged feet and with long arms to match, his length ball came at you at waist height, and he had a deadly yorker. He may have looked like a lumbering giant but it was something of an optical illusion. With the leverage he got from that great height, he could be very quick. And he bowled next to nothing that was loose.

Formidable though all these men were, my most painful experience at the hands of a West Indian fast bowler came from someone I never encountered in Test cricket, Sylvester Clarke. He could be very rapid on his day and, as with Mikey, bowled me some deliveries I never quite saw. Playing for Surrey he bowled me a ball at the Oval in 1984 that I started to defend only to realise that it was still climbing. As I tried to get my hands underneath it, the ball caught my thumb (which I had carelessly left sticking out) and took the rubber off the end of the glove and my thumb-nail with it. Ouch! At least there was no need to rip off the glove to check the damage. Not that the Surrey boys were remotely sympathetic. The ball had flown to third slip and, as they kindly pointed out, I was out and in a position to survey the damage in the comfort of the pavilion.

On another visit to the Oval, I pulled him one bounce for four to the square leg boundary, managed to avoid the Clarke stare as he followed through, and prepared for the next ball. It was pretty much the same length as the previous one but, without the action changing much, suitably quicker. I got in position to repeat the shot but the ball seemed to be thudding into the keeper's gloves having passed me at head height before the bat was anywhere near it.

You need things to run for you against such bowlers and they did in Jamaica, where rain cut three hours off the fourth day and a strained rib ruled Marshall out of the later stages. It was a mighty task facing us on the fourth morning when we were 32 for three – still 125 behind – with Gooch, Athey and Boycott all gone. These were big wickets. Boycott had saved the previous Test in Antigua by indulging in his favourite hobby of batting all day while Gooch had played brilliantly in the first innings, really getting stuck into Croft especially on a pitch which in the early stages had a bit of moisture within but which flattened out to become a beauty, albeit quick and bouncy. Unfortunately, his 153 had been a lone hand in a team score of 285. Infuriatingly Croft had bowled me behind my legs.

In the second innings I walked out to bat feeling better than at any stage of the tour and was absolutely determined not to miss out on my last chance for a big score. I was so determined in fact that I talked to myself more during that innings than any other, urging myself to keep going and not give my wicket away. I'd never talked to anyone that much before – ever! It was a rigorous and vigorous process, and in itself fairly exhausting, but it was something I felt I needed to do. I think it proves that there was a little more steel within me than I showed. I had a long partnership with Peter Willey, always a good man in a crisis, but even after he fell an hour into the last day, and even after I had reached a hundred, I kept on at myself, knowing the job was not done. It was only after I'd got through the second new ball in company with Paul Downton, who batted heroically through the last two sessions, that I felt we could breathe more easily.

I used to find it frustrating playing blocking innings but even I would acknowledge that sometimes it was required. To someone like Boycott, whose philosophy was to never get out, I was viewed as a wastrel who started an innings as though I had already got 30 to my name before I'd done the hard graft of getting my eye in. Perhaps because he was in such close proximity, some of his seriousness rubbed off on me when we were batting together, and we shared some fairly lengthy partnerships. His presence gave me a subconscious feeling of security. Although there were a few bizarre occasions – such as the one in India – where he opted not to pass on advice, he was usually a very useful person to talk to and a great analyser of a situation. The major drawback to batting with him was that you had to be ready when he thought a quick run was in the offing – one for him, of course (he had done me in cold blood against Jamaica just before this Test match). Despite his reservations about my casual approach, he used to say he'd like to be able to bat like me. I am happy to take him at his word on that!

Whenever I came in for criticism in my early days I was invariably compared unfavourably to Boycott. Why could I not be as single-minded as he was? The same argument was later applied in relation to Gooch. They in effect talked to themselves through every innings, steeled to avoid any mistake.

If talking to myself worked so well in Jamaica, why did I not try it more often? All I can say is that it was not my style. I found it hard to be bloody-minded all the time and the figures simply did not mean enough for me to try. It would have been too much. Should I have been able to work out for myself how to perform at my best? Yes, but that's not the person I was. Ironically, in this second career of mine as a broadcaster, the balance, I like to think, has veered more towards professionalism but admittedly with the odd lapse and with the proviso that it is still meant to be fun. It suits me beautifully to keep it that way.

The summer of 1981 was of course the summer of Beefy. Amazing though some of Ian's feats were, the idea that he won the Ashes single-handedly that year was something of a myth. Although we would undoubtedly have come second without him, one should pay full tribute to the vital contributions from others such as Bob Willis, Chris Tavare and John Emburey to assist in the tipping of the series on its head, but IT Botham did the most important, eye-catching bits. Beefy lost the captaincy but found paradise, and for a long time after that it seemed to most people including himself that there was nothing he could not do.

Ian was absolutely full-on in those days. He was a hugely charismatic figure, truly bumptious in and out of the dressing room. He was literally unstoppable: physically at or near his peak, he was never injured during this period (or if he was, he played through whatever niggles were affecting him). Nor did he show any sign of weakness. He has always insisted that he did not have insecurities but even he must have had the odd doubt flit in and out of his mind at the start of that series when nothing went his way. That day he walked back through the Long Room at Lord's to absolute silence from the members would have hurt and would remain in his memory for ever. If there were doubts then, I would say he hid them well. It was a great trick to master. When he gave up the captaincy and freed up his mind and when the circumstances presented themselves at Headingley for him to play not necessarily the best but the most iconic innings of his life, the results were simply awesome to behold.

The story of Headingley has been told so many times it has attained the status of legend. The excellent documentary that told the tale again on its 30th anniversary reminded us all of various things that had maybe slipped our minds in the interim. For one thing, I confess I had forgotten that there was a political backdrop to all this with the miners threatening to strike and the country in some low dudgeon. In other words, for us to lose to Australia would have merely added to the mood of general depression whereas the miraculous escape at Headingley and the subsequent wins at Edgbaston and Old Trafford were enough to raise the spirits of at least the cricket-loving public.

Even with Mike Brearley back at the helm, that game at Headingley still did not go to plan. How we let the Aussies get 400, God only knows, though *Wisden* gives us clues, referring to dropped catches from Botham and Gower in saying that 'England . . . suffered for their ineptitude in the field'. This was Headingley under cloud cover and we all know what that meant in that era: uneven bounce and movement for the seamers. It is certainly what I recall from my innings in the game. One ball from Geoff Lawson rose from a length to hit me in the armpit and not for the first time in my career I had a feeling that I might be keeping the slips interested.

By the Saturday night we were staring defeat in the face but, no worries, with the rest day now due there was a party at Beefy's to help take our minds off it all. In those days he and Kath were living at Epworth, an hour or so from Leeds, and we headed there as soon as we could after play had finished for the day. I vaguely – that's the best I can do – remember finding myself in the front row of a rugby scrum by the beer tent at one point thinking 'what the f*** am I doing?' and then it was dawn and time for a quick kip. A couple of pints in the pub at lunch with Beefy in full flow and it was time to head back to Leeds.

Ian's innings was just outrageous and utterly fearless. Even so, the ball was still doing things and with Dennis Lillee, Terry Alderman and Lawson it did seem just a matter of time before someone played the part of the vet and administered the lethal injection. Somehow Beefy, as the boisterous puppy, continued to elude the vet's attentions and although his 149 not out was the headline, one should never forget the hand played by Graham Dilley who helped him add 117 for the eighth wicket or Chris Old's part in adding 67 for the ninth. With everyone checked back into the hotel rooms vacated in anticipation that morning, the stage was set the following morning for the 'Goose', Bob Willis, to play his part.

Forget the story of Lillee and Rod Marsh putting a bet on England at 500–1. While accepting that betting against your own team is never to be recommended or condoned, those odds were irresistible to anyone who has ever placed a bet on anything! I can tell you that there is no bone in either of their bodies that would not have been trying to win that game and I daresay that up until the final moments neither would have considered defeat as possible.

The key move on Brearley's part was switching Willis to the Kirkstall Lane End. Goose stayed in his trance as the wickets kept coming, wheeling away from every celebration in a great, energised arc and remaining as pumped up as I had ever seen him for a long time even after the game was won.

For the rest of us, it was an edgy time to say the least. There was a nervy atmosphere around the ground as events unfolded, noisy as the wickets fell but deathly quiet in between. In the field one was aware that any mistake could cost us the game but that was in its own way exhilarating. It would have been worse for those in the dressing room, who were powerless to contribute. In contrast to the first innings the catches stuck and when the final wicket fell it was just a whirl of frenzied, disbelieving celebration.

Whatever our commitments the following day, and I was due to be playing a NatWest Trophy match against Surrey at the Oval (which thankfully was washed out by rain that next day), we were going to stay to continue those celebrations for a while. The tricky thing was that all the champagne was already on ice in the Aussie dressing room. We sent our young dressing room attendant in to ask for it back, and although he was given understandably short shrift initially it did make its way into the victors' hands and down our throats before the M1 beckoned.

From then on Ian was in his element. Kim Hughes's team did not lie down – far from it – and indeed they should have won the next Test at Edgbaston and thus gone 2–1 up in the series but for Ian's final spell with the ball, a last throw of the die from Brearley, which saw Beefy take five for one in 28 deliveries.

At Old Trafford, Ian's 118 in the second innings was technically a better knock than his Headingley tour de force and just as thrilling. The Ashes were Beefy's and England's.

As events unfolded during the series – and let us not forget that all too often we were up against it in those matches before another Botham miracle got us over the line – we were riding that clichéd rollercoaster of emotions. The thrill and the joy of victory was usually tempered by sheer relief. Only as the dust settled did we really begin to realise that we had actually been involved in something incredibly special – for some extraordinary reason the public seemed to rather enjoy what we had done and the reflected kudos was there for all of us to bask in.

Cricket became mainstream, but by today's standards that albeit welcome reaction to our success was relatively low key. Compare the celebrations to the 2005 Ashes and you quickly get the drift. There was no open-top bus parade through London or any massive

Trafalgar Square gathering. I have to say I thoroughly enjoyed the 2005 jamboree, and being at the centre of that day in Trafalgar Square as one of the comperes on the stage with 10,000 people in front of us, the atmosphere was simply stunning. It matched the buzz one gets from walking out to bat in a Test at Lord's, though what you don't have to do in a Test at Lord's is assess in an instant just how paralytically drunk Andrew Flintoff is and therefore how to phrase a question to him that might just elicit a cogent answer. Somehow, and I don't know how he did it, Andrew, despite his acknowledged all-night bender, managed to come up with enough words in about the right order to give the crowd yet more to cheer.

In 1981, we just went back to our counties and finished off the season. In years to come the legend of '81 would grow and the stories would be retold time and time again. If ever an England team, as was all too often the case, found itself in trouble, then 1981 would be evoked, but seldom with the same results. The game went back to its normal pattern of ups and downs, and in the next few Ashes series the little urn went back and forth, as it had done for 100 years. What of course made 2005 so special was that it followed an unusually long period of total Australian dominance.

What Ian did in 1981 was transform not only a series against Australia but his own commercial potential. The marketing men began to see him as a prize in a way that other players – myself included – were not. The money in cricket had improved a lot since Kerry Packer's arrival in 1977 but it was still relatively small beer. Thanks to Beefy's heroics, that now changed – mainly for him, though perhaps his celebrity drove things forward for the rest of us as well. If anyone was looking to do a deal with a cricketer – and after 1981 maybe more of them were – Ian was well out at the front of the queue. This reached its height with the involvement of Tim Hudson, a cricket nut whose entire reputation rested on his former career as a Los Angeles disc jockey, and whose wealth derived mostly from his wife Maxi's business acumen. He somehow convinced Botham that he could transform his earning power on both sides of the pond. Er, he couldn't. That episode showed the fun and flamboyance of Beefy but the highlighted hair, multi-coloured jackets and the faux country-house cricket matches at Birtles Bowl, quickly proved an unhelpful distraction.

For me personally, the 1981 Ashes changed very little because I was hardly a major performer. I played in the first five Tests, so witnessed at first hand the drama of three famous England victories, but apart from scoring 89 at Lord's I did little of note except show a penchant for getting out in the twenties (I did it six times). The pitches favoured the bowlers a fair bit. The ball nibbled around quite a lot and I was batting, as I felt it, out of position at three. Although it became my favourite place to bat later, in this series it felt like an experiment and that seemed to affect the way I batted. So batting was not always easy, and Lillee, Alderman and Lawson were quite handy in those conditions, but I didn't get down about it because for once I was making runs in county cricket. I probably thought a score for England was just around the corner.

Within a few months, I was to be in need of a good commercial adviser. Fortunately, I had just the person in Jon Holmes, who was my agent then as he is now. I was put onto Jon by Mike Turner at Leicestershire who, at around the time I was starting with England, thought he would be the ideal person for me. As I have said, Mike took a very paternal interest in my welfare, and I think he wanted to put me on to someone who would take a broader view of my interests than just spiv the occasional kit deal (which in those days was pretty much all that was available). Jon, who had briefly been a journalist, was working for a financial adviser in Leicester and had just set up his own sports management business on the side. At the time he met me he had just one client, goalkeeper Peter Shilton, who lived in Jon's neck of the woods around Nottingham.

Jon has always been very convincing and very sensible and I'm proud that we've stuck together so long. As a sportsman there's a temptation to chase the dollar and keep questioning your agent as to why he hasn't got you more work, but thankfully we haven't operated like that.

Jon never once went to Mike Turner and said you're not paying David enough and, to my discredit, nor did I. I was naively happy with my lot. In any case, after three years playing for England, I didn't feel as though I could go making demands of Leicestershire. You can imagine a Phil Edmonds, who loves a deal, saying to Middlesex, 'I assume you're using me to market your club. What are you prepared to give me?' Stupidly, naively, nicely, I never got round to that. As far as I was concerned, things were good. I had somewhere to live, was living within my means, and enjoying my cricket. After I became an England player, whenever I was back at Leicester there would have been enough solid professional souls to keep me firmly grounded and I had no intention of setting myself apart from them in any case. I had never heard of things like image rights — I cannot even be sure the term had been invented then — but there is no way I would have gone to the club asking for more money on the grounds that I was an asset to them in marketing terms and should be rewarded as such. Asking for extra pay while your senior colleagues remained on less would have seemed wrong and could possibly have become divisive. So, in an involuntary, unconscious way, it probably suited me the way things were.

The abiding principal with Jon was that I would play the cricket and he would do what he could behind the scenes in terms of finding decent contracts. We did some deals that were pretty good by the standards of the day. We had a good relationship with bat-makers Gray-Nicolls, where my liaison was primarily with Jock Livingston, who would always be there to welcome me to the

Robertsbridge factory with a selection of great 'made to measure' bats from which to choose the ones I hoped would be properly productive for that season. We did a deal with Patrick at a time when boots were things even the top players were expected to buy themselves and tied up with Sondico for pads and gloves. Lyle & Scott pitched in with those distinctive golfing sweaters in the purest cashmere. It was a shame that my golf never matched the quality of the knitwear. Indeed one day I was invited to play with the Gray-Nicolls team, including Jock and the father figure of the firm literally, John Gray, and turned up thinking I could at least look the part. We began at the short ninth, a par three, and as I prepared for my first tee shot, I was aware that members of the golf society who had just finished their round were all watching from the picture window of the clubhouse. To a man they seemed to think it was hilarious that the tee shot popped a mere 20 yards into the rough, though one of them did recover in time to notice that the hastily played recovery shot did actually make it to the green, where I probably three-putted!

There was a watch deal with Ebel – I still have that timelessly (excuse the term, it kept perfect time) elegant timepiece to this day. Eventually we did a deal under the revived brand name Open Championship (I think Kenny Barrington had once endorsed the name for his whites), which brought bats, pads, gloves and cricket clothing all together into one contract.

Sponsored cars became the norm. Beefy had his deal with Saab and on one track day at Thruxton managed to roll two of them, walking away unscathed and undaunted both times. Saab were delighted – it just proved how strong and safe their cars were! I went through an assortment of vehicles from local garages. One time a local Mitsubishi dealer provided one with my name plastered on the side in sticky letters, which those of mischievous disposition would rearrange. After the end-of-season party that year during the final away match at Canterbury, it took me a few days to notice that my car was being driven by someone called 'avid rewog'.

The great thing was that Jon was a genuine sports fan who wanted to help. He was not just thinking of his cut – not that he took a huge cut, certainly nothing like the 33 per cent some of the big marketing companies in other sports like to extract from their clients. Jon's involvement in football taught him how to negotiate and to know what a good deal was, but first and foremost he was a mate, who was there as a sounding board, on the social side of things as well as in business. When I was going through a thin patch, he'd be there over dinner urging me to score runs.

It was on Jon's advice that I resisted joining a rebel tour of South Africa in 1982. The idea was for a team of English players to go there at the end of an India tour and the money I was offered looked very attractive – in the region of £50,000 for a month's work compared to around £10,000 for four months in India – and there had been surreptitious talk about it among the players for some time. I think the first tentative offer had been made during the West Indies tour and by the early weeks of India the whole scheme was gaining momentum. The feeling was that there was nothing the TCCB could do to touch us if we did decide to go. In those days before central contracts, we were free agents (or thought we were) during the winter months when we were not involved in an official tour.

I never got as far as committing myself to going but in purely monetary terms it was highly tempting. I'd done that tour of South Africa as a schoolboy and had an enormous amount of fun. My memories of the place were only positive. When we arrived, we weren't given leaflets outlining the iniquities of apartheid: 'By the way, this is how we do things here. You might not like it but we think it works for us.' So when you get an offer to go and play there again, and for very decent money, you are going to consider it. As a young sportsman you do have an insulated view of the world. I can't think of any English cricketer I knew whose first reaction would have been, 'You must be joking. It's an abhorrent regime. We're not going anywhere near the place. Human Rights is the most important thing in the world. I will not even consider it.' Even if you had a deep understanding of apartheid, there was always the argument that sport may be the way to break down the barriers.

That said, alarms did begin to ring for me. We only had to cast our minds back to the Jackman Affair in the West Indies the previous winter to know how highly charged an issue South Africa was. By the time of the first Test in Bangalore, Boycott (who was one of the chief orchestrators and on a mission to recruit as many good players as he could) wanted to know who was in or out. I phoned Jon and told him what was happening. The whole matter was of course highly secret and we hoodwinked the team management – including Keith Fletcher, the captain, who was the only player who did not know what was going on because he'd have been duty bound to tell the authorities – by setting up a bogus chess club as cover for our meetings, a ruse we were very proud of. If a word was needed about South Africa a phrase such as 'How about some chess?' was the code for another clandestine meeting. Amazingly, no one seemed to notice we didn't seem to have either chessboard or pieces and, equally strangely, no one not in the know ever overheard these conversations – despite the fact that we could all clearly hear anyone's chats from other rooms as the sound travelled all too easily via the air conditioning vents!

It was such a potentially important matter that I felt I needed a second opinion. Jon was very clear that I should not touch the tour with the proverbial barge pole. It would be a highly political issue, he said, and I should think carefully about the moral ramifications. He wasn't sure what action the TCCB might be able to take but warned that the risks were high that those players who went would suffer some sort of consequences. Joining the tour might do nasty damage to my career, he argued. I was only 24 years old and had plenty of time left. Why jeopardise things? We are moving in the right direction, he said. Just carry on playing for England and things will be fine.

Shortly after speaking to him I ruled myself out, and was absolutely right to do so. I cannot say in all honesty, however, that I did so solely because to go would have been to affirm apartheid. I did not go chiefly because it might have adversely affected my England career. I'm very glad I took the decision I did because I can look back on it now and say that even if it wasn't 100 per cent for socio-political reasons, we got it right.

All that Jon said proved to be spot on. Those who went on the tour — Boycott, Gooch, Emburey among them — were banned by the TCCB for three years.

Beefy also opted against going, although I believe it was a pretty close-run thing. As I understand it, he would have been offered more than anyone else in the first place, understandably would have been tempted by the money, but needed to consult with his advisers, Reg Hayter and Alan Herd, to make sure there were not other angles that he was yet to consider. For someone of his status, there would have been rapidly burgeoning commercial opportunities associated with him being part of the official England team, and it seems that those advisers did indeed convince him not to go. Somewhat disingenuously, Beefy then came out with the quote, 'I could not have looked Viv in the eye,' in his column in the *Sun*, adding a veneer of respectability to his decision. It was not the last time he would be offered money to go in that direction, and he never succumbed — or maybe Ali Bacher couldn't meet his demands! Thankfully for Ian, the subsequent sea-change in the political scene in South Africa means that we are all allowed to visit the new South Africa, allowing us to make the most of the game parks, the vineyards and, in his case, to sample the delights of those fantastic golf courses that he so loves – and which I shun for the simple reason that if I cannot play it like Seve Ballesteros then I'm just not going to play it at all!

Jon used to joke that he could sum up his advice to me on a postcard in two sentences: 1) concentrate 2) don't go to South Africa. More broadly, he felt that by keeping out of trouble and maintaining a clean-cut image, I wouldn't go far wrong. He would argue that this was proved by subsequent events. When Beefy's image was sullied slightly with revelations of his drug-taking, some sponsors were less keen on his involvement and I was among the beneficiaries, picking up deals that had been intended for him (at reduced rates, I hasten to add!). For instance, as captain against Australia in 1985, I acquired a deal with Wiggins Teape Stationery earmarked for Botham. It was nice enough in its way, although the nicest part came when the chairman, Athol Angus, offered me a bottle of pre-war port for every hundred I scored in the series. As I managed three, this turned into a handy little perk, and a better one still when Tim Stanley-Clarke, who worked for the Symington family in Portugal, owners of Dow's Port and several other notable brands, obtained three bottles not pre-dating the Second World War but the First. I've still got them. The problem with such treasure is choosing the right moment to uncork them. Tim – a great practical joker nicknamed 'Filing' for obvious reasons – became a good friend and the facilitator of many trips to Portugal in search of port and cricket.

If Jon performed a good service in keeping me away from rebel tours, his most important contribution came towards the end of my playing career when he prepared me for a move into television and newspaper work. It was thanks to his hard work talking to the likes of Brian Barwick, then the head of sport at the BBC, that the switch was pretty seamless. That was just really good career planning.

*   *   *

Although I was left out of the last Test of the 1981 Ashes series at my favourite ground, the Oval, it proved a minor blip. I'd not had a great time, England led the series 3–1, and the selectors wanted to have a look at Paul Parker of Sussex. I was still taken to India and Sri Lanka that winter, and was much less concerned about the state of my game than I had been the previous year when I knew I was out of sorts. As it turned out, I was actually setting out on a very settled phase. I scored steadily for England for the next three years, and the eighteen months leading up to my appointment as captain was the best sustained spell of my career.

I certainly did not look to alter my method much. Ed Smith wrote an article in 2012 saying that I was brave for not changing my game through the difficult times, when I was being criticised for the 'carefree' way I batted; that while most batsmen cut out risky shots as they matured, I kept faith with my favourite strokes. I applaud him for what he says, but to call it brave suggests it was a conscious choice to carry on taking risks and be entertaining. The truth, as is so often the case, lies somewhere in between; I did not want to change the way I played largely because I couldn't.

There were times when, yes, I was guilty of going against the professional grain. I remember a 1983 World Cup match against New Zealand at the Oval – as I've said, my favourite ground – when I got into the thirties and found myself facing the part-time medium pace of Jeremy Coney with a packed off-side field. Maybe he did it deliberately; maybe he reckoned that I would be unable to resist the challenge of piercing that field. If so, he was right. I duly tried to go over the top, miscued slightly, and was caught at extra cover. I just wanted to play shots; I didn't want to be shackled. But I ended up trudging off thinking, 'Damn, I've missed out there.' Allan Lamb, meanwhile, got his head down and scored a hundred. Should I have done that myself? Professionally, yes. But as a batsman and entertainer, as an 'amateur' if you like, I was prepared to take the risk.

As a general rule I wasn't going around urging myself to brave it out. Yes, in the early days, you do have to be careful not to listen to every word of advice that comes your way about how to play, or you'd end up thoroughly confused. But it really was just the way I operated: I needed to play shots to get myself going; quite often, I felt it was the only way. 'Trust your instinct and hope you survive,' was for me as good a philosophy as any.

The tour of India in 1981–82 was a desperate experience, and witnessed some of the most tedious cricket imaginable after India went 1–0 up and looked to sit on their lead. We came to realise there was little hope of ever forcing a result, and in three of the remaining five games the first innings was not completed until the fifth day. If India bowled 12 overs an hour, England replied with 11 and at the most turgid points that over rate slipped even into single figures. Although I did not score a hundred, I did pretty well with 506 runs in the seven Tests on the tour (we also played a Test against Sri Lanka for the first time). I might have done better still had I not been twice run out in the Tests – and, bizarrely, six times on the whole tour. Nor was it always a certain Yorkshire opening batsman's fault either!

However mundane the cricket was on that tour, spending four months in India is always an extraordinary and eye-opening experience. The experts tell you to quickly de-Westernise yourself and to try and adopt local perspectives when viewing the myriad and sometimes shocking scenes of everyday life on the sub-continent. To go from the overstated opulence of the Taj Mahal Hotel in Mumbai, or the Oberoi Grand in Calcutta, and within yards be confronted by scenes of utter poverty, is an immense test of one's humanity. They tell you to do your best to ignore what you see, and in time you do become inured to these stark contrasts. It helps to read something like Dominique Lapierre's wonderful *City of Joy*, which at least gives you an impression that there is something about the human spirit that allows even the poorest of Calcutta's slum-dwellers a vestige of pride and self-respect. On a tour of this nature, you need people with strong stomachs and a will to embrace the way of life and the rules of the country in which you are a guest. 'Good tourists' were the ones who retained a sense of humour and were able to see their way through the bulk of those four months with equanimity.

We were always made to feel welcome, but the truth is that in those up-country towns, away from the comfortable refuge of the big cities, our accommodation could often be described as basic. I remember one early morning departure at 4am from Calcutta, to get to Jammu, up in the far northern reaches of India. Although Jammu itself is on a large flat plain, you can see the foothills of the Himalayas in the distance. When we arrived at 6am, it was still very cold. As the team checked into the hotel, we all discovered the single-bar electric fires in our rooms but the act of the England team simultaneously flicking the switches in the desperate quest for heat led to the obvious result ancient fuses pinging everywhere.

At the end of our stay, the hotel laid on a party for us, in a marquee at the back. For entertainment, there was a four-piece band doing its best to come up with some vaguely recognisable versions of some classic Western hits from the 1960s. When they needed a rest, there was a gramophone player and a Bee Gees LP. Entering into the spirit of the whole thing, John Lever, definitely a 'good tourist', had been to the local market and equipped himself with a lovely floral dress, an enormous bra and a fetching black wig. When he flounced his way in to the marquee that night, it was an entrance to behold. Always a good mover, his dancing drew admirers from all round the room. This would have been entirely good fun but for the fact that one tall handsome turbaned gentleman appeared to take a genuine fancy to our left-arm swing bowler, or should I say 'swinger'. JK's cries for help were cruelly ignored by the rest of the squad but I'm happy to say all survived intact to tell the tale.

The following winter in Australia was much more satisfactory, even if we didn't regain the Ashes (we lost 2–1, which was probably a fair reflection of the relative strengths of the teams, although with more luck with the umpiring we might have levelled the series in the final game at Sydney) and didn't make the finals of the triangular one-day series. But on a personal level I did well, scoring more than 1,000 runs in Tests and one-dayers, and being player of the series in the preliminary stage of the World Series Cup. Failing to make the finals was not a complete disaster as we then had time off to do whatever we wanted for a few days, which in my case meant flying to Hayman Island where I learnt to scuba dive on the Great Barrier Reef – not a bad place to start.

It was in this Test series that I first moved up to No. 3 on a serious basis. Before that, I'd mainly batted four or five for England. At that time, the No. 3 spot had become a bit of a poisoned chalice. Whoever went there never got runs. If someone was told they were to bat there – and a few people were – their response was probably something along the lines of, 'Oh really. Are you sure?'

But now this position was to become mine for the next few years. With time and experience, it was certainly the place to be. If you were not an opener by trade, but intent on making runs, then the earlier you got to the wicket the better. But you had to believe it would work rather than thinking, 'Someone's got to do it . . . I suppose it had better be me.' England had had some great No. 3s over the years, from Wally Hammond to Peter May to Ken Barrington, so it was a privilege to fill the same shoes.

I started with an innings of 72 at Perth which – even if I say so myself – was a cracker. That day I felt like I was going to get 200. I've told many people down the years that that was the innings in which I played my best. My feet moved like nothing before or since. I just got into position and hit. Everything clicked: I felt pin-sharp all the time. I didn't get the big score I should have done only because of a minor misjudgement: I clipped the ball in the air through midwicket just long enough for John Dyson to dive and get his fingers under it just in front of square. It was a very fine catch. For a lot of that tour, it felt like my bat only had a middle.

Once I became full-time captain, I tended to prefer batting at No.4, although in fact during the 1985 Ashes when I had my best series I went back to No.3 and it worked really well. Coming in at No.4 gives you that bit of breathing space which you need if you're captain, otherwise you are no sooner walking off from fielding than you're strapping on your pads and watching how the openers are shaping. It is quite common for someone to drop down the order after becoming captain. Clive Lloyd did it and so too Viv Richards. Nasser Hussain stayed at No.3 for a while but eventually moved down a place. Michael Vaughan was opening the batting before he became captain but then moved down to No.4, though he later moved back up again, largely to suit the needs of the side. These things are not of course always a matter of sound cricketing sense – where you bat often comes down to superstition. If you're going well in a particular position, you want to stay there; if you're not, you don't.

My good form in Australia in 1982–83 helped establish me as captain-elect. During the previous summer, when Bob Willis was appointed captain in succession to Keith Fletcher, I was made vice-captain and the message had gone out from Lord's to Mike Turner that I was seen as a future Test captain who needed all the experience of leadership that could be mustered, and Leicestershire duly appointed me vice-captain. In fact, shortly before Willis was confirmed as captain I was asked to lead MCC in an early season fixture against the Indians and there was speculation that I might get the top job there and then. But the powers-that-be were merely having a look at me for the future. They'd identified me as someone who had every chance of being around for a while, possessed the right pedigree to be captain, and – ahem – was not entirely stupid.

Graham Gooch, an ally of Fletcher's at Essex, naturally defended his mate at this juncture. He described me as underprepared for captaincy, and when it was announced that Fletcher was being replaced by Willis, Gooch was also critical about that decision, thinking captaincy ill-suited to someone whose main job was to bowl fast.

As it turned out, I did not have to wait long for my chance to lead England. With Willis suffering a ricked neck, I had to deputise in the second Test of the second series of the 1982 home season against Pakistan. As baptisms went, it was fiery. In the field, I found it interestingly difficult. It is like that moment when you pass your test and take your own car on the road by yourself for the first time. You know what you should be doing but it does not all quite feel right yet. With experience it becomes that much more instinctive and natural. The good news is that everyone was willing me to do well and I had players coming from all directions with ideas and advice.

Forced to follow on and then bowled out by the part-time swing bowling of Mudassar Nazar, we lost heavily. It was poor batting against a ball that may or may not have been tampered with. I was oblivious at the time to any suggestion that it was, but when he was batting Botham apparently showed the ball to umpires David Constant and Dickie Bird after becoming concerned that one of the quarter-seams (at 90 degrees to the main stitched seam) was raised. Nothing came of it, Donald Carr, the TCCB secretary, later declaring himself satisfied at the ball's condition.

Our capitulation was lent an air of farce by events the previous evening when several of us ate out in St John's Wood High Street. Robin Jackman ordered duck and insisted the rest of us did the same. What harm could it do? Superstition? Bah!! Next morning Jackman, nought not out overnight and with three runs needed from our last wicket to avoid the follow on, was promptly lbw to Imran Khan without scoring. Then when we batted again, myself

126

and Allan Lamb, who had also partaken of the aforementioned duck, were also out for nought.

What? Cricketers superstitious? Surely we can rise above mere coincidence rather than elevating a simple menu to the status of game-changing event. Having said that, I did spend all of my career thinking about lucky bats, lucky gloves, lucky shirts, putting the left pad on first, and of course there were the colour-coded socks . . . blue for England, red and/or green for Leicestershire, blue and/or yellow for Hampshire, or traditional grey marl, the official cricket sock, if all others were in the wash! It all started with my mate Tim Ayling, a tennis and squash coach in Leicestershire and a near neighbour. Popping round to his shop one day, either for a cup of coffee or glass of red wine, I spotted all these very comfortable looking walking socks, and thought, quite reasonably, that they would be both effective and fun, and once I'd started wearing them it became all part of the ritual.

Little did I know that something so harmless as a blue sock would later become a bone of contention with the England coach and chairman of selectors. There was a Test match at Trent Bridge during which, at a time when I'm sure there were more pressing matters to focus on, Mickey Stewart took me aside to ask me if I really had to wear blue socks. I asked him why and he said, 'Because I've had letters about it.' So what, I thought, and told Mickey that I didn't really think it made a jot of difference in the grand scheme of things. No sooner had I got rid of Mickey than Peter May caught me coming up the stairs to the dressing room without shoes, blue socks thus plainly visible. 'Er, what colour are those socks, David?' was all he said. I thought, 'Is this a trick question? Is the man colour-blind? Is there a hidden agenda?' Apparently not. It just seems that someone breaking 100 years of tradition with a pair of socks bugged them. I loved them, found them genuinely comfortable, and blithely carried on. This deep flaw in my character later manifested itself in a different form when I went through a period of wearing the most lurid and ludicrous sweaters – off the field I hasten to add.

I did better in my next games as stand-in captain in Pakistan in 1984, when Willis was sidelined from the last two Tests through injury, though he stayed with the team to offer encouragement. On the face of it, it was a tough situation. We were trailing 1–0 in the series, we were down to 13 fit men – although even we bore haggard appearances as we'd all agreed not to shave for the duration of the tour – and one observer not unjustly described me as leading 'a demoralised rump of a team'. But by this stage I felt fairly at ease with the role and – though I did not consider it at the time – virtually sealed my promotion with an innings of 152 in Faisalabad (when I wasn't feeling well and dropped myself down the order) and 173 not out in Lahore. I wasn't often accused of really applying myself like I did in Jamaica in 1981 but in these two games that was certainly the case, and we emerged with creditable draws from both games. We even had a brief sniff of victory in Lahore before Pakistan put up the shutters.

By this time, I was returning home to a large modern house in Ratcliffe Road, Leicester that I now shared with Vicki. She had originally moved in with me in my first flat in Ratcliffe Court and as the finances improved over the years, we moved steadily down the same road in the direction of the club. Each move must have saved me half a minute on the journey to Grace Road and the last one took us literally next door to the Coach House, a move which meant all we had to do was take the furniture out of one door, manoeuvre it to the other side of the fence and carry it into our new home.

It was to be two months before I received confirmation of my appointment as England's official captain.

6

IT'S NOT ALL ABOUT THE CRICKET

It would be hard to deny that team discipline is stricter today than it was 20 or 30 years ago when I was playing. I had a great deal of fun during my England career with the likes of Ian Botham and Allan Lamb, and I make no apology for that. It was the spirit of the times: it was the way they – we – were. Things are run very differently today but I would still argue that not much is gained by trying to hammer square pegs into round holes. Not everyone benefits from preparing for a Test match by spending hours in the gym or pounding the roads. This, of course, was the basis of my differences with Graham Gooch and Mickey Stewart. Equally, though, I'd concede that as the game became more professional, some changes were inevitable.

My view is that anyone mature enough to be picked for England ought to be mature enough to know what sort of lifestyle suits them best, and in most cases they do. To me there never seemed much to gain from nailing Botham and Lamb behind their bedroom doors at 10.30pm the night before a game. They would simply have fretted over what they might be missing. There was in fact an attempt during the 1985 Ashes series when I was captain to impose a 10.30 curfew. To be absolutely clear, that was 10.30pm rather than the much looser regime espoused by legendary Hampshire

129

captain, Colin Ingleby-Mackenzie, during the club's champion-ship-winning year of 1961. He merely asked his men to be in bed 'by half past'. Interviewed by a young TV reporter, the following exchange also took place:

TVR: 'To what do you attribute Hampshire's success?'

CI-M: 'Oh, wine, women and song, I should say.'

TVR: 'But don't you have certain rules, discipline, helpful hints for younger viewers?'

CI-M: 'Well, everyone in bed in time for breakfast, I suppose.'

Much though I would have loved to have emulated Ingleby in all sorts of ways, for he was a man with great natural charm and an ability to motivate players almost effortlessly, our curfew was more an attempt to make sure there were no accusations against the team for being a little over-social during the Tests. I have to say I did not really believe in it; I suspected that it would achieve little other than drive players who weren't quite ready to go back to their rooms to carry on drinking, or socialising, somewhere out of public view – and for those of us who were already doing our teeth, ahem, it was almost an insult. I even recall taking the mickey out of my own curfew by standing at the bar at what was then the Westmoreland Hotel close by Lord's at 10.28 and checking if any of my colleagues would like one more before bedtime. Disgraceful! As I also recall, Botham had a terrific series that summer, so whatever time he opted to go to bed seemed to work quite well for him. Of course, he achieved many amazing things on the field with what would today be called unconventional match preparation.

A lot of it was harmless – and very good – fun but one tour in particular attracted much adverse criticism. The tour of New Zealand in 1983–84 became known as the Sex, Drugs & Rock 'n' Roll tour, and as its nickname suggests there probably was some sex and possibly some drugs. There was some partying, for sure. Those who thought that New Zealand was a quiet, unassuming little backwater full of sheep farmers should seriously think again. The cities may not be Los Angeles or New York but things happen. There was good wine and some good-looking women and there's a house on the hill in Wellington that has seen many a party that we experienced only a little of on our tour. On the night of our visit most of the team was there at some stage, although quite when everyone left is less clear. A birthday cake was also baked for someone in the squad to a recipe that was not quite as innocent as it seemed. It certainly didn't follow Mrs Beeton's original recipe. Fortunately A C Smith, our old-school manager, who in his playing days would certainly have enjoyed a glass or two of Bollinger but who in his latest position of responsibility had revised his definition of a racy night out to include wearing a brightly coloured cravat, beat a tactful retreat and left the rest of us to it. It all just seemed to be a good idea at the time.

Newspaper reporters who had not been sent to cover the cricket were soon hot on Beefy's tail – he was after all the most obvious target, being the only one of us who lived his life on both front and back pages of newspapers – though he was blissfully unaware he was being followed. He was subsequently obliged to admit that he had been on cannabis, and was briefly suspended from playing. There was a bit of wacky baccy on that tour, though personally it was of little use to me as I can't stand the stuff – it makes me go dry in the mouth and unable to speak. After we had been soundly beaten inside three days in Christchurch, it was alleged that players were taking cannabis in the dressing room, which was total rubbish. No one is that daft and anyone writing such stuff must have had a pretty healthy imagination. It was all a great shame, not least because my mother had come out to New Zealand to visit an elderly relative, and was in Christchurch for that Test. She didn't have much to watch, certainly not much that was any good from an English perspective.

Bob Willis, the captain, was also good mates with Beefy. Bob was part of some of the fun; indeed during the party on the hill he had found a delightful and imaginative way of making the most of a rocking chair – apparently made for two – on the balcony that overlooked the city, but he kept himself at arm's length from the rest of it. He was – is – a strong character and as his vice-captain I certainly didn't feel I had to be constantly feeding him ideas. He had more than enough of his own, as he does now. A valid criticism of his captaincy would be that he sometimes got a little immersed in his own game, though I wouldn't make it a strong one.

Allan Lamb had joined the team in 1982, though I had known him for several years before that while he was qualifying for England at Northamptonshire (he was born in South Africa to English parents). Despite our different backgrounds and upbringings, we got on well from the start and not living far apart we saw a fair bit of each other along with our respective partners. He and his wife Lindsay seem to have been at each other's throats for 30 years; both are noisy, fun, and give no quarter. He was also a very good friend of Lynn Wilson, the then Northamptonshire chairman, of whom more shortly.

There may have been resentment in some quarters at a 'South African' coming into the England side but it was never an issue for me. Allan was a bloody good player and I was very keen he should qualify for us. Once he took his place in the team, he, Beefy and I spent a lot of time together. They certainly knew how to enjoy themselves, and I could never really keep up. Lamb was an absolute livewire, your original Duracell bunny who never ran out of energy. Sadly, the bare figures of his Test record don't show how good or courageous he was, but the runs he got against West Indies should count double. On that measure alone, he was among the best batsmen of the time. It was something of a surprise that he didn't do better in Australia, because he had a technique that should have been suited to those conditions. He was maybe more polished as a player than he was as an individual, but there was no doubt he was a charmer, a talker, and great fun to be with. We once went on a holiday together with the girls around the Champagne region of France and to hear him mangling French words with his still broad South African accent was truly hilarious. However, as I was driving and he was the one reading the map, the main problem was that by the time I had worked out what on earth he was trying to say and what I should be looking for on a signpost we were already well past the turnoff.

As suggested, he loved a party and my fortieth birthday was no exception. My wife, Thorunn, and I shared a joint fortieth – despite the fact she is of course much younger than I! – and invited all the usual suspects, with the theme, in a deliberate reference to my past, 'Out of Africa'. Tim Rice brought his band (well, it was Bill Heath's band really, Whang and the Cheviots), sang his heart out and also brought the most stunning present, an original edition of *The Life and Explorations of David Livingstone*. Robert and Babs Powell joined us; Robin Smith came as a Zulu with a rather short loincloth, and a neighbour, Jerry Dugdale, accessorised his safari outfit with a genuine, live, thankfully non-venomous, snake. That caused a stir or two among the ladies! We had friends from the cricketing world, from the BBC, from *They Think It's All Over* and of course our circle of friends in Hampshire, with roast meat from Robinsons of Stockbridge and wines from the Gower collection – which rather dwindled as the night wore on.

It was mid-summer, in the days when we had summers, and the most gorgeous, balmy night. We had a swimming pool, which was open for business, but if you have a pool and Lambie you also have an open invitation. Many of the guests took to the water voluntarily but any that did not were rounded up by Lambie (obviously years of experience on Lindsay's family sheep farm in South Africa were put to good use) and unceremoniously dumped in the water. It mattered not if the girls were still wearing their gorgeous silk numbers – though they might have been given at least seconds to take off anything so valuable and vulnerable – in they went! My sister-in-law, Kris, read that race very early and locked herself inside the house.

In the early hours, by which time Lambie reckoned he must have got 98 per cent of our guests properly wet, the party wound up. I had arranged for a small fleet of taxis to be on standby to take people back to the Potters Heron Hotel and as they all left we were handing out bin bags for them to sit on in the cabs to try and protect the seats. To no avail, it seems; when the bill arrived from Abbey Cars it included a sizeable amount for drying out said cars.

As for Beefy . . . well, the words 'Botham' and 'room service' do not belong in the same sentence. Even nowadays, you won't catch him staying in his room unless he's been beaten with a club into doing so. I could tell some horror stories about nights out with him – if only I could remember all that had happened. Often, I'd wake up the next morning vowing to myself that I really must keep safer company. Take this for A Day in the Life of Ian Botham. A Saturday in Taunton – what a surprisingly social town that is – and Ian is 'resting' a bad back during the day while Somerset take on Leicestershire. 'Resting' means lunching in the pavilion with sponsors and seeing off numerous bottles of wine in the process. When we come off the field at 6.30pm Beefy is showing no signs of wear whatsoever and suggests an itinerary to Brian Davison and I which involves a ride in the great man's Saab to Yeovil for a benefit barn dance for Hallam Moseley and an even quicker journey back to Taunton to unwind at the Four Alls pub with a few games of pool and a quantity of Fosters. Davo and I bounced off the walls of the alleyways back to the County Hotel and collapsed at God only knows what time. All I know is I arrived at the County Ground the next day for the Sunday league match feeling an utter shambles, to find Botham lying in the bath in the Somerset dressing room with a cigar in one hand and the *News of the World* in the other, looking as right as rain. Roger Tolchard, our captain, wasn't happy to see the state I was in, but fortunately, although we lost, I made fifty so couldn't be held entirely responsible.

Although I don't think it was Beefy's prime motive on that occasion, he was a master at 'taking out' key members of the opposition. There was a famous time when Surrey visited Weston-super-Mare, and Sylvester Clarke, one of the most feared fast bowlers on the circuit, was taken under Beefy's wing for the night, and between them I can only imagine how much whisky might have been demolished – 'Silvers' was partial to a little scotch! Much to the gratitude of Beefy's Somerset colleagues, Clarke was unable to bowl the next day.

After that New Zealand tour, the dynamics of touring became completely different. When I first went to Australia, we were allowed to have fun and not censured for it, certainly not by the press. When we stayed in Sydney at the Sebel Town House, you could come back from dinner at around 11pm and there was a good chance of finding in the bar a rock star (it was a popular haunt of rock 'n' roll stars) and a 100 per cent chance of finding a cricket scribe. We'd have a drink with them, and could stay past midnight without anyone giving a monkey's. If you made a prat of yourself, you would get an avuncular arm round your shoulder from Peter Smith of the *Daily Mail* advising you not to do it again, and promising to steer you through it. Peter was special in that respect. He had your interests at heart and you could trust him implicitly. Up until New Zealand, no one was ready or required to make a link between whatever might have happened off the field the night before and what happened on the field the next day.

After that New Zealand tour, which was very much a watershed for the change in relations between players and press, everyone had to be more aware of what they did in public. This made Beefy in particular more cautious about whom he might spend his time with on tour, and he often later turned his hotel suite into a refuge where he could enjoy himself in company with a few hand-picked allies. But it did not really curb our enthusiasm for enjoying life.

Looking back now, I would concede that a more dedicated approach to training and early nights might have brought better results, but there is that conundrum as to whether you live to play sport, or to live with it. Mine was an era where a lot of people who happened to be very good at the game were also very good at enjoying everything that came with it. It wasn't just Botham and Lamb; there were plenty more besides, including J K Lever and Geoff Miller to name but two. County cricket was played in a very social atmosphere, and so was the international game. The Australians were no different from us and nor were some of the West Indians.

Inevitably there would be some collateral damage but I don't think there were many occasions where some impressionable young team-mate was left at a huge disadvantage because of a night out with Botham or Lamb. And if he didn't like it, no one was forcing him to do it again. It's a complete fallacy to expect sixteen blokes to stick close together every night of a long tour; they are bound to divide up along lines of age, interests and experience. There will be those who like going out and those who don't. This is the way all touring sides work: on a bad tour you call them cliques who mutter darkly about what the others are doing wrong, and on a good tour they are just groups. Going back to the principle that most players know how to balance their own lives to get the best out of themselves, many would have the discipline to choose their moments to cut loose. Bill Athey, for one, knew that if he had one drink he'd probably have plenty, but would simply choose evenings when there was no cricket the following day. Simple! The rest of the time he'd be on water and early to bed, as disciplined as you'd hope anyone would be today.

I certainly would not say that I fell in with the wrong crowd. Your friends are your friends and they were very good company. Nor was I often led unwillingly to where I did not want to go. We had many a good night on tour all around the cricketing world with all sorts of interesting and entertaining people. It was hardly compulsory to be out and about with the same crew night after night or even to carry on as late into the night as they did. Even if they felt invincible, it didn't stop me raising the white flag of surrender. I'll still do that now if I have to. Even more so. If mine is the first face that people see on TV at 10.30am before the start of a Test match, it's probably best that it doesn't show severe signs of having been 'Bothamed'. The technical term for that, I believe, is '*oeno*phylactic shock', defined as a 'serious allergic reaction' to drinking far too much wine in the company of a legendary England all-rounder. (See also Flintoff, Andrew!) The least I can do is pitch up feeling bright, keen and sober. It's not quite like batting where you don't get a second chance but you are expected to set the tone for the day ahead. I don't tend to go too mad and it's been 20 years since my last all-nighter.

On tour with Sky TV in South Africa we had ODIs on consecutive days in Johannesburg and Centurion. After the first, I rang Ian and suggested a 'quiet one' as it would be a slightly early start the following morning. It was quiet enough – but just a long night. Supper was peanuts in the bar at the Sandton Towers with Mike Procter and somehow I failed to notice how the time passed as we then raided Ian's minibar and found his only good use for room service. As dawn broke it seemed a good idea to have a shower and change into work clothes and Beefy drove us to Centurion. I was so ill that I could barely make it down all those steps at Centurion that take you from the upper levels and the commentary boxes down to the field. I had to do a pitch report and when I got the cue from John Gayleard in my ear just managed to crouch down without toppling over, caressed the grass lovingly, and croaked the words 'it looks all right to me.' 'I guess that's as good as I am going to f***ing get,' was all I heard as John realised that this was the end of my assessment of the turf. It had brevity, if nothing else, to commend it.

I can't deny that England's Test results declined during the Eighties. We had some notable victories in the Ashes and also won in India, but New Zealand and Pakistan not only beat us in series for the first time, but did so home and away. Losing to West Indies was essentially par for the course. But I would say all this had less to do with a decline in our abilities and more to do with the rest of the world catching up – probably partly as a consequence of so many overseas players broadening their experience in county cricket, in a way that only happens on a much smaller scale today (although some people still get agitated when the likes of Phil Hughes or Vernon Philander prepare for a Test tour with a stint at a county). We suffered, too, the loss of several key players through the rebel tour of South Africa that I have already talked about, though I would still maintain that there were not many weak links in our side. That said, we were a good side but not a great one.

To an extent, of course, having fun fed off playing well. If you were feeling good about the way you were playing, you were more ready to savour life than if you were struggling with your cricket. Combining the two made life feel doubly good and you did not want it to stop.

Of course, even Botham and Lamb had a serious side. They may have had this free-and-easy reputation but they were ferocious competitors. I was probably a little more serious than either and – as I've already pointed out – there was within me a little more steel than I usually showed. I just found it hard to be steely and bloody-minded all the time. Some days you had to force yourself to be good and on others you could do well without going to all that trouble. I'm afraid there is a sad truth that your innate charac-ter will out in the end. Fears, worries, weaknesses . . . you can only do so much to overcome them. The impression of me being a bon viveur – and I would still insist this was not an entirely accurate impression – served a purpose both within and without. In my mind it lessened the hurt of failure. It was a way of saying, 'Well, okay. There's always tomorrow.'

With the exception of the odd flight in a Tiger Moth, I rarely committed offences serious enough to get into hot disciplinary water. In fact, I'd argue that the Tiger Moth incident was a bit of harmless fun that should never have been treated as anything else, certainly not the act of high treason the management paraded it as. I would concede, though, that I had a gift for getting into the kind of scrapes P G Wodehouse had so much fun writing about. I think they caused as much amusement as official opprobrium. I don't really know why this was. I suppose that, just as I sometimes committed errors of judgement on the field that led some to wring their hands and shake their heads ('Oh, no, Gower caught down the leg side . . . not again'), so I made some mistakes off it that might have been avoided had I thought things through a little more carefully in advance, and how they might look to others. But let's face it, why would you?

If some of these incidents seemed as though I was being wilfully subversive or casual, all I can say is that they were not meant as such. In the overly casual category was my rather major misjudgement as captain of England at Lord's against the West Indies in 1984. Towards the close on the fourth day we had, largely thanks to Allan Lamb, batted ourselves into a good position and the pundits felt we should be cracking on despite the light failing rapidly. When the umpires offered the light to Lambie and Derek Pringle, they looked to the balcony for guidance. With none forthcoming, they took it upon themselves to call it a day. They might or might not have taken advantage of a tiring attack to add more runs, and I could try and pull the wool over your eyes by suggesting that I felt that the two batsmen were best placed to make the decision out in the middle as to whether they were capable of continuing in the conditions – bearing in mind that West Indies did possess the kind of bowlers you didn't always want to face in good light, let alone bad. I have to admit now that it would have been better had I been outside on the balcony directing my troops rather than sat inside, as I was, watching the tennis from Wimbledon on the TV – though I'm not sure I would necessarily have come to a different decision than the two batsmen out in the middle.

Of course, when I eventually declared early the next morning, setting a target of 342, West Indies proceeded to cruise home as the ball stubbornly refused to swing in the way it had earlier in the game. Even then, I had declared later than Peter May, the chairman of selectors, would have liked; he had urged me before play began to declare to leave myself a full day to bowl out West Indies – or eat into it by no more than half an hour. I looked at the clear skies and flat pitch and was more reticent, but he was entitled to his opinion, as was everyone else. If nothing else we had the best view of Gordon Greenidge's extraordinary innings. He always felt that he was as good as Viv Richards and on that day you would have believed it. Nowadays, in the commentary box, whenever there is a chance of a fourth innings chase in a Lord's Test match, I know that the graphic with the highest successful run chases in a Test at Lord's will be on that screen in seconds and that Nasser Hussain and Michael Atherton will be chirping, 'Who was captain in that match?' All I can say is that it still grates that they knocked off the runs with 11 overs of the final hour still to spare. At least we got them to the final hour!

Another time I was guilty of taking my eye off the ball came in a Sunday league match at Cheltenham. On this occasion I would say that we were genuinely bloody unlucky. It had been hammering down for most of Saturday and overnight and was still hammering down all through the Sunday morning to the extent that I left my Leicestershire team at the hotel enjoying the lunch-time jazz band and went off to the College Ground to check on conditions. It was hardly a shock to see the ground under water. Both sides were convinced that there would be no play – so it seemed a shame not to accept the kind invitation from Roger Moore, no not that one but the chairman of sponsors Duraflex and a Gloucestershire committee man to boot, to join him in his tent for a glass or 12 of Pimm's. There was also a fabulous spread of cold meats and lobster and the two girls serving the Pimm's, one of whom came for dinner later, were among Cheltenham's finest. While we got stuck into the Pimm's, the weather outside began to morph into sunshine and wind, and the College Ground's famed draining properties came into play. Not that most of us noticed. The first clue that something was afoot was when Mervyn Kitchen, one of the umpires, stuck his head around the tent flap at around half past four and informed me that we might start a ten-over slog at ten past five. I genuinely thought he was joking but he quickly disabused me of that notion.

I attempted to knock up on the outfield with little success and duly delegated the toss to Nigel Briers. We decided to bat first, chiefly on the basis that it would allow nine of us more chance to try and sober up. I went in at No. 3, charged at my first ball and somehow managed to hit it over long on. I followed up with several air shots before deciding (for the first and last time in my career) that the reverse sweep might be a good option. I might even have made contact with one! Somehow we managed to muster 77, which proved to be plenty, Gloucestershire falling short by seven, which in the context of a ten-over match consti-tutes a thrashing. It was ironic that one of the few of our players who hadn't touched a drop, Gordon Parsons, went for 14 in his only over. I'd like to think that our successful defence owed some-thing to my leadership but anyone keeping a close eye on my shambolic fielding at cover would know that could not possibly have been the case. In honour of our triumph, I duly led the troops straight back into the tent.

In 1986, I was criticised for missing the first warm-up match of our West Indies tour in St Vincent. I was captain but took the match off for what I considered to be the very good reason that, following the death of my mother a week before the beginning of the tour and on the assumption that I would be involved in all the cricket from then on, I could do with a few days off. She had been ill for some time with asthma, though seemingly not critically so, but the drugs she had been taking had apparently weakened her heart. It was a terrible shock and perhaps had I been in a calmer state of mind I would have delayed my departure for the tour. But with the help of my mother's sister Liz and her eldest daughter Jane we had arranged a funeral; I had also left instructions for someone to sell the house and auction the contents – something I now regret doing. At the time, my overriding emotion was to not sit around moping, and I thought getting on with my cricket would be the best thing to do. But once I actually got to the West Indies I realised how emotionally drained I was: my mind had been racing and my body with it, and I knew I needed to sit out the first game just to get myself straight.

I also knew there would be few opportunities to miss later matches. For the same reason, Botham also did not play. The management had no qualms about this as the Windward Islands were probably the weakest side in the Caribbean. However, events and my trusting nature conspired to make life tougher than it should have been. On the third day of the match, Beefy and I agreed to go out for a sail on a yacht owned by a Scandinavian friend of mine called Bjorn, who had skippered me on a fantastic holiday through the Grenadines on a previous visit. What had been intended as a short excursion turned into a long one when we swam out to Bjorn's boat only to find the engine had broken down and it took him a couple of hours of tinkering to get it going again.

Eventually we headed off but as we did so the radio powered up and we heard the latest score from the match . . . and it was not good news. The boys were collapsing in the second innings. By the time we returned defeat was all but inevitable and I was blamed by the press for not being at the ground to urge on my team in their hour of difficulty. It was deemed to be poor form to be on a yacht at such a time. What made the situation all the trickier was that we had taken along with us on the boat a photographer and friend in Graham Morris. His pictures of us drinking beer on deck only served to support the charge that the captain was indifferent to the plight of his team, which of course was not the case.

Such mishaps have a habit of sticking to your CV and with the tour turning into a disastrous 5–0 'blackwash' my credentials as leader inevitably came under fairly intense scrutiny when we got home. It was not hard to look lost for inspiration when playing West Indies and because I was not one for waving my arms around in the field the press had begun to ask who was in charge of the team. Even Peter May himself was lured into asking me, with extreme polite-ness, if I could possibly be a little more demonstrative.

I was given one more chance and invited to captain the team against India at Lord's. My response was to get some T-shirts printed off for the team to wear, one of which had 'I'm in Charge' printed on the front, while 11 others (to include the twelfth man) said, 'I'm Not.' I hope you can guess which one I wore. It was meant as a bit of a joke against myself and certainly not as a dig against the chairman of selectors. No malice was intended and the other players took it in good spirit by wearing the shirts during practice. Had things gone well and we'd won the first Test of the summer against India it would have been a masterstroke; unfortu-nately we didn't and within minutes of the game finishing Peter

May was informing me that I was no longer England captain. It was a poignant moment handing over the T-shirt to Mike Gatting: 'I guess this is yours, now.' I don't know if he ever tried to put it on but if he did it might have been something of a struggle!

On England's most successful tour of Australia of all time (Ashes, Perth Challenge, World Series Cup, all won) in 1986–87, there were more shenanigans. Our first match of the tour was at Bundaberg, a sugar farming centre from where the famous Bundaberg Rum originates. The night before the game, Mike Gatting had quite rightly led the team meeting with words along the lines of, 'Tomorrow we need to get straight down to business (against a Queensland Country XI) and start the tour on a positive note.' We had a reception at the Salter Oval to attend and for some unearthly and horribly misjudged reason I stood next to Ian at the bar and went with him rum for rum. It was never a contest: at the end of the reception he and Lambie dragged me to the bus before dragging me off it at the other end and leaving me under the shower. They then headed to the bar, where they ran into three 'Cane Cookies', or sugar farmers, one of whom was a loudmouth. Beefy nutted him, at which stage Lambie headed for cover behind a sofa, emerging rapidly when he realised the other two Cookies were not looking for a fight but actually applauding Beefy for sorting their mate out.

The following morning we were in the office, up before the beak, with Botham and Lamb saying they were fine thank you very much, while I, as a recently deposed captain and senior player, was apologising profusely and admitting that I should have known better. The game was delayed due to overnight rain so I did not have to bat until the afternoon, thankfully, and when the game was delayed again the following day, we found a seaplane to do a tour of the area. The pilot had no qualms handing over the controls to Beefy, who then took great delight in performing a series of gentle aerobatics, buzzing the hotel and anywhere else where there might be people unused to low flying vintage seaplanes. Perhaps this helped give me ideas on our next visit to Queensland four years later!

Contrite though I was, we had not quite got the hang of this early night thing by the time the Test series began. We, as members of the older guard, were a bit suspicious of the new management team of Gatting and Mickey Stewart, who had been brought in to instil more discipline into training and preparation. In hindsight, this was a necessary step on the road towards the kind of fully professional England setup we have today (although I would again add my usual riders about the need for accommodating different personalities and their different needs). Mickey was certainly passionate about what he was doing; he had been brought up in sporting terms to work hard and train hard, and couldn't understand why anyone wouldn't want to go to the nets. I was in slight personal disarray at this point. Having been captain, and been a very different kind of captain to Gatting, playing under this new system took a bit of thinking about. Could I be my old self, or did I need to change? Like most of the squad, I had started the tour in terrible form and Australia was delighting in telling us how bad we were.

The night before the Test, we held our traditional team dinner, towards the end of which Mickey got up and said that he liked to think that once we'd finished the meal we'd head back to our rooms for a quiet night ahead of our big day tomorrow.

Beefy goes: 'You what? I'm not going to bed to stare at the ceiling for two hours. No way . . .'

Lamb: 'Eh Mickey . . . hang on a moment, China. I can't sleep at this time of night . . .'

Me: 'I'm with them . . .'

Mickey relented a little, saying that he understood that each of us had to do what we'd got to do, but he hoped we'd all still be having an early night.

We furtively slipped out. It was not a planned mission but one thing led to another and we ended up in the Pink Parrot, a night-club under the Hilton Hotel where we were staying. We were still there at 2am when the penny dropped: 'Hey, haven't we got a Test match tomorrow? We'd better go.'

It was irresponsible and my seafaring ancestor Erasmus would probably have had me keel-hauled and left to the sharks. But in fact it wasn't a problem. The adrenalin kicked in, I scored fifty, Lamb also got runs and Beefy, typically impervious to any effects of a late night, hit a typically destructive hundred that set up what turned out to be a decisive win, much to the horror of all those Aussies who had written us off.

Back in Brisbane in 1990, I got myself involved in another interesting nocturnal adventure, this time in the middle of the match. Tony Greig, who was commentating for Channel 9, approached myself and Allan Lamb and said that 'the Boss' – meaning Kerry Packer, the head of Channel 9 – would like to invite us to dinner. I'd not really met Kerry before and neither had Lambie, and we agreed it would probably be interesting. As it happened, come the Saturday night of the game, we were already in a bit of trouble in our second innings. I was one of three wickets to have fallen but Lamb – acting captain in the absence of the injured Gooch – was still batting. But Greig assured us that everything would be fine. A couple of cars were to take us down to the Gold Coast where we were to dine with Kerry at Jupiter's.

At that stage, there was nothing wrong with this. We were not driving. It was up to us how much we drank. The food was delicious, as was the wine, and Lambie, with the day to come in mind, was uncharacteristically restrained. But the crunch was this: Kerry Packer was a gambler, Jupiter's was a casino, and the only thing that was going to happen after dinner was that Kerry would be playing the tables and the men in the party would be expected to be his supporters. Packer's gambling was legendary, as was his generosity to his friends if he won.

Whereas that was not why we hung around, we were aware that he did not like his guests bailing out on him early either. He took over one blackjack table to himself, gave the girls present some money to play on another and began. After an early run of good form, the cards went against him and he tried everything to change his luck, asking for new cards, changing croupiers, anything. He was in no hurry to get to bed. He was immersed in retrieving his losses and there was some rugby on TV he wanted to watch at 2.30am. But we had to get to bed and at around midnight finally dared to make our excuses and left.

Compared to some of the nights we had this was nothing too serious. We were probably safely in our rooms by about 1am. But the story got out because the porter on the back door of the Hilton Hotel sold the story of our late return. Lambie was in more trouble than I was because he was acting captain and still batting and – as it happened – was out quickly the next morning. That didn't look so good but I honestly don't think the evening affected him adversely. We should have just had the balls to say to Kerry earlier in the evening, 'We've got to go.' He wouldn't have minded. If only he'd had a better night on the tables, we could have slipped the night porter something to keep it quiet.

I would defend myself more over my decision to walk out of a press conference at Lord's in 1989 when I was restored – briefly to the England captaincy. We'd already lost the first Test to Australia and now had a couple of bad days. By stumps on the Saturday we were seriously up against it after a tough day in which we'd been smacked around by Geoff Lawson during a big partnership with Steve Waugh, and then lost three early wickets. Emotions were running pretty hot and looking back on it now it might have been better for me not to have been obliged to do a press conference that night. In today's game, admittedly without rest days, it would not happen and it was mere convention that dictated I should front up soon after the end of a testing day.

You could argue that I should have known that it was part of my job to be at that conference but there was another little factor. I had got in the back of my mind that I had to be at the theatre at 7.30pm – I'd been invited by Tim Rice to see *Anything Goes*, his latest West End show – so, having tried to compose myself as best as possible, I started out with the thought that a quick interview might be handy and with the intention of getting through the questioning as amiably as I could, but England were heading for another defeat and the assembled media were not to be placated by any show of levity. Phil Edmonds, a former ally, who was now writing a newspaper column, wanted to know why I'd bowled Neil Foster from what he described as the wrong end. In fact, Foster had only been given the end he wanted. The grilling wasn't long but I'd walked in knowing it was a duty to be got through and that there was really not much I could say.

Those that have played with me – and sadly those that have lived with me – know that every so often my fuse will blow in a surge of emotion and impatience. It blew now. 'I'm off,' I said. 'Mickey. Over to you.' The look on his face was priceless. I got up, strode purposefully out of the room and down to the Grace Gates, hailed a cab and headed for the West End. Once I was among friends, and in a different atmosphere, the pressures of the press conference evaporated and I had a very enjoyable evening.

Sadly, that was not the end of it. The next morning I got a call from Ted Dexter, the chairman of selectors, who suggested I might have to rebuild a few bridges. So even though it was supposed to be a rest day I ended up going to the Hurlingham Club to speak to a BBC crew in an attempt to get in some good PR. I apologised for my outburst and generally smoothed things over, although the best piece of diplomacy was scoring a century the next day. Sadly, it wasn't enough to prevent us going 2–0 down.

*   *   *

My most notorious escapade, though, came nowhere near a cricket field.

I had first gone to St Moritz to do the Cresta Run shortly before the West Indies tour of 1986. Allan Lamb and I have a very good mutual friend by the name of Strong, Simon Strong. He met Lambie at a golf day early on in Allan's career and they found that they had all sorts of mutual friends, all of whom seemed to love their sport, many of whom actually had a talent for sport and all of whom seemed to know their way round a jug of Kummel. Leonardo's, in the King's Road, was a frequent haunt and very soon I too was part of this set, comprising city boys, property developers, all sorts, and including the rakish 'Bungalow' Bill Wiggins, who counted as one of the property men but was soon to be more famous for squiring Joan Collins. A lesser known attribute, given his reputation elsewhere, was that he was also a decent left-handed batsman.

Anyway, we had the odd skiing trip to Verbier, staying with Bill and Reena Price, and being taught to ski by Lassie and Rod at Mountain Air. Having skied once at the age of ten, this was very much starting afresh and after a day or so sliding uncontrollably on some of Verbier's few gentle slopes, with a bit of hiking with skis on shoulders to get to lunch thrown in, by the end of the week they thought we were ready for Tortin. I have just googled 'Tortin' to refresh my memory. Top of the page comes, 'The world's scariest ski runs; terror at the top'; lower down, 'Ten ski runs to try before you die.' I can tell you that if you start with Tortin you might not get to the other nine! The terror at the top is a very narrow snow bridge and if you negotiate that all you get for your trouble is a steeply inclined, massive mogul field. God only knows how the novices made it down, though much of it did not involve what you would call normal skiing, or even skiing at all. Bliss is the piste that lies at the bottom.

Strongie's next cracking wheeze was to suggest that we try the Cresta Run. He had driven bobsleighs in St Moritz and had been a member of the St Moritz Tobogganing Club for some years. He thought, rightly as it happens, that Lamb and I would quite enjoy it – and the lifestyle that comes with St Moritz. Dare I say it, Cresta riders do have a reputation for making the most of their time in that town. The timing of our visit was interesting – we pitched up the week before the tour of West Indies in 1986, me as England captain, Lambie as arguably one of the finest players of West Indies style quick bowling at the time. Reckless? Foolhardy? Bonkers? Probably. Believe it or not, the board in those days had no say over what we did outside the contractually prescribed dates of a tour. The *News of the World*, bless them, found out and asked Peter May, then chairman of selectors, what he thought. The gist of his response was, 'I'd rather they didn't.' My man Jon Holmes also had to answer questions on my behalf. 'What's he got himself into now?' was the gist of his reaction. Actually, this was early January and over the years – I don't know what it is about January – Holmes would get used to having to help me escape various scrapes, as we shall discover. For the record, the Queensland Tiger Moth was another January incident. In the meantime, our excuse was that we were merely altitude training and sharpening our reflexes for the West Indies bowlers by sliding down an ice track on a skeleton toboggan (a glorified tea tray) at 60mph.

We survived the trip and coped with the Cresta better than we coped with the West Indies that year and returned to St Moritz most winters if only for the odd long weekend until our final trip in 1990.

This was around the time I was splitting up from Vicki and spending quite a bit of time living out of the spare room in Simon and Charlotte's house in London, from which I would occasionally flit up to Leicester to check on the house, pick up my mail, and avoid flying objects. Simon's friend Mark Horne also came with us and out in St Moritz was Lynn Wilson, a hugely successful builder, chairman of Wilcon Homes and the chairman of Northamptonshire, and his two sons Nick and Giles. Lynn was a big mate of Lambie's and someone whose hospitality we'd often enjoyed over the years. Lynn was a charming gent and a real god-send to Northants. When he died in 2008 he bequeathed money to the club that enabled them to finally purchase the freehold to their Wantage Road ground.

The Cresta is an extraordinary club. It's incredibly sociable (as well as incredibly expensive). You are up at the crack of dawn to get on the ice and won't be staggering home to bed until the small hours, but despite the lack of sleep it's amazing how quickly you sharpen up on a mixture of fresh air and fear before sliding down on your 'wagon'. Although a skeleton toboggan is a reasonably hefty piece of kit, by the time you work out the physics of it all you are connected to the ice only by a couple of thin blades. The club was run by Lt-Col Digby Willoughby, secretary of the St Moritz Tobogganing Club, who gave every new rider the famous lecture – the death talk – before they signed the disclaimer and headed off to begin their first run from Junction. He also threw his infamous Nikolaschka parties from his room at the Kulm Hotel which acts as the club's unofficial headquarters. In essence these involved drinking shots of vodka in a very strictly prescribed fashion, with penalties for any error, elbows not horizontal, that sort of thing, which meant another shot before the next round or a spell outside on the balcony in minus 10 Celsius, with the predictable result that everyone got totally smashed very quickly.

On this particular night Lamb and I made our excuses early and left Digby's party to join up with Lindsay and attempt to introduce food into the evening – a novel concept – back at our hotel, the Eden, a short walk from the Kulm. Setting out for a nightcap, we bumped into Simon and Mark much the worse for wear from Digby's drinking games – Mark was in fact curled up asleep in the snow beneath a car! – so diverted to help them into bed before heading off for the Palace Hotel.

It was at this point that things started to get silly. I lost Lambie but picked up Chris Lander and Brendon Monks of the *Daily Mirror*, who were there to do a feature on the Cresta Run, and Lynn's two sons. We'd been across the frozen lake a couple of nights previously on a horse-drawn sledge that had taken us to a restaurant on the other side, so we knew the entry point, and we now decided to take out the hire car we'd brought with us from the airport for a spin on the lake. As the only person insured to drive, I was the one behind the wheel, and we duly spent I don't know how long whizzing round the lake, skidding, sliding and spinning. It was all good fun. Eventually, we dropped off Lander and Monks, and went back for one last spin – in both senses of the word.

Bad idea. Ironically it was literally the last run that brought disaster. Having decided enough was enough, we were heading home but made a crucial navigational error. Whereas I thought I was crossing the middle of the lake, where the ice was a good 12 inches thick, I had actually veered towards the top end where the water runs off the mountains and into the lake. I only realised this when the colour of the ice in my headlamps changed from brilliant white to grey. Already doing 50 or 60mph, I had a decision to make, so I braked. Hmmm. The car skidded to a halt – perfectly in the middle of the grey strip of ice. There was a sort of cracking sound – actually no, it was indeed a genuine cracking sound. I opened my door and saw water where I was hoping to see just ice. At this stage it seemed a good idea that the three of us abandon ship and we waded to the thicker ice. Optimistically I wondered if I could get the car onto safer ice, and had one go at reversing it, but not surprisingly it didn't work. So we removed any valuables or weighty items, such as the snow chains, out of the boot and tramped back across the lake into town. There was nothing more we could do.

The next morning I woke early and rang Heinz, the manager at the Eden, and asked him if he'd mind doing me a favour. Could he have a look at the lake and see if there were any cars parked on it. Naturlich. He phoned back five minutes later. 'Mr Gower, zer is no car on ze lake.'

'Right, okay, thanks Heinz, that will be all.'

I conveyed the news to Strong and Horne that I had lost – well, sunk – our car. We convened a crisis meeting over a horribly hungover breakfast. We took advice from one of the senior and more sober members also having a late breakfast and were urged to contact a lawyer, Urs Nater, who had just set up a practice in St Moritz but who would not be available until he had finished racing on the Cresta at the end of the morning. Recovering our poise, we headed for the Sunny Bar at the Kulm, where the Cresta meets after racing for lunch, prize-giving . . . and more champagne! Eerily, as Simon and I walked on to the balcony we were aware of people looking at us. Somehow rumours had got around that we'd gone down with the ship. That evening, in a moment of religious fervour, we went to church to give thanks for what had been a lucky escape, and the Rev Lester Brewster, the Anglican vicar of St Moritz and chaplain of the St Moritz Tobogganing Club, got the service off to a fitting start with the hymn, 'For Those in Peril on the Sea'.

Urs, God bless him, sorted things out. We were allowed to take a train back to Zurich and leave the country. He persuaded the police there was no one in the car when it went down and made sure no one (i.e. me) would be prosecuted for endangering life. But then the bills started coming in – the Schweizer Polizei charged 5,000 Swiss Francs to salvage the car and prevent any further pollution of the lake; Herr Budget in Zurich decided his car had gone down in value by 20,000 despite my protestations that it would have been perfectly preserved in the cold waters of the St Moritzsee, and Urs's bill came to 3,500. Let's call it £15,000, and as clause 39(c) on the rental agreement disallowed driving off proper roads, the bill was all mine!

That was not quite the end of it. When I next saw him, Lynn Wilson was not a happy man. His more than sobering feeling was that I had nearly killed his children. What could I say? Even though Nick and Giles had been pretty calm about it all at the time, I had been driving and it had been my mistake. No one had been hurt but something could have gone horribly wrong.

Nor was Jon Holmes amused. I'd rung him from Switzerland at the time to tell him what had happened. 'You're going to like this one,' I began. He was staying with Gary Lineker at the time and the two of them were apparently convulsed with laughter as I told the story. Once he'd put his sensible hat back on he was 'not impressed'. I then came up with what I thought was a clever idea for recouping the cost. I'd do a Hamlet cigar advert . . . as the car sinks into the icy water, I'd sit on the edge on the lake and light up my cigar as 'Air on a G String' played in the background. *Happiness is a Cigar called Hamlet*. I didn't actually smoke, but that might add to it. But Holmes would have none of it. No way are you profiting from your own stupidity, he said. Shame, I thought, but there was no shifting him.

Although in common with the rest of the male species, I like to think I qualify as a perfectly competent driver, this was not the only time something large and mechanical nearly drove me to a sticky end. Some years later, while commentating on the 1995–96 tour of South Africa, we were in the Shamwari Game Reserve just near Port Elizabeth, with a few days off before Christmas and the Boxing Day Test at St George's Park. I was joined there by Thorunn and two-year-old daughter Alex, and friends of ours, Greig and Christina Macpherson and their baby and my godson, Matt.

We'd been doing our two daily drives into the park with our designated driver, Lucky, and had got to know the terrain pretty well. One evening after dinner I suggested we might do a night drive and that I would love to drive the Land Rover. Greig and Christina were up for it while Thorunn, pregnant with daughter-to-be number two, decided to stay at camp. I had driven open-top Defenders before at Londolozi and Phinda, and had no qualms about taking the wheel again. Lucky, bless him, blissfully unaware of my previous misdemeanours in St Moritz, after a moment's hesitation, agreed to navigate from the passenger seat and for a while, at least when the terrain was reasonably flat, all was well. I had noticed that the brakes weren't exactly, to coin a phrase, efficient but at this stage it didn't seem to matter much.

We then started on the ascent to the top of the escarpment that is the highest point of the reserve. I followed the winding track until I unfortunately found myself faced with a wall of rock and a lack of lock on the Defender's steering which meant I had to back up. The bad news was that this was the moment that I realised just how totally ineffective those brakes were. We started heading back down the hill, tail-lights first, not that they exactly shed much light on our rapidly worsening predicament. We didn't have long to think about all this, just long enough for Greig to shout, 'Jump!'

which he, Christina and Lucky duly did. A couple of seconds later, my uncontrolled descent of the hill came to an abrupt halt and I found myself looking up at the stars at an angle of approximately 45 degrees, wondering how that had happened. This is one of those times when you can veer towards believing in either God or guardian angels. The car had stopped thanks only to a combination of two things: one, the long wheel-base of the Defender which meant that the chassis was now wedged on the corner of the track, and two, and infinitely more important, the large and very solid termite mound that the rear end was now lodged against!

I was completely unhurt, though somewhat shaken, but immediately my thought was, 'Where the hell are the others?' I called their names. Greig and Christina both responded quickly but it took three or four increasingly frantic shouts before Lucky – who we can now say was indeed aptly named – finally confirmed he was still with us. He had damaged an ankle and had come to rest in a thorn bush but, let's face it, it could have been worse. Christina meanwhile had a long gash on her shin which she has never let me forget.

What to do next? Greig started scrabbling at the earth under the chassis to see if we could clear the way to somehow drive the car back onto the road. I'm afraid to say that it struck me immediately that this was never destined to be anything more than a futile gesture. It looked as though we would have to walk a couple of miles back to camp. The only consolation was that this was still early days at Shamwari and the only lions they had were still in a separate part of the reserve. However, before long there was a vehicle heading up the hill towards us driven by the park manager who had seen our lights and feared poachers. He was able to give us a lift back and make arrangements for the Defender to be tugged from its resting point in the morning. I slipped into bed quietly and chose an opportune moment the following day to give Mrs Gower a clue as to how close she'd come to being a single mother.

7

AN ASHES WINNING CAPTAIN

As England captain I experienced all available combinations of personal and collective success and failure. I scored no runs and lost the series. I scored no runs and won. I scored runs and lost, and scored runs and won. I don't need to tell you which proved the most satisfying, particularly as the opposition when I scored runs and won was Australia. While failing to score runs in defeat has little to recommend it, I actually found the worst combination was scoring runs and losing, as this was what happened shortly before the two times I was sacked as captain.

I don't know if 'going through the card' like this is unique but it must be pretty rare. While it would obviously have been ideal if I could have scored runs and led England to victory in every series I played, at least at the end of it I was well placed to understand the full gamut of emotions a captain can go through. Captaincy is a pretty constant talking point in the commentary box and whether things are going well or badly for those at the helm I generally feel I know something of what they are going through.

Although I endured three very bad hammerings as captain – losing 5–0 twice to West Indies and 4–0 to Australia can only be described as hammerings, I'm afraid – I did also enjoy two of the most exhilarating series wins available to an England player, beating India in India and Australia anywhere. Before the 2013 Ashes, only six Englishmen in 100 years had savoured the pleasure of leading England to victory over Australia at home, and only four had ever done so over India in their own back yard. I consider myself very lucky and privileged to have those two achievements on my CV – even if they did produce the only five wins on my captaincy record.

Of course, given how strong they were at that time, beating West Indies would have been best of all but England weren't alone in failing to manage that. West Indies didn't lose a series to anyone between 1980 and 1995 and you only had to cast your eye down their teamsheets to realise why. Those two 'blackwashes' were serious tests of character for all of us who were on the wrong end, and as captain I was just glad the experience didn't tip me over the edge completely. As Andrew Flintoff discovered when his team went down 5–0 in Australia many years later, it can be a pretty harrowing experience. At least most people stood by me during my two years as captain from 1984 to 1986.

The basic principle, in my book, is that as leader you should try to create an atmosphere that allows people to relax enough to perform at their best, and only when they don't do you intervene. I had players coming to me at various times saying they liked how this approach worked, while others would occasionally whinge because you were treating someone differently. You deal with people as they come to you and tackle problems as you spot them. I think players understand that captaincy is hard; it is all encompassing, time-consuming and draining, yet so fulfilling and joyous when you win. Although I would say that the best captains have been autocratic and self-sufficient, it also makes sense in this ever more demanding of jobs to make the most of the management team that is now standard. It is safe to say that backroom staffs are much bigger today than they were back in the 1980s!

I wasn't a dictatorial captain. I envisaged an open house. My approach was to get everyone involved so that they felt part of the team. It is a captain's job to communicate a sense of common purpose and reaffirm the collective spirit. I can get on with, and talk to, all manner of people but sometimes players would go with their issues to Mike Gatting, who was a very good vice-captain to me, and he would then come to me. It doesn't matter how it's done, as long as it works. You have to have the right blend of authority.

I thought there were times when it was important to show that as captain you were able to rise above things when they were going badly, and not lose perspective. This was largely natural but also sometimes consciously done. When we were playing West Indies, it was a case of showing my team that I wasn't about to commit suicide. Inevitably, my head sometimes went down but I tried to make sure it happened off the field rather than on it. You've somehow got to carry on being cheerful in those situations. People think you should wear black if you're losing but it rarely helps. Of course, if you dare to smile, or share a joke, you risk accusations of not caring. It's not a question of not caring, but working out how to deal with the situation.

I always tried to work with my players rather than necessarily telling them what to do. I would encourage a bowler to set his own fields and choose which end he wanted to bowl. Call it radical, but I thought he knew more about the business of bowling than I did. Generally, I found that if a player was given responsibility he responded well to it; that if you treated him like an adult, he was more likely to actually behave like one. Other regimes around that time, of course, thought it better to treat players like schoolboys in need of constant discipline. I disagreed. Mike Gatting, for one, said he appreciated the faith I showed in him, not only by appointing him my deputy in India but by letting him bat where he wanted to at

No. 3, whereas previously he had rarely been trusted to go in higher than five (he invariably batted three for Middlesex). Phil Edmonds was a similar case. He had been regarded in the past as difficult but I'd had no problems with him before and had none when he played for me. Graeme Fowler also appreciated being allowed to make decisions for himself. He said that it was the first time he had been given a choice about what he needed to do to be ready for a game.

Chris Cowdrey once said that he thought Graham Gooch and I wanted to captain as we played. Maybe he had a point.

I pre-supposed everyone to be equally capable of looking after their own games until I found out otherwise, and of course not everyone had the strength of mind or self-sufficiency to do so. Some need encouraging, others need a sharp kick up the backside, and perhaps I wasn't always firm enough with those who needed guidance. Maybe that was a failing. Certainly for some, treating them like an adult proved to be an over-promotion.

A newcomer to Test cricket obviously needs more help than a veteran. I would encourage people to come forward with ideas – not something that required a second invitation with the likes of Edmonds, upon whom I could unfailingly rely to approach me within the first half dozen overs of any innings in the field and whatever the conditions with the words, 'Captain, I am not averse to an early bowl' – but this is less likely to happen if they are in their early twenties and have played for England only a handful of times. The more you play, the more you learn to question decisions and strategies, but I could never see the advantage of treating your players like paid servants, or lackeys waiting for instructions. People can accuse you of being laissez-faire, or captaining by committee, but I always thought the more ideas the better, as long as the captain makes the final call.

Creating the right kind of relaxed environment for players to perform well, and asking everyone to think like a captain, has been very much the approach of modern England sides from Michael Vaughan onwards, and it may be no coincidence that they have enjoyed such great success. One of the big improvements in the English game has been the development of emerging talent through the England Lions and England A programmes, and without wishing to shift responsibility I think that had the younger players of my era been better prepared for Test cricket fewer of them would have needed help. At the risk of using a base statistic without qualification, between 2004 and 2009, four England players scored hundreds on Test debut. During the period of my entire Test career – spanning 1978 to 1992 – none did so.

I wasn't a great one for rallying speeches or up-and-at-'em tirades, but I did occasionally blow a fuse. The storm soon passed. I'd have a complete rant and then return to my usual even-tempered self, hopefully without having created too much ill-feeling in the interim. When I had a rant it was generally a means of issuing a wake-up call. The one I recall with most satisfaction was the explosion at tea on the final day in Delhi on the 1984–85 tour of India. India only had to bat the day out, Kapil Dev was still in and there was an air of resignation creeping in. I had my say, declared angrily that the game was far from f***ing over, and apparently woke a few up. I'd love to say that it was that rant which won the game but Kapil getting himself out, or falling victim of a cunning plan to be caught at deep midwicket, did help.

If blowing your top is your only trick apart from being cool and considered then it soon loses its meaning. For precisely this reason, Mike Brearley rarely went in for shouting, although he may have made an exception in Edmonds's case. You can only rant so often. Nasser Hussain was a much stronger and more volatile character, and by all accounts wasn't averse to a rant, but his was an era when England needed someone to beat them round the head and toughen them up a bit, ready for Michael Vaughan's lighter touch. The approach of both men, naturally as it came to each, was entirely suitable to the state of the team at the time.

I had my incendiary moments too as captain at Leicestershire, but I was leading them for the most part at times when I was also England captain, and it was often hard to be fully in touch with all aspects of how the team was performing when I was away so much. I'm afraid captaining England does leave you rather pre-occupied. As a club perhaps Leicestershire needed more guidance than I could realistically offer, although I did lead them to the Benson & Hedges Cup in 1985, which was our first trophy for eight years and highly satisfying for all concerned. A couple of years later they gave the captaincy to Peter Willey, who was more of a clenched-fist type. It was quite normal in those days for counties to be led by people who spent a lot of their time away with England – Botham captained Somerset and Gatting was in charge at Middlesex, for example – but it was difficult to juggle both roles. Gooch gave up after his first two seasons as Essex captain because he said his game was suffering. Today no county would dream of making a regular England player captain because they'd rarely see him.

I know that Clive Lloyd, a man whom I both admire and respect, once said something about how I was too 'self-centred' to lift the spirits of a losing side. To be honest I am not quite sure what he meant. If he meant self-centred as in selfish, I'd be upset. That whole 1985–86 tour was horrendous, starting with my mother dying the week before we left and later the sub-plot surrounding our South African rebels, who had just returned following three-year bans, to the great agitation of some politicians in the Caribbean. At the start of the tour, I tried to concentrate on the cricket and failed. I was self-centred to the extent that I allowed myself to be worried and isolated. It was my problem. Perhaps a better captain would have risen above it all better and would have somehow kept things going.

I wasn't the only one pre-occupied with my own problems. Graham Gooch, rather overly affected by the posturing of some very minor politicians on the matter of South Africa and the rebel tours and by the threats of a very small minority among the Caribbean public, was hankering to walk away from it all and to go home ahead of the final Test. As he was the man at the top of the order with the best ability to cope with the West Indies quicks, I thought I should talk him round and encourage him to stay. Just letting him go without doing so would have been too weak, I felt, and without him the team would have looked even weaker for that final Test. It is never an easy one to judge when a player is disaffected for whatever reason. Maybe I could have let him go and left him to ponder his future.

Whatever one might say about West Indies being an easy side to lead, Lloyd was a very good captain and excellent in the way he brought together the various elements that make up the West Indies cricket team, remembering that the history of cricket in that region is one of inter-island rivalry and jealousy. Clive was very much a unifying force. Jeff Dujon said that when he first joined the West Indies side Lloyd took him out for dinner and assured him he was a big part of the team. He made him feel valued and in no way subservient. Little gestures like that make a big difference. This was a clear instance of a new player being treated like a grown-up. Lloyd had a great knack of taking people under his wing, but in those days West Indies had a stable group of players and perhaps that allowed him to treat the rare newcomers they had as special. Some of our England sides of that period saw such a high turnover of players that such a policy would have simply been impractical. 'Is that Langan's? David Gower here. Table for eight please, tonight. We have some new lads playing tomorrow.'

I would love to have captained England at a time before the media held so much sway, but unfortunately the press grew ever more influential during my career, to the point where in 1988 the Test and County Cricket Board (as it was then) felt obliged to appoint its first full-time media relations officer. After the Sex, Drugs and Rock 'n' Roll tour, the team was hardly likely to be short of company on tour and I remember at an early stage of the India tour the following winter being asked at a press conference how I was going to moderate the players' off-field conduct. I said it would all depend on how well newspaper editors controlled the imaginations of their reporters. I had a regular tormentor from the *Sun* who wrote as if fuelled by pure vitriol, although the tabloids weren't alone in putting the boot in. The correspondent of a respected broadsheet breezily suggested that while I went into hospital for shoulder surgery in 1989 I might like to book in for a lobotomy at the same time.

In the West Indies in 1986 we were often ripped to shreds by people who weren't even in the Caribbean, and even if they were there, some of the stories were such that we were left wondering if we were actually on the same tour as them. Private lives were once regarded as respected territory but no more. Before the first international match of the tour in Jamaica, when I was fully expecting questions along the lines of, 'How do you hope to compete with these boys?' I was truly astounded to be asked: 'Is it true you are having an affair with Paul Downton's wife?'

Utterly bonkers of course– though Ali is a lovely girl there was absolutely zero foundation to such a suggestion. As far as I understand it, kissing the bride chastely on the cheek for a wedding photo does not constitute having an affair. If it does, then all I can say to Paul now is that I am deeply sorry! I cannot for the life of me fathom where it came from – the question was linked to reports that all was not well with my relationship with Vicki, which was in fact true, and I daresay that a bit of digging might have unearthed some other suspects but definitely not

Ali. My mother's death had brought Vicki and I closer together briefly but she was not due to come out on that tour, although she came under such siege from the press at home that in the end we decided it would be best if she did. Even that did not go smoothly. The day she arrived a newspaper ran a story alleging I'd been cavorting with an air hostess in a pool in Trinidad, leaving me with yet more fire-fighting to do, although, to my shame I ought to admit that there was at least more truth in that story than in the previous one.

The Downton story was so preposterous that it was easy to laugh off. Had someone however asked some weeks later: 'Is it true that a cake was produced at the resort in Barbados for someone's birthday which had a little bit of cannabis in it?', then the answer would have to have been: 'Er, what, er, that's true, but . . .' But fortunately no one did. On that one, I might add, as captain I was kept out of the loop and was blissfully, well soberly, unaware!

By and large, press conferences are a tedious ritual. Even today's England players, who are generally treated more kindly than we were, have hinted at their frustration at being asked to do so many, but they are hardly going to go away. The best thing for a captain to do is to keep cool and maintain confidence in his judgement, even when the side is doing badly. There is nothing to be gained by moaning about what is being written or said. It rarely helps your mood to find you have been written off as a hopeless duffer. Unfortunately, emotions do come into it and for all my good intentions I did get riled by some lines of press conference questioning, and some of the articles written about me. Perhaps the best thing to do is regard a press conference as part of the game and play it accordingly. Publicly affirming your belief that you are going to do well in a series or tour doesn't do any harm, even if it sometimes leaves you looking a trifle foolish if you end up getting hammered. Before that West Indies tour we genuinely believed we could make a major improvement on how we'd done in 1984. In fact, things turned out worse.

The 1984 series was arduous enough. Against an attack led by Malcolm Marshall and Joel Garner at the top of their form, our batting struggled to make headway and we did not top 300 once. I managed an unbeaten 57 at Headingley but mustered only 57 more runs in nine other innings. I'd felt quite comfortable with the captaincy in the games I'd done in Pakistan but this was another magnitude of challenge altogether. Things actually started quite well in the first ODI at Old Trafford, where we got into a very strong position only for Viv Richards to play one of the most astonishing one-day innings I've ever seen. By the time he and Michael Holding had put on more than 100 for the last wicket, the game had been well and truly turned on its head. Through that summer, things just kept chipping away at our confidence and belief that we could win even one game. We quickly realised that if we were going to win a game we'd have to play out of our skins. Sadly, that never happened and as the defeats kept coming so did the changes to the team as we desperately sought ways to improve.

Fortunately, I managed to rationalise it all by telling myself that no one else could have done any better had they been in charge. Alternatives, in fact, were few on the ground with some senior players serving bans for touring South Africa. Graham Gooch and John Emburey might have strengthened our side had they been available but had either of them captained the side there would have only been differences in style, not substance.

In hindsight I don't think I could have done much different, except perhaps delay my declaration even longer than I did at Lord's and make sure that at least we came away with a draw. I have talked about why we came off for bad light when we did on the fourth evening. What I haven't discussed was our performance the next day, when West Indies chased 344 with such incredible ease. We were simply dreadful. The bowlers didn't bowl to their fields and our fielding was nothing special either. I had a rant that day, I can tell you, although I saved it for the dressing room at tea when the doors were shut and I spoke loud and clear. That was a game in which I experienced a whole range of emotions, from elation and satisfaction through to disappointment, fearfulness, and eventually hopelessness and anger. It was the worst day of the series.

I think that even the press understood my dilemma that summer and during the Test at Old Trafford, where we went 4–0 down, I followed my formal press conference with an impromptu heart-to-heart with certain senior journalists in which I frankly said: 'What do you want me to do? What can I do? We're trying, but they are just better than us.' There may have been decisions of mine you could have quibbled with but the bottom line was that if you had been assembling a composite XI you'd rather have had nine of their players than nine of ours. You might have kept Botham at a pinch but I could hardly have even picked myself on the form of that series.

My desperation to achieve any sort of victory, however small, had been evident at Old Trafford when I asked Paul Terry if he would go out to bat despite his left arm having been broken earlier by a short ball from Winston Davis. He generously agreed. My original thought was that he could help Allan Lamb get to his third hundred of the series. We were getting thumped and I wanted Lamb to get another hundred for his sake and to show that some-one could achieve something striking even against a side as mightily strong as West Indies. When the ninth wicket fell Lamb was on 98. He duly got the two runs and he and Terry duly started to walk off but by then the thought had occurred that perhaps they (or rather Lamb) could get the 21 runs we needed to avoid the follow on. So I waved to them to stay out there (of course, this was what I hadn't done at Lord's when Lamb and Pringle were batting together!) It was a foolhardy idea and it didn't work. Unable to defend himself, Terry was promptly bowled by Garner. That was me clutching at a wisp of straw.

Early that season I went down with blood poisoning, which put me out of action for three weeks and had a lengthy impact on my game: my average was lower that summer than in any other season bar 1980 since I became an England player. I grazed the knuckle on my right index finger while playing for MCC in the champion county game at Lord's and within a few days it was plainly badly infected. My lower arm began to swell up nastily and I missed the final day of our championship match at Chesterfield. Back home I tried a glass of champagne but the instant I took the first sip I had this searing pain in my finger and arm. The doctor was summoned, took one look and I was immediately admitted to a private hospital in Leicester for treatment. I spent the week there on the strongest antibiotics available, with needles being inserted every four hours to first administer the drugs and alternately to check my blood. I am not exaggerating to say it was touch and go but I was so out of it that I had little idea of the severity of my condition.

I was only confirmed as England captain for the West Indies series after making my comeback and 24 hours later I celebrated with a hundred at Worcester. But my finger, which initially resembled a burnt barbecued sausage, remained very stiff and sore for a long time afterwards and even a year later I was sent for a medical check-up to see if the infection was still lurking somewhere in my system. Mike Turner said he was told by a leading specialist that had I suffered the same condition a few years earlier I might easily have died.

I was very happy the selectors stuck with me for India, although, like I say, I'm not sure how much choice they really had. With a tour, you have more of a chance as captain to stamp your mark, pick the players you want and generally set your own tone.

There was no still Gooch, Emburey or Willey because of their bans and Botham had also opted to have a winter off after years without a break. He was inevitably a big loss but we didn't arrive in India wringing our hands and wondering how on earth we were going to cope without him. We just had to get on with it. Chris Cowdrey snuck on the tour in his place. Chris was of course a great mate of mine and I was delighted he was with us but I would have to deny fervently that he was there just to keep me company! We originally saw him having a role in the one-dayers, which in those days were interspersed with the Tests, but when it came to picking a side for the Tests we realised we could do with him to balance the side by bowling a few overs and he was just the man to put at short leg. So he played, with famous consequences for his father's driving when Colin in his excitement drove down a one-way street in the wrong direction after hearing his son on the radio commentary dismiss Kapil Dev for his first wicket. Chris had in fact rung me before the tour concerned that he wouldn't be able to go because he was carrying a hamstring strain and might not be able to bowl for a couple of weeks. 'Good', I said. 'We'll see you on the flight.'

We picked people to do a job. We left out Chris Broad – I was happy to have him but was outvoted on a panel chaired by Peter May and also including Alec Bedser, Phil Sharpe and A C Smith – and if I'd held out to win that battle I would probably have lost another elsewhere. Broad was perceived as good against pace, and not so good against spin, while Tim Robinson – who was then uncapped – was rated as good against spin and a solid accumulator, so we went with him to open alongside Graeme Fowler.

In exchange for Robinson I got my way on two semi-controversial choices in Gatting and Edmonds. Gatting hadn't done much against West Indies and had made slow progress in his Test career since beating me to a place on the 1977–78 tour, but he was a very good player of spin and would be an excellent vice-captain. He was ambitious and others said later that by giving him a lift up I had opened up the possibility of him one day replacing me, which is what eventually happened, but I certainly wouldn't make an issue of that. He was a very good lieutenant for me and scored a lot of runs for us on this tour, and I was grateful on both counts. Vitally, Mike scored a double-century, as did Fowler, in our big win in Madras.

We were recalling Edmonds for his first tour since falling out with Brearley in Australia six years earlier but to me this wasn't an issue. My attitude was that he was clearly the best left-arm spinner in the country and that in India we might need someone who knew how to spin the ball. As it happened, he developed the yips at the start of the tour, where he would take his three paces to the stumps, stop and have to bowl from a standing position. He was strong enough to do that but it didn't look great and I began to fear that I might have to send home my main spinner in a straitjacket. It got to the stage where I went to see him in his room in Rajkot prior to the first Test but I'd barely started to speak before he cut me off. 'Dave, if you've come to talk to me about my bowling, don't . . . I'll be all right.' So I left him lying on a horrible mattress, reading some piece of high literature by a dim electric light in our flea-ridden hotel . . . and fine he was.

He didn't cure it overnight but recovered to play a vital role, he and 'Percy' Pocock, who was himself making his first Test tour for 11 years filling the off-spinner's role vacated by Emburey, getting through more than 500 overs between them in the Tests and giving me a lot of control. Life was rarely dull with Edmonds around. He always liked to be involved and also played a valuable innings in the final Test, sharing a century stand with me that sealed the draw we needed to win the series.

We built up a very good spirit, perhaps precisely because we were such an inexperienced, enthusiastic team. I'd like to think it was partly down to me too but I know a lot was due to the characters of the people involved. Apart from myself, Cowdrey and Gatting, there were other survivors from the Young England tour of West Indies in 1976 in Downton and Allott. Fowler and Lamb were great, two cheeky, chirpy chappies, while Pocock, who was excited to be back playing for England at such a late stage in his career, was full of ideas. (I still get emails from Percy now, incandescent about something we've said, or failed to say, about spin bowling on commentary!).

India can be a difficult place to tour but because you have to make your own entertainment you are thrown together in a way you aren't in, say, Australia. I think India is an absolutely fascinating country and later in the tour I left Gatting in charge for our match against East Zone and went off tiger hunting with Tim Robinson (cameras only – no weapons). But given the vast crowds that cricketers attract, moving around can be difficult and not everyone is keen to leave the hotel. But we had a lot of fun. There was one famous evening in Hyderabad where we were staying at a hotel on a lake, which had an ornamental fountain in the middle, and we took to the water in shikaras, the local version of gondolas. We challenged the press (with whom relations were good on this tour) to a race round the fountain from the hotel jetty, but the race had the added spice of Pocock and Fowler, both of whom had good arms, taking up positions on the roof of the hotel, several storeys up, and pelting the teams with oranges and plastic bags full of water.

It could have been all clean, harmless fun but one of the water bombs unravelled as it left the hand and dropped onto the floor of the open air restaurant below, landing next to a Swedish scientist who had the shock of his life and was quite put off his biryani. Although the incident was hardly life threatening, he was understandably riled. When I got back from leading my gallant men to a glorious win in the shikara races I was confronted by the Swede wanting to know who was in charge. 'Well, I am.' He wanted a full report to go to our authorities, so I found some headed TCCB notepaper, borrowed a typewriter from Chris Lander of the *Daily Mirror* and duly reported myself to the authorities. With him mollified, the next man to deal with was the hotel manager, who was concerned at the damage to his shikaras, some of which had suffered from the odd broadside ramming. In his case a cash payment was enough to bring the matter to an amiable close.

Our sense of togetherness was probably all the firmer for the tragic events in the early weeks of the tour in which Mrs Indira Gandhi, India's prime minister, and Percy Norris, the British Deputy High Commissioner were assassinated. These appalling incidents obviously shook us badly. Mrs Gandhi was killed within hours of our arrival and Percy Norris was shot dead in the days before the first Test in Bombay, only hours after hosting a party for us the previous evening. While these crises brought us together, it would be trite to say that they somehow made us determined to fight all the harder and show how British we were. That's just nonsense.

With Mrs Gandhi's death, the tour was halted before it had even started. We expressed our deepest sympathies to the Indian people at our opening press conference – to the alarm of some of the Indian journalists who had not yet heard the news – and then spent the next few days using the High Commission in Delhi as our daily refuge. We then received a kind offer from Sri Lanka to go there and play a couple of games until the mourning in India was over, which, with no disrespect intended to India, seemed the best solution to our problem because there was no chance of any cricket in India until life got back to normal. The nine days we spent in Colombo can only be described as a fairly hedonistic mix of cricket and partying with diplomats, business folk and tourists, and did as much as anything to forge team spirit.

While the death of Mrs Gandhi was terrible, we felt one stage removed from it. That was not the case with Percy Norris, whose generous hospitality we had only just enjoyed. High Commission functions were a common feature of tours in those days and were approached with mixed feelings. Some could be highly social and fun, others were painfully formal and dull and would leave players exchanging furtive glances about when it was okay to make their excuses and leave. We had set out with some reluctance but this one was very much the former, which only made our host's death all the more poignant. The players were understandably spooked and a crisis meeting was promptly called to discuss the tour's future. The High Commission assured us there was no specific anti-British motive to Mr Norris's death and we were not targets, but I wasn't going to say we're staying without giving people a chance to speak, although I hoped that by exuding an air of calm the players might be persuaded that I viewed the risks as low. Some of them needed convincing but Tony Brown, the tour manager, was quite belligerent, saying that the team was staying and any player wanting to go home could take his passport. It was a slightly confrontational meeting but although Allan Lamb was keen to take possession of his no one actually left or withdrew from the Test. But when, the following day, with the HC's advice that we were safe to carry on pretty much as normal albeit with a lot of security in attendance, Gatting and I went round the rooms one by one to inform the players that we were going down to the ground to practice, it was Graeme Fowler who said: 'Practice? What sort of practice? Target practice?'

I wouldn't put down our defeat in the first Test simply to unease but it was a factor: people certainly weren't as focused or as settled as we would have liked. We were given repeated assurances about heightened security around the Wankhede Stadium but that didn't stop us casting an anxious eye around the place as we took the field. In choosing to bat first, I might have had half a mind on the thought that if we were indeed targets it might be best if only two of us were out there rather than 11! Mind you, few of us batted long enough to come under serious threat.

Losing the first Test was my worst fear following our experience on the 1981–82 tour, where the series descended into futility as India sat on their early lead. But what was outstanding was that we had enough guys keen to do well that they weren't fazed by our position, and we went on to win the second Test in Delhi thanks to a great last-day performance and the fourth in Madras on a wicket with enough pace and bounce to help Neil Foster, who bowled beautifully, to take 11 wickets. We had almost given up in Delhi but fine bowling from Edmonds and Pocock and a couple of brainless shots (one of which cost Kapil Dev his place) brought us six wickets in the penultimate session and set up a manageable run-chase. Smog, rain and some bizarre tactics from India's captain Sunil Gavaskar, who seemed to lack any urgency in search of the win he needed, led to the third Test in Calcutta being drawn amid the kind of tedium familiar from our previous visit.

My form was not great but I made runs in the final match when they were needed to save the follow on, draw the match and preserve our lead. I hadn't been playing well against Laxman Sivaramakrishnan, who bowled India to victory in the first Test, although in Delhi I was given out to what I considered a shockingly bad piece of umpiring. Siva was bowling from round the wicket, turning the ball in from well outside my off stump, and hit me on the pads in line. Anyone with any idea about angles must have known that the ball was going down leg. I later had a quiet word with the umpire, P D Reporter, with whom I got on very well and who took my remarks in the friendly spirit in which they were delivered. Unfortunately, we'd already had issues with umpiring in the first Test, when I felt a lot of decisions went against us, many made by a large fellow by the name of Swaroop Kishen, whom I knew from previous visits to be a bloody good umpire. I thought he just had a bad game but we weren't happy and this view duly went into my captain's report. This was supposed to be a confidential document but somehow the contents became public. I had told the players before the tour that dissent towards umpires would not be tolerated – a couple of players had overstepped the mark in Pakistan – but now unfortunately I had no choice but to state we did not wish to see Mr Kishen again. Nor did we. In fact, the umpiring in the last three Tests was perfectly acceptable.

Sadly, some of the gloss was taken off our triumph by having to return home via Australia for a one-day tournament to celebrate the 150th anniversary of the founding of Victoria. As an excuse to stage what amounted to a mini-World Cup – at least in the eyes of the promoters – this must rank among the thinnest, but we were expected to give it our best shot and there was no shortage of harrumphing when we failed to win a game. After three months on the subcontinent, we were emotionally spent and with a week off before our first warm-up fixture, a period earmarked for preparation felt temptingly like an opportunity for some well deserved down-time. I popped over to Hobart with Vicki to visit Brian and Caroline Davison for a few days and left the rest of them having a riotous time in Sydney. This proved to be a big mistake because when I returned it was impossible to get things going again. We'd experienced something similar at the end of the previous summer when we played our first home Test against Sri Lanka. Though relative newcomers, they showed they possessed some fine players by having the better of the game but after our high-octane meetings with West Indies we struggled to raise ourselves for the contest. This time, however, it was worse; we lost to a NSW 3rd XI at Manley and only just saw off the 2nd XI at Sydney University.

By the time we got to Ballarat and Bendigo in Victoria we had no idea where we were and we were also down to 12 fit men. It was all a bit of a struggle.

The glory of India receded further in the memory as I struggled for runs in the early weeks of the English season. I had passed fifty only three times in 11 Tests as official captain and was still awaiting my first hundred, and my form became a fairly lively topic of debate. Should I be allowed to go back to concentrating solely on making runs? Although I would not have thought so at the time, the concerns being expressed were entirely reasonable. The Ashes were important and the country wanted them regained.

Mercifully, the selectors kept faith and deliverance was at hand in the one-day international at Lord's. I took a steepling catch from David Boon that somehow stuck, just the sort of moment that convinces you it is your day, and then rode some rather generous luck in the early stages of my innings to score a hundred as we chased down more than 250. I had a particularly close escape on the short boundary in front of the Tavern, when a pull shot only just had the legs to clear the rope, and I would have to concede that I hadn't played brilliantly, but at the end of the day I finally felt like I was back in some sort of nick.

On the back of that day hinged what turned out to be my favourite summer. I didn't get many runs in the first Test at Leeds, made 80-odd at Lord's, where Australia levelled the series at 1–1, but after that things just got better and better – for me and the team. I can't really put my finger on why my form hit those heights that summer but maybe it had finally sunk in that I should make the most of the feeling that I had seldom if ever been in better form. Form is impossible to define but when things click, they click, and there were other incentives in my mind too. I was after all captain of England for the first time in one of the game's most historic contests, and at something of a peak physically.

We also had Botham back in the team, and playing his best, and our rebels were available again, while Australia had lost Terry Alderman, among others, to their own rebel tour of South Africa. Gooch and Robinson, our openers, both topped 475 runs in the six Tests, Gatting exceeded 500 while I finished with 732, which was apparently an England record at home to Australia and, according to one onlooker, the most 'by a batsman who was as dispirited and as close to the plug hole as Gower was only three months ago.'

Perhaps one of the secrets of my success was an absolute chance encounter that led to me finding the best bat I had ever used. Wandering into the office at Grace Road I found Mike Turner Junior, son of the chief executive and a club player himself (this is no time to quibble about his talent as such!), who showed me a new bat he had just received from County Sports. I picked it up, and bounced a ball on it, and straight away thought, 'This bat is too good for you, sunshine!' It was extraordinary. I'd never felt a ball ping off a brand new bat like this before. And so, I offered him any number of my bats in exchange for his. He ended up with a couple of beautiful Gray-Nicolls and I got to work changing the stickers on his. I ought to say at this stage that Gray-Nicolls, who had supported me from my early days as a fledgling county player, had produced for me any number of brilliant bats but it was just a quirk of willow that made this one too good to ignore.

The innings at the Oval was the favourite of the three hundreds I scored, even though the double-hundred at Edgbaston was statistically my best ever and was made in a situation in which we needed to score runs quickly because time had been lost to rain. The pitch in Birmingham was an absolute featherbed, as was the one at Trent Bridge, where the game ended in a dull draw. If the bowler somehow managed to get the ball head height on either of them, you were going to have plenty of time to deal with it, and I remember spending a lot of time batting in my floppy white hat. There wasn't a lot of that going on the previous summer, or the following winter, against West Indies, I can tell you.

But going into that Oval game was to stand on the edge of a beautiful dream. It could have gone wrong were we to lose the game. You don't really want to think about playing for a draw, though a draw would have been enough to seal the Ashes. Win the game though and you not only win the Ashes but win them properly, comprehensively. We knew a good first day would take us a long way towards our goal and so to personally score 157 before stumps, having gone in early at No. 3 with so much at stake, was fantastic. I had one bit of luck early on where a ball from Craig McDermott took the shoulder of the bat and flew over the slips, but apart from that I look back and think, God that was great. I've got some video footage which I would look at any day you like to cheer myself up. That was the apogee.

Later, as we were bowling Australia out, there was a decision to be made about the follow on. As ever, I was happy to hear everyone's views, with some arguing that following on was the only way Australia could get back into the game, but I felt we hadn't taken much out of ourselves with the ball, and were in complete control, so I said, 'Thanks guys, it's my decision, they're following on.' And we went on to win by an innings. It was all simply marvellous.

I have some treasured photographs of the occasion, the scene on the balcony with Botham showering me with some unpronounceable Australian beer, and me receiving a replica of the Ashes urn which was so tiny, only a few inches tall, that the crowds below could not possibly have known what it was I was holding had not Peter West of the BBC said, 'The Ashes!' I was rather hoping to take the urn home and place it on my mantelpiece but the strict instruction was that this was one of MCC's official replicas and had to be sent straight back to Lord's. No matter. There was no taking away the gorgeous feeling of being an Ashes winning captain, a simple joy that came with knowing that, as a cricketer, it was moments like this that you played for.

As for my opposite number, our careers had developed at much the same time, and much the same pace. I'd always got on well with Allan Border, and in amongst the fray we always seemed to find time for a bit of light banter, at odds maybe with the stereotypical version of the way any Australian would play a Test match. The fact that we did not subject each other to full-on Neanderthal sledging does not mean that this was anything but an intense contest. As it happened, four years later, that all changed as far as AB was concerned, and he ditched the concept of friendship among foes, for all-out enmity. That, simply, is not something I could ever see myself doing but it certainly worked for him.

I said on the Oval balcony that I was sure West Indies would be 'quaking in their boots' at the thought of playing us next. I was only being half-serious, if that, but I was quite optimistic that we could put up more of a fight than we'd managed at home. After all, we were at full strength again. I'd been in the job more than a year and we seemed to be making progress as a side.

As it turned out, the tour of the Caribbean was, as I've already suggested, my hardest time as captain. It was possibly one of the toughest assignments any England captain has gone through because we were totally outplayed by a superior side and our batting, in particular, was given a working over the like of which has rarely been seen. In one sense we improved on 1984 in making two totals of more than 300 but in our other eight innings we never exceeded 200. It wouldn't be an exaggeration to say that some of us were shell-shocked long before the end. The pitch on which the first Test was played at Sabina Park was disconcertingly uneven, prompting John Woodcock, the distinguished and long-serving correspondent of the *Times* to write, 'I have never felt it more likely that we should see someone killed.'

I took a battering from Courtney Walsh in the match against Jamaica beforehand – Walsh at this stage could only get into the West Indies side for one of the five Tests – but got some runs in the Tests, three half-centuries and 370 runs in all, representing riches indeed against such a venomous pace attack, some members of which seemed unconcerned at the prospect that Woodcock's fear might actually be realised.

It is amazing I scored as many as I did. My mother's death had naturally taken a toll and things with Vicki had not been good for a while. Other factors militated against us. The long break between the end of the English season and the beginning of the tour in January left us starting cold (compare and contrast to England's sluggishness in their new year series against Pakistan in 2011–12) and the practice facilities in Antigua, where we spent much of our preparation time, were terrible. Nor, as I've also pointed out, did the press help create a climate of calm. It was quite a lonely time. The confidence that brimmed over against Australia fast evaporated and I was left putting on a front, giving the impression that everything was okay even when it wasn't. Inevitably, sometimes the mask slipped. I've never known such concerted outside pressures on a touring side and you don't make your best decisions in those circumstances. I look back on that tour and think, yes, I would re-do things.

The team was perhaps not as shrewdly selected as the one for India but there could be no quibbling with the rights of Gooch and Botham to be there, even though they both experienced difficult tours. Botham was under intense scrutiny from the press pack, for whom anything he did was the big prize, while Gooch, as I have described, spent much of his time fretting over the fuss made in the Caribbean from relatively minor politicians about his South African connections; the West Indies had not let their rebel players return and there was considerable hostility to those in our side who had been let back in. There was a demonstration when we arrived at Trinidad airport but the overall level of protest was not significant and he should have taken a leaf out of Peter Willey's book and brushed it off as a fuss about nothing.

If my boat trip with Botham during the opening match in St Vincent created unhelpful press coverage, the decision to declare net practice optional in the wake of a defeat in the third Test in Barbados spanning little more than three days was nothing short of a PR disaster. I would still maintain that, while possibly not the finest decision ever, frogmarching the players down for punishment training on net pitches that were sub-standard before the game began and now next to useless was hardly going to rebuild confidence. Net practice is not the solution to everything but in the light of such a defeat perhaps we had to be seen doing something, even if it amounted to little more than a show of contrition.

As it was, we arranged two days of nets and made the first one non-compulsory. My mistake was in being among the six players who opted out, but after all that had happened I just felt I needed some time off, to get away from things, and try and get a fresh perspective on what was happening. That being the case, I could hardly compel everyone else to go to work without me. Of course, when the press learnt of my non-attendance, and also that I had spent some of the day wind-surfing, they let me have it with both barrels, which I suppose on reflection was not a surprise.

Whatever the critics' views, my own feeling is that I was the victim of something of a perfect storm. On top of all the issues I have mentioned so far was one more problem. Just when I needed my main man, the world's leading all-rounder, to be at his ebullient and brilliant best, he wasn't.

Beefy's role as a strike bowler rather than a stock one had worked well at home against the Australians but he was simply not in the right form or fitness to fulfil the same role now. Having four months off before the tour had hurt him, not because he had let himself go physically but because a marathon charity walk from John O'Groats to Land's End had inflicted a toll on his body from which he'd yet to recover. True to my beliefs, I allowed him to do what he thought he had to in preparation for the Tests. Given the toll on his body, it is understandable that he was not exactly full on in the nets but it became an issue for others in the squad who were being expected and asked to do more. Such are the risks of attempting to treat people differently within a team. By the time we were getting ready for the fourth Test in Trinidad his casual attitude to bowling in the nets had created a hostile mood among some others in the camp but, more importantly, his bowling with the new ball had let us all down. I admittedly pandered to his whims and allowed him the luxury of too many slips and gullies to sustain his dream of peppering Gordon Greenidge and Desmond Haynes with sheer pace.

Now I should have been the first to realise that the plan was not working. I was in my usual position at cover and therefore well aware of the number of times that I was picking the ball up from the edge of the field. Those slips and gullies were having a lovely quiet time of it. Loyalty to my mate – and belief in him – left us all in the lurch.

It was an interesting discussion on selection for that fourth Test and Ian held on to his place only by a whisker. I went to see him in his room at the 'upside down' Hilton on the edge of the famous Savannah to inform him of how close he'd come to the axe. As with Edmonds in Rajkot the previous winter, it was not a long conversation and he accepted what little I had to say. Things did improve but by then damage was already done.

I only caught on to the ill-feeling at a late stage and had blown my top about it at a specially convened meeting. I felt angry at what I viewed as a whingeing attitude but in truth I also realised that it was not only my temper I'd lost control of but the entire tour.

At the end of it all, what was hardest to take was not that we had yet again been beaten by one of the finest cricket sides of all time, but that we had been unable to put up more resistance. As captain, you are honour bound to take the blame but I honestly don't feel that even the finest captains in England's history would have changed the result of that series drastically. It was an object lesson however as to how the dominance of one side and the extreme pressure created by that dominance can expose every little weakness and every crack in the unity of the opposition. I felt at the start of the tour that we were a pretty spirited group but ultimately we were as powerless as Canute against the waves.

8

YOU WIN SOME, YOU LOSE SOME

The role of England captain is a great honour and privilege and when it goes well there are few things to beat it. But it is in the nature of the relationship that it rarely ends well. Few holders of the post have been fortunate enough to go out on a great high. Michael Vaughan and Andrew Strauss were among the most successful captains England have had, yet both withdrew from the fray beaten men after home defeats coincidentally to South Africa. Both had great records but would have dreamt of happier endings. Vaughan tried to get back into the Test side purely as a player without success, while Strauss quit altogether, his energy drained by the all-consuming nature of the job.

I had a different problem when the captaincy was taken away from me in 1986. I was 29 years old and, though fairly demoralised by a string of losses, had no real wish to stop playing altogether. But the re-integration of a former captain into the team is not a simple matter. As the man who has been used to making all the decisions, it is hard to adjust to your new role. Doubts swirl around you. All you really want is to feel involved and receive the precious assurance that you are still valued, still important. Equally, the new captain has the challenge of clearly showing that he is now the

184

man to follow while being mindful of the need to get the best out of the man he has just replaced. The last thing he wants is an ex-skipper mooching around feeling sorry for himself. The Prime Minister has become a backbencher and if the situation is not handled right he can quickly resort to what backbenchers do, namely whinge.

As it turned out I played another 29 Tests back in the ranks – in two spells broken by a brief return to the top job in 1989 – and in those games topped 2,000 runs at an average of nearly 46, which was slightly higher than my overall career figure. As a lifelong Monty Python fan, I have always tried to follow Eric Idle and 'always look on the bright side of life' but it was a far from straight-forward journey and I spent the months following my demotion in a state of some emotional turmoil.

I returned from the Caribbean feeling very low. Those who knew me well, such as Jon Holmes, said later that they had never seen me lower. I knew that I had failed to lift the team, even if we were up against an incredibly strong West Indies side, and my self-belief had probably been more thoroughly tested than anyone's. The series had not ended pleasantly, with Viv Richards voicing his displeasure in pretty vehement terms at what he saw as our time-wasting tactics towards the end of the final Test in Antigua. He had struck a brutal 56-ball hundred earlier in the game and, so close to a 5–0 clean sweep, was in no mood to be denied. What he expected us to do – throw in the towel at tea?! – I have no idea but he got his win anyway.

One tries to be gracious, even in the face of such a massive thrashing. The recurrent theme throughout that tour, in a musical sense, had been the Trinidadian calypso, Gypsy's 'Captain the Ship is Sinking'. Its true relevance was to recent tricky times in Trinidadian politics but by the time we were halfway round the Caribbean the rough seas in the lyrics were all mine. Crowds were singing it at me and the BBC used it as the soundtrack over their under-standably disparaging report put together as the series was lost. Despite the dark subject it is a typically upbeat and catchy piece of music. My mood by the end of that Antigua Test was far from bright and breezy but it did inspire one final sardonic comment at the post-match presentations: 'Ladies and gentlemen; the ship has well and truly sunk.'

People at home were fairly upset too. There had been a big disparity between the expectation and the reality of the tour: the public, like the players, were hoping for an improvement on 1984 and when it wasn't forthcoming the inquest became all the more searching. The calls for the team to be given a full-time manager, a regimental sergeant-major who could restore respect and pride, were one manifestation of that. So be it. If you lose 5–0, there are going to be demands for change, as Duncan Fletcher found many years later.

I knew my future hung by a fairly thin thread but no sooner had I got back than I dunked myself into a deep tub of hot water with my county. I had taken a week in Barbados to 'gather my thoughts', with the help of a bottle of Cockspur and a 2CV-driving blonde. Now there's a combination and I have to say that as an antidote to three of the toughest months of my life it largely worked. When I got home there was the usual pile of mail to deal with and I sat down a couple of days later to tackle it. I thought I was going well and then the phone rang; it was an irate Mike Turner on the other end. 'Where are you?' he asked. Ah, yes, Leicestershire's pre-season cocktail party. I'd clean forgotten. Insisting I was just on my way, I hurried into a suit and down to Grace Road, but Charles Palmer, the club chairman, was neither fooled nor impressed. It was an honest mistake on my part but he saw it as an unforgivable sin and bizarrely it seemed to rankle so much with Charles and the club's committee that the ill-feeling lasted through the summer.

Disappointingly, they – and not me for once – dragged their heels in deciding whether to award me a benefit for the following season, though as it was due, on the ten-years-as-a-capped-player convention, and as there was nobody else queuing for one, it should have been a done deal. All because I missed the first Everards of the season!

As it was already mid-April and the season was upon us, there was little time to ponder and all one could do was get on and play, desperately trying to find the appropriate enthusiasm and regain one's good humour. As luck would have it, within a few days I found myself playing a championship match at Old Trafford and who should I be up against? None other than Patrick Patterson, the Jamaican fast bowler who had bowled at the speed of light at Sabina Park in the opening encounter of our Caribbean nightmare and had rather set the tone for our travails there. Great! It was one of those times when I started as though wearing a blindfold, so much so that James Whitaker strolled down from the other end and said, 'Look, Captain, don't you think you should stop batting as if you've only got one arm?' – or something of that ilk. I looked at him, said nothing and took guard for the next over from 'Patto'. (God knows why I should refer to him with any sort of affectionate nickname but he was, as with so many of those West Indies quicks, a very nice guy. He called me 'D'.) At the end of the over, 16 runs to the better as something finally kicked in, I went to find James again. 'That any better?' I asked.

Around mid-May, I was told I was being retained as captain for the two one-day internationals and the first of three Tests against India. As a vote of confidence, it had barely half a heart in it, especially as it came with direct instructions from Peter May to be publicly more demonstrative. That actually irked me more; cool, calm and undemonstrative was okay in winning the Ashes, but now the way to success depended on my waving my arms more!

Peter had been one of England's finest captains but I was disappointed that in this instance he was merely endorsing what the press had been saying rather than empathising with his captain. All the players were also given the message to show more pride in playing for England. I have a very simple theory about things like pride and team spirit; whereas it is the job of any captain to create an atmosphere in which his players can thrive, to those watching all one sees are the basic results of the games. If you win, your team is the paragon of team spirit; if you lose, it has no pride. Look at England in the last few years: win the Ashes and beat India to go to No. 1 in the world and team spirit is not an issue but lose to South Africa in the quest to stay top and you end up with Kevin Pietersen finding it 'tough to be me' in a dressing room apparently filled with fake Twitterers! As ever, the truth is much more prosaic – and it is that psychological ups and downs are perfectly normal in any dressing room. So, more pride it was then, but where it was going to come from was hard to fathom – hence, I suppose, my printing of the 'I'm In Charge' T-shirt. It seemed the easiest way to show that, yes, I was listening to what the selectors were saying.

The one-day series ended 1–1, though we lost on the tie-breaker of run-rate, with a match-winning score of 81 in the second game more than compensating for my duck in the first, but the terminal blow to my reign came with India's five-wicket victory in the first Test at Lord's. Given the short-term nature of my retention as England captain, and that India had only ever won one Test match in England before, the news after the game that I was to be replaced by Mike Gatting, my long-standing deputy, was hardly a surprise. It did not lessen the hurt. If I was low before, I was even lower now.

There was no formal explanation for the change but neither was one really needed and nor did I hold this against Peter May. We'd lost our last six Tests and not many captains survived that. Peter was a lovely man and in his heyday as a player doubtless a quiet but authoritative presence. He was respected as a brilliant batsman and his reputation as a captain was strong, even if he showed himself towards the end of his England career sensitive to criticism (mind you, who doesn't?). By the time I met him, he was the epitome of a middle-aged English gentleman, polite, thoughtful and encouraging. He wasn't forceful in selection but was confident in his own opinions. The problem was he didn't gel with our generation and it created a gap in communication and attitude that could not be bridged. When Chris Broad made his debut at Lord's in 1984, May had gone up to him before the game and said, 'Peter May, Brian, welcome.' Brian was of course Broad's first name but not the name he used. May's attitude towards the timing of my declaration later in that same game also hinted at a view of the game acquired in a different era. Like Ray Illingworth later, Peter came to the chairmanship too late. If Ray was ever going to do the job it should have been ten years earlier. The age gap between him and Mike Atherton would have been the single biggest factor in consigning that relationship to failure. A love affair it was not and although I will have everlasting respect for the captain who got me started, Michael would no doubt have a different view.

As it happened, I'd injured my right shoulder diving into the wall in front of the Lord's pavilion attempting an over-enthusiastic stop and was unfit for the next Test at Headingley. This was probably a blessing in disguise as it gave me an opportunity to take stock of my new situation. I scored some runs on my return to the side at Edgbaston, where we drew the final game of a series in which India already held a 2–0 lead, but my appetite for getting up in the morning and going to play cricket was wavering and I allowed myself to toy with the idea of pulling out of the first Test of the following series against New Zealand. Thankfully I stuck at it and scored runs in each of the three games, following

189

half-centuries at Lord's and Trent Bridge with a hundred at my favourite stamping ground of the Oval, though rain thwarted our push for a series-levelling win.

I found the whole summer something of a struggle and before the Oval Test it was agreed with Leicestershire and England that I should be given time off from the last three weeks of the county season. By this stage there was no disguising that a traumatic year had left me mentally and physically exhausted. At the same time, Leicestershire announced that Peter Willey would replace me as captain, an understandable move on their part given my frequent absences and the potential distraction of my benefit season, now eventually confirmed for the 1987 season.

Throughout that season and the subsequent winter tour of Australia and beyond, I was very fortunate to have such a good relationship with Mike Gatting. As I have said, a new captain has to be sympathetic to the feelings of the man he has replaced, at least if he wants to get anything out of him. Mike was certainly that. We understood and respected each other well and that played a big part in what proved, in the end, to be a successful transition back into the ranks.

Just as I had to work out how to accommodate Bob Willis in my team when I became captain, so did Mike with me. The biggest problem is the lingering respect the new man may have (I hope) for the old, who is bound to have strong opinions about how things should be done. If the new man discounts them, it's a slap in the face. If he listens to them too often, he risks turning himself into little more than a puppet of his predecessor. With Bob, I told him straightaway that I'd value his input and wanted him to offer whatever advice he liked. That was my solution to that problem, although as it turned out Bob's career was coming to an end and he didn't play many games under me.

When we went to Australia in 1986–87, Gatt named John Emburey as his vice-captain. There was obviously no way he or the management team would even consider me in that role, so it was hardly a shock but nonetheless I still felt rather out on a limb, isolated. To their credit they soon found me a niche on the tour committee as a voice but in no way a power on selection and tour policy. This was a shrewd move as it was enough to give me a fillip and a renewed sense of worth, while in no way lessening their authority. At the time I rather needed any encouragement I could get as I'd had, to put it mildly, an absolute shocker in the warm-ups, finishing up with a pair in the last game before the first Test against Western Australia. Gatt was very good about things. On the first morning in Brisbane, he asked me where I'd like to bat in the Tests – I'd been expecting to bat at three – and suggested he should go in three and me at five, which given my poor form was probably the best plan, although he'd not been making many runs himself. I was not about to turn him down and the switch was to work well for both of us.

There was something else I had to adjust to. Mickey Stewart had now joined the team as manager (what we would today call head coach or director of cricket). It was a job that could have gone to Illingworth, who was sounded out about it, and had it done so things might have turned out differently for me over the final years of my career. As it was, Illy only took on the role after I'd retired in 1993. As the inaugural appointee, Mickey had to make what he could out of the post, and in Australia he worked well with Gatting. I would give Mickey absolute credit for his dedication and profes-sionalism, qualities he imbued from an early age in Alec, his son, and which were the key to why Alec was so good for so long. He they – loved the game. Mickey was good in Australia. It was only later, when he worked with Gooch that he seemed to become more dictatorial.

I've already spoken about how the 'old guard' viewed with suspicion the arrival of a football-style coach. From my point of view, it only heightened my sense of disarray because the way the team was run bore so little relation to how things had been when I was in charge. Did I have to change the way I was in order to fit in? Was I in fact too long in the tooth to do so? That was partly why I went along with the minor revolt in Brisbane, where we resisted attempts to have us tucked up in bed by 10pm on the eve of the match. Fortunately, to their credit, Gatting and Stewart moderated their stance and cut the likes of myself, Botham and Lamb some slack while the younger, less experienced players such as Bill Athey, Chris Broad and Gladstone Small were told what to do and when. That some of us were accommodated in this fashion counts against us but the arrangement actually worked well for all concerned.

The 'old guard' played their part in a great winter in which we completed a clean sweep by retaining the Ashes and winning two one-day tournaments. For Botham it was a difficult tour because the media interest in everything he did for once cowed him into retreat, with his hotel suite becoming his refuge for much of the time. But he remained bullish on the field and played a famous innings in the first Test in Brisbane, for the most part taking on the bowling while wearing a white floppy hat; his hundred laid the platform for a big victory. He also took wickets in the win in Melbourne, when only half fit, and was man of the finals in the triangular one-day series with Australia and West Indies.

I started the Tests with a fifty in Brisbane but it was not until my century in the second game at Perth that I felt the pressure that had been bearing down on me lift. As with the centuries at Sabina Park in 1981 and at Lord's in 1985, I batted with a sense of anger at my recent inability to put together a big score. There was that extra need to prove something to myself and others. I'd had a dreadful net two days beforehand but on the morning I began batting I'd had a gentle practice session and felt much better. For once, the mind felt free – and the runs flowed. I ended up with more than 400 runs in the series to reinforce my affection for Australian bowling.

Lamb had a quieter tour, but contributed forties to the two Test wins and played an amazing innings to win us a one-dayer against Australia in Sydney, where he took 18 off the final over from Bruce Reid to steal a game we appeared to be losing. What made that performance all the more astonishing was the party we'd had the night before at the flat we were sharing in Bondi. Lambie had got some local friends of his to do the catering and they baked some little cakes mischievously sprinkled – we later discovered – with cannabis. No wonder they seemed to go down rather well. George Michael even pitched up to that one. We'd met him in a nightclub a couple of nights earlier. As I recall he spent most of the evening sat quietly in a corner. It was a cracking night. Fortunately the game the next day was a day-nighter so we had plenty of time to recover.

The home series with Pakistan in 1987 was less productive for me. I played all five Tests but averaged less than 30 and was probably fortunate to retain my place as Pakistan won the only game to produce a positive result in a series liberally soaked in rain. From an early stage, I'd let it be known that I intended to have a break from international cricket the following winter – my first since first playing for England nine years earlier – and to my mind it was no coincidence that for Leicestershire I played more freely than I had done for a long time in the weeks after the last Test ended. Even before it began, the impending sabbatical had a beneficial effect. Perhaps I was also motivated to sign off from my benefit season with a flourish. To my mind, the break was an essential restorative if I was to continue playing for another five years, which I wanted to do. I still felt at that stage that things had been getting on top of me, which may sound a little weak, but it is genuinely how I felt. I knew there was a risk attached to giving up my place but I also knew I needed to refresh my mind and rest my body. The attitude of the England management was well, fine, I could take the winter off but it was all or nothing. It was certainly due to be a busy winter with the World Cup in Pakistan and India, a tour to Pakistan, the Bicentenary Test in Sydney and more Tests in New Zealand.

Perhaps if I'd been madly in love with one-day cricket I would have convinced myself that the winter off could wait and made myself available for the first World Cup to be staged outside England in late 1987. It proved an eventful tournament with England only narrowly losing to Australia in the final in Calcutta. But the joys of the limited-overs format had rather faded for me by this point. I'd played it happily enough, and with some success, in the early Eighties but somehow it had become a chore.

What certainly didn't help was that I was increasingly handicapped in the field by a problem at the top of my right shoulder where tendons and bone rubbed against each other in excruciating fashion – which left me with only the palest imitation of an over-arm throw and hardly made me an asset in the one-day game. I'd undergone an exploratory operation earlier in the year, although the surgery did not actually happen until 1989.

The 1988 season was a tumultuous one for English cricket. Mike Gatting, relatively fresh from his winter contretemps with umpire Shakoor Rana in Faisalabad, was sacked after dallying with a barmaid in his hotel room during the first Test of the summer. The Test and County Cricket Board accepted his denials of impropriety but sacked him anyway. Playing against a side as strong as West Indies, the last thing you needed was any sort of distraction. You were more than likely to come second but if you were to have any sort of chance you needed your team to be stable and playing well. We had neither of those things (I made an unbeaten 88 in that first Test, which we drew, but was hopeless thereafter and was left out for the final match; so much for a winter's rest).

The barmaid was a big misjudgement on Gatting's behalf and would not have gone down well with the likes of Peter May, who was a stickler for proper behaviour, but removing him as captain destabilised the whole enterprise and led to an extraordinary chain of events that was to have big consequences for me. Embury briefly took over the leadership before being replaced by my good friend Chris Cowdrey, who was unenviably parachuted in on the back of a great season leading Kent but was not necessarily a good enough player for such a stiff assignment.

Chris kindly wanted me alongside him at Headingley even though I was out of nick, which, if little else, enabled me to reach 100 Test caps and 7,000 runs, but that was the last either of us saw of the action. His part in that action saw him sustain a broken toe and before he could tell the selectors whether the damage was sufficiently serious to prevent him playing at the Oval, they informed *him* that he was unfit and brought in Graham Gooch as the fourth captain of the summer. Allan Lamb meanwhile was given until the morning of the game to declare his fitness. There were obvious double standards at work but when Chris later complained (entirely reasonably) about shabby treatment, he was fined. What he didn't realise at the time was that he would recoup the money many times over telling superb after-dinner stories about his extraordinary week as England captain.

So far so shambolic but there was more drama to come. Gooch's connections with apartheid South Africa led to the winter's tour of India being cancelled and left the new captain with no opportunity to make the kind of mark that would have made his retention a formality. Instead, with Ted Dexter replacing Peter May and given wider responsibility for the state of the English game, Gooch's prospects nosedived. Dexter, as he famously told the world, thought Graham had all the charisma of a wet fish, while he seemed to hold some affinity for me. He was certainly more my type: a bon viveur and a non-conformist, he also had been, in his day a crowd-pleasing cricketer of the front rank. He spoke up for me early on.

So it was not a complete surprise when, in the spring of 1989, he got in touch and asked if I would be willing to lead England again in all the home internationals against Australia. I said I'd love to, thank you. I even surprised myself how keen I was to take up the reins again and promptly celebrated with a career-best double-century against Glamorgan in the opening championship match of the season.

And why wouldn't I be keen? The Australians didn't appear to be particularly strong at that point. Yes, they'd won the World Cup 18 months earlier, but they'd just been hammered in Tests at home to West Indies and hadn't won a major Test series for more than five years. They didn't hold the Ashes, England did – even if we had been recently put through the ringer ourselves by Viv Richards's side. With a new chairman of selectors and new captain, though, we were embarking on a fresh start.

I didn't know it, but things were actually about to get a whole lot worse.

I only found out later that I wasn't the first-choice captain. Dexter and his England committee had wanted to return to Mike Gatting but had been blocked from doing so by Ossie Wheatley, who as chairman of the TCCB's cricket committee had the power of veto over the appointment of the national captain.

Wheatley, a former Cambridge blue and captain of Glamorgan, felt that to recall Gatting would have been premature given his past behaviour. Basically, he was saying, 'We can't have this man captaining England. His face doesn't fit. He isn't a decent chap. He doesn't wear the right tie.' As if Gatt's sacking over the barmaid incident hadn't already done so, it smacked of Old School mind-less rationality – as did the fact the decision was kept secret.

It is remarkable the truth didn't come out earlier than it did, especially given the capacity for leaks in those days. I was blissfully unaware of what had happened for more than three months and only found out when John Emburey told me after Gatting had signed up for another rebel tour of South Africa, news of which eventually broke on the day Australia reclaimed the Ashes at Old Trafford. Emburey and Gatting were big mates and Gatting had obviously confided in him.

'You know you weren't first choice, don't you?' he said.

'Well, actually I didn't,' I replied.

'Well, you weren't.'

'Okay . . . It doesn't matter.'

But it did matter, even though it wouldn't have stopped me taking the captaincy. I would still have wanted to do the job, and would still have been optimistic of doing well as a player and captain. It mattered because when I found out the Ashes were heading back to Melbourne and the pressure was at its height. I was left nursing a grievance that only helped further erode my relationships with Dexter and Stewart, the England manager with whom I was supposed to be working hand-in-glove.

Like a detective drama, there was a clue there if you could be bothered to look for it. When I joined Dexter for a press conference at Lord's for my unveiling as the new captain (wearing, as I recall, a horrendous grey jacket), the question was asked: 'Was this a unanimous decision?' And Dexter employed a deft use of words, something along the lines of: 'He is our choice. This man is our choice.' So someone, it seemed, had an inkling as to what had gone on from an early stage. Those in on the secret should have realised then, if they hadn't already, that the story would come out in the end, and that when it did they would be left looking the worse for it. It turned out to be a horrible summer, not least because the whole season was riddled with lies, damned lies and bloody poor statistics!

When I first agreed to take on the captaincy again, I thought my experience – of playing, captaining and dealing with the media – would stand me in good stead. Despite some of my experiences in the Caribbean in 1985–86, I didn't expect to have to deal with the sort of stuff I did. It turned out to be a very fraught few months and a big test of one's inner strength, or lack of it. Dexter had said he wanted me as captain to set the tone and style of the team. I wished I could have met his demands but as events turned out I doubt I did.

Of course, we didn't realise that Australia were going to be quite so good; that Mark Taylor and Steve Waugh would score so many runs, that Terry Alderman and Geoff Lawson would be quite so effective with the new ball (Lawson took my wicket seven times in six Tests that summer), or that Allan Border would have changed so completely. Border had been a friendly foe in previous meetings, uncompromising on the field but congenial off it, but the only words I got out of him for three months were 'heads', 'tails' or 'we'll bat' (he never bothered to put us in). We had a proper argument about their use of a runner during the one-dayer at Trent Bridge where Ian Healy had an injured knee and out came Dean Jones to sprint like a March hare. That was quite irritating but then Healy forgot himself and ran a sprightly two, which suggested that his ailment wasn't life-threatening. My protests were upheld by umpire Dickie Bird but Border was livid.

Border eventually apologised for the way he'd behaved but only after he'd won the Ashes and I'd invited him over for a barbecue during Leicestershire's match with the touring side a few days after the decisive Old Trafford Test. 'Sorry mate,' he said. 'I had to be a bit of a shit.'

Unwittingly, I exacted a revenge of sorts that night. Reaching for another bottle of champagne, I thought I'd demonstrate the technique for opening champagne called *sabrage*. This is traditionally performed with a French cavalry sabre, the blade of the sabre being slid along the side of the bottle to break off the collar with the cork still attached, but as the trappings of captaincy with Leicestershire or England disappointingly failed to include a sabre I was obliged to attempt the manoeuvre with an axe. I'd done it many times since first seeing it done in a seafood restaurant in Queensland. Normally the neck of the bottle comes off with a clean sheer but this time a shard of glass flew off and caught the triumphant Australian skipper on the side of the face, leaving him with a tiny gash. Sorry mate. No worries.

I might add that he was in considerably less danger than I was with Lambie on one of our visits to Geoff Merrill's Mount Hurtle vineyard in the McLaren Vale. Wine, as they politely say, had been taken, rather a lot of it I suspect, when we found a bottle of champagne and an axe. Lambie persuaded me to hold the bottle on my head and – with zero style or technique – took a long horizontal swing at it, taking off the neck (from the bottle, not me) a third of the way down. I was grateful still to have a scalp and all my fingers.

A frosty relationship with my opposite number was far from the worst of my problems. When previously I had been captain, I had largely been on my own, but now with the arrival of Mickey Stewart I was part of a management team of two rather than one. It was nice to have the moral support but Mickey and I were different animals. I didn't dislike him but I didn't exactly like the way he worked; it wasn't a huge divergence of views but just enough to be important. To be fair to him, he did a lot of good work with people who enjoyed the way he operated, but what he did wasn't for me.

My mistake was telling Mickey when I started that I would run the cricket and he could run the net sessions. What this meant was that I was taking total responsibility for the way that 1989 Ashes series went. Perhaps it was a reaction to the last time I'd captained: I wanted to show that, yes, this time I really was in charge. The danger with this approach, though, was that if things went badly wrong (as of course they did) I was making it hard for anyone but me to carry the can. There could be no hiding behind differences with the coach. I never went so far as to say, 'He's got to go.' I just said to myself, 'I'm going to ignore him,' which is a horribly flawed position to take. At one point during that summer, Dexter asked me to let Mickey have more of a say in press conferences, which shows how I was treating him I suppose. Ostracising Mickey was my biggest political error, making it clear that I didn't really want him there while pretending to work with him.

We had some perfectly decent selection meetings, me, Mickey and Ted, though we came up with some wrong answers. Those meetings established that our ways of thinking were different and that we weren't going to agree on selection and tactics, and as the series went on these get-togethers became more laboured. It was the same with net practice. Things were not quite as they should have been. Injuries cropped up left, right and centre, which didn't help, and selection became a merry-go-round. I certainly wouldn't suggest that the fault was all theirs. I had my failings and did things that I regret.

It was my fault as much as Mickey's that things didn't turn out better between us or that we were unable to operate as harmoniously as Duncan Fletcher did with Nasser Hussain and Michael Vaughan, or Andy Flower with Andrew Strauss and Alastair Cook. We simply had cultural differences. For the most part, we worked cordially and respectfully, and as I say Mickey did a lot of good stuff with other players. There was no shouting or swearing. We'd come off the field at lunch or tea, and Mickey would say, how about this or that. It wasn't unworkable. It just wasn't a marriage made in heaven.

In return for Stewart being relegated to virtual assistant coach, I was kept out of the loop on anything that did not pertain directly to the games. I'd invited this, of course, little realising the importance of what I might be missing out on. It took me almost three months to find out I'd been the second-choice captain and knew nothing of the planned rebel tour until it was coming out into the public domain. We'd feared that another rebel tour might be in the offing and talked of contracts that might bind players to England – an early version of central contracts – and in the end letters were sent out asking about availability for the winter tour, but this came too late to make a difference. I know that it is in the nature of these things that the captain is often the last to hear because the players have to keep it from the authorities, but why could Stewart and Dexter not tell me? They were the authorities. I still don't know the answer to that one and that they deliberately kept me in the dark was one reason why, after that, things between us broke down completely.

For all that, my relationship with Ted was better than it was with Mickey. I am not one of Ted's harsh critics. If were to see him now I'd be as friendly as you like. Back then, everything was full of emotion, ambition and principle; none of us felt we were doing wrong but we just ended up opposed. With time, you re-think things and accept you could have done things differently. It does not stop me liking him. I defended him steadfastly after the 1992– 93 tour of India, when, after a 3–0 whitewash in the Test series (we didn't win), there were the usual media calls for the resignation of the chairman of selectors. Quite simply, it was hardly his fault. I said so on the line to BBC Radio 4's *Today* show, listeners to which heard something from me that they had not heard before, namely the words: 'For f***'s sake.' Gary Richardson had pressed the question for the third time, 'Surely the chairman's position must be in question?' I thought I had done my best to put the microphone out of harm's way but had not realised that the back of the radio mics used then were as live as the front. It's different on the telly! Anyway the truth is that the team got badly beaten because they played badly and were unlucky that a couple of players ate the wrong food the night before a game.

Going back to the 1989 Ashes, the bottom line was that we were beaten horrendously by a very good side that grew in confidence as the series went on – and as their confidence grew ours was sapped further and further.

Things got off to a horrible start at Headingley, where we picked the wrong team by not going in with a spinner (how many teams have made that mistake at that venue?), an error compounded by my foolish mistake at the toss. I'd called the situation right in similar conditions at Old Trafford in one of the Texaco Trophy one-day matches a couple of weeks earlier, when a slightly green-looking pitch might have tempted some to bowl first, but failed to do the same now, opting to bowl when my instincts told me batting was not a risky thing to do. The pitch again looked greenish but did nothing for the bowlers. I'd allowed myself to listen to the committee view, particularly in this instance Dexter. I'd felt I'd betrayed my own thinking. Those errors set the tone for the summer. Australia made a huge score but after replying with more than 400 ourselves we should have saved the game. Left to bat out 83 overs, we failed by a distance.

The press hostility started there and hardly let up for the rest of the summer as we continued to get hammered. Dare I say it, the media, like us, had not anticipated Australia playing as well as they did, and demanded explanations. Our inadequacies were as good a place to start as any. I felt that it didn't matter what I said, I'd get slated anyway. Even so, I over-reacted with my walkout on the Saturday of the second Test at Lord's – which I've already described – if only because it was a bit early in the piece with four and a half Tests to go. Was I going to keep on walking out of press conferences if I objected to the lines of enquiry?

After that, I badly needed to make amends by scoring a hundred, so the innings I played at Lord's on the Monday must go down as one of the most satisfying I played for England. I was contrite but also annoyed, annoyed at myself and the situation we as a team found ourselves in. Wanting to do well is one thing; needing to do so as a matter of urgency brings a different dimension. It wasn't one of my most fluent innings but one of those occasions where sheer determination got me a long way. I couldn't often play like that, but that day I did. We still lost the game but considering our near-hopeless situation did well to set Australia over 100 to win and make them sweat to get there.

We came off second-best in a rain-affected third Test in Birmingham and by the time of the next game at Manchester the problems were multiplying fast. Even before news of the rebels broke, even before we had surrendered the Ashes, I was in trouble for flicking a V-sign at a barracker. I was fielding at silly point at the time and the ball had dropped just short of me; in trying to reach it I'd ended up on my knees. That's when I heard someone behind me shout words to the effect: 'C'mon Gower!' It was nothing really offensive, but what riled me was that – for once that summer – I'd done nothing wrong. I'd not dropped a catch. I'd not sledged the batsman. Nothing. I didn't turn round or try to identify who the person was. It was all over in a second; I just made the gesture and did my best to get on with the game, not thinking for a moment that anyone would even notice. I certainly didn't regret it once I'd done it and thought no more about it until late that evening when I was surprised to take a call from an agitated Dexter asking if I'd seen *News at Ten*. As I was out with friends at the time – this was Saturday night and the next day was a rest day – I hadn't. It transpired that my V-sign had been picked up by Mark Austin, the ITN sports reporter, and his cameraman and they'd stuck it on the news as evidence of how the pressure was getting to the England captain.

As far as I was concerned, it was an editorial error, as it was making a very large mountain out of the tiniest of molehills, mischief-making pure and simple, though Mark has always said that he didn't think it would do any harm, but Dexter didn't quite share this view. He wanted me to apologise and smooth things over. I was dumbstruck. Who was I supposed to be apologising to? And what for exactly? After my walkout at Lord's I'd agreed to repair the damage by giving a television interview the next day, but this time I said no. I told Dexter I'd got nothing to apologise for and we'd got enough problems on the field without getting embroiled in trivia such as this. If he wanted to do something about it, go ahead, but I was not getting involved. I'd arranged to meet Chris Kilbee, my old school friend, for lunch on the Sunday, but sensing that some newspapers might be keen to get a reaction from me to the ITN story we slipped over the border into Cheshire and I left it as late as I could before returning to the hotel.

The news that three of our team, plus six of those who had featured earlier in the series, had signed up for a rebel tour of South Africa was rather more deserving of headlines. Gatting's decision to accept the captaincy of the rebels came as a shock and provides a salutary instance of a failure to re-integrate a former captain. Gatting said later that one of the reasons he joined the tour was because he felt forgotten and unwanted when he was out of the side (he missed matches that summer through injury and a family bereavement); there was no doubt also some lingering resentment at his treatment the year before, which you could understand. I felt rather guilty about this but Dexter and Stewart had even more cause for regret because they were more responsible for the general welfare of players and should have been checking on how he was. I was in the middle of captaining an Ashes series, though I'd concede that any of us could have made a call at any time just to say, 'How are you?'

That so many players were ruled out of consideration for the rest of the series hardly mattered in the sense that the rubber was now dead but it did affect my decision to stay on as captain. With several changes to the team inevitable, switching captains would only have created further unnecessary turmoil. I could entirely understand why people might think I should resign at that point, because we'd failed abjectly to put up a decent fight. I certainly wasn't enjoying the situation but friends loyally encouraged me to keep going – even in my dispirited state I could see that the chronic injury list and defections to South Africa were hardly my fault – and I sensed that if I did quit I would probably have to surrender my place in the side as well, and I felt there were things I could still do. Besides, Dexter and Stewart didn't want me to resign, even if I strongly suspected this was chiefly because there were so few alternatives. No doubt their faith in me had slipped a long way – my faith in *them* had slipped – but probably we all reasoned that further bad results might as well go on my record as anyone else's.

Geoff Lawson has since said that the fifth Test of that series at Trent Bridge – which Australia won by an innings and plenty – was the only easy Test match he ever played in, and described our lack of spirit as unbelievable. But was that really such a surprise, given all that had gone on?

It was also said that we had forgotten our sense of national pride. That was rubbish. As I said before, national pride – or at least the absence of it – is something that only ever comes up when a team is losing. If your team is winning, and you are performing on a personal level, no one questions your ability or motivation. But when you're getting badly beaten by, say, West Indies, you have enough on your plate dealing with four nasty fast quick bowlers without bringing national pride into it, however you are supposed to do that. If thinking about the Union Flag or the Queen or Britannia, or the Second World War, or Dunkirk, helps you give

205

that extra something, then fine, go ahead. I'm sure there are people who when they play for England see Union Flags in front of their eyes. David Bairstow was one, Ken Barrington too, probably Alec Stewart. But not everyone will feel like that. Your motivation might be national, personal or plain selfish; maybe you just don't want to let down the ten other blokes in the dressing room.

To my mind, your own game has to come first. You can be as proud of your country as you like, but if you don't look after your game you won't be in the team long and you'll be doing your flag-waving from beyond the boundary. If I got a hundred but then started to play more extravagantly and lost my wicket, it was because my personal pride was satisfied and my desire to entertain beat my sense of responsibility towards the ethic of grinding down the opposition (sorry, Graham).

As it happened, as we gathered before the third Test in Birmingham, Ted Dexter did attempt to appeal to some sense of national pride by handing out printed sheets of verses he had written to the music of 'Onward Christian Soldiers', under the heading, 'Onward Gower's Cricketers.' On this one, I am sorry Ted, it was a weird idea and I'm pretty sure we never sang the words, as Ted asked us to (in the bath the night before the game!)

We continued to be plagued by injuries to the end, and the situation was so chaotic ahead of the Oval Test that Dexter, Stewart and I reached an impasse on who to pick. The original face-to-face selection meeting had been rendered obsolete by injuries so a conference call was needed at the weekend and with six different names being put forward for the two remaining places, exasperated we had to re-convene the next morning to see which names each of us might be prepared to give ground on. By this stage we were no longer on the same side, just three people in jobs that required them to speak to each other.

*   *   *

Even my sacking turned into a farce. In the immediate aftermath of the series, I resisted the urge to resign and awaited the contact from Dexter and Stewart that I was sure would come. Someone was going to carry the can for the disaster and it was more likely to be me than them. Sure enough a few days after the Oval Test match, I was summoned to Ted's house in Ealing to meet them and no sooner had I walked in the door than they said, 'Right, we think we'd like a change of direction . . . we want a new captain.' I said, 'Fine. Okay. How do you want to do this?' They said that they didn't want to announce anything straightaway, probably because whoever they chose to succeed me would need ratifying by the board. As it happened Leicestershire had a week off and I'd been invited to spend the weekend with Paul Symington and Tim Stanley-Clarke from Dows Port at the Quinta do Bomfim in Portugal, so I told Ted and Mickey I'd be well out of the way and would leave them to sort things out.

I declined their suggestion that the blow could be softened for public consumption with an announcement, when the time came, that I had resigned rather than been sacked and that my impending shoulder surgery was ruling me out of the winter tours.

Of course, as with all these things, someone got wind of what was afoot. We had already seen that with the Gatting veto. Even so I was surprised to take a call at my bolthole way up the Douro Valley from John Etheridge of the *Sun*. How he tracked me down there I've no idea but he said he was in Portugal and ready to come and see me. I said, 'John, I've got nothing to say. I don't know what you guys have heard but this is in the hands of Stewart and Dexter. You should be speaking to them.' He said that if I didn't talk to him he'd get on the train to the Douro and doorstep me until I gave in, and if I didn't cooperate he'd be writing something anyway. Surely, he said, it would be better if I got some of my side of the story across. After weeks of anguish, the prospect of having my peace shattered or that of my hosts didn't appeal, and I relented, quite a generous act given that the *Sun* was a newspaper that had spent the summer putting a dunce's hat on my head. The headline at the top of the resulting two-page spread – he's prolific that Etheridge – was 'DAVID GOWER OPENS HIS HEART TO THE SUN'. Bollocks!

When I caught the plane back from Oporto the media were there in force and I knew things were still not going my way when the kid sitting next to me on the plane tipped his Coca-Cola all over my lap. Shortly after my return, Graham Gooch was unveiled as the new captain. The King is dead. Long live the wet fish!

You could have made a film about the 1981 Ashes, about how England dragged itself out of the economic mire and everything was great again thanks to the Royal Wedding and Botham's heroics – in fact, someone did make a film out of it – and you could equally do the same about the 1989 series, only in reverse. It would make pretty unsavoury viewing and would have been the cricketing equivalent of Toby Young's *How to Lose Friends and Alienate People* with the credits undoubtedly rolling to a soundtrack from *Monty Python's Flying Circus*.

9

'YOU DO KNOW YOU'RE NOT
GOING TO INDIA, DON'T YOU?'

On the day Graham Gooch was unveiled as England's new captain, I was officially informed that I would not be needed for the West Indies tour. Given how my recent conversation had gone with Ted Dexter and Mickey Stewart at Ted's house, when they'd said they wanted a new leader, this was no great surprise. It was evident they would like me to disappear into the shadows. They wanted to make a statement about the future direction of the team and what that statement was became plain when it transpired that Ian Botham also did not have a seat on the plane. Mickey sometimes liked to call us 'champagne' cricketers (it was not a compliment) and for us the bubbles had gone flat.

For all the many failings of the team – England hadn't won a Test against anyone but Sri Lanka since the 1986–87 Ashes, let alone a series – the pair of us were seemingly cast as scapegoats. I had scored almost 400 runs in the 1989 Ashes – second only to Robin Smith on our side – yet I was now not deemed good enough to be among the country's seven best batsmen. How did that work?

Although I felt uneasy about what the future might hold under the Gooch–Stewart regime I had no inkling as to what trouble lay ahead. It took a while for the realisation to dawn that here were two men with diametrically opposed views to my own about how to run a cricket team. For the most part, they did not want me in their side at all and, even when they did pick me, they seemed burdened by serious reservations. From late 1989 until I finally announced my retirement four years later, I appeared in only 11 of the 39 Tests England played.

There was not much I could immediately do about my relationship with the new England hierarchy but I did do plenty about those things I could affect. In what I described as my end-of-decade clearance sale, I got a new girlfriend, a new shoulder and a new county.

As I've already suggested, relations with Vicki had been on a downward slide for quite a while. We'd lived together at three addresses on Ratcliffe Road in Leicester for ten years and at some point there had been an engagement of sorts. It was in fact more of a ring than an engagement; dare I say it, a rather beautiful ring, an antique diamond solitaire. This will sound terrible but the 'engagement' was probably more of an acknowledgement on my part that Vicki merited some sort of long-service award and we never got round to actually planning a wedding. Things bumbled on sometimes very happily, sometimes not – but the relationship was under severe strain simply from the nature of what I did, the long absences and the temptations that came my way. Such an existence hardly encouraged you to settle down and get married. Every now and again you made a mistake, got found out, and tensions rose. She came to tolerate her life with me less and less and there was an underlying malaise from 1986 onwards. By 1989 things had deteriorated beyond the point of no return.

At this point I need to backtrack to explain that I had met Thorunn Nash, the future Mrs Gower, at the VAG Sparks Ball in London in the autumn of 1985. She was with her partner – usefully also called David – while I was without mine. Vicki didn't want to make the journey – it was one of those less happy times, I suspect – while I had to attend as VAG (Volkswagen Audi Group) were one of my sponsors. I had been driving Audis for some years by then, having a lot of fun with the legendary Audi Quattro, which was drop-dead gorgeous to look at and mighty quick and with that rally bred four-wheel drive system even I could just about keep it on the road most of the time. At least I never rolled one like Beefy did with his Saabs! Sparks has remained one of my favourite charities ever since and not just because they inadvertently helped introduce me to my wife. The funds they raise for research into medical conditions affecting babies and children have been exceptionally important.

Thorunn came over to ask me for a dance as a bit of a dare to wind up a friend of hers who was a cricket fan. I was immediately taken with her, decided on the spot that she was yet more beautiful than an Audi Quattro and was more than happy to take her for a few spins round the dance floor. I had no intention of letting her go so that one dance became several. I joined their table towards the end of the evening, said hello to the other David and all their friends, and quietly found out what I could about the stunning blonde up and down whose back I had been running my hands for thirty minutes on the dance floor. Her father, sadly the victim of a heart attack that summer, had been a Major in the army. Her mother came from Iceland. More importantly for my immediate future I discovered that she worked as a dental nurse and PA to Chris Bone, a dentist in Knightsbridge with his practice in Hans Road just behind Harrods. That was all I needed to know and a simple bit of detective work with a BT phonebook followed by a deep breath and a slightly shy phone call secured me a lunch date the following day.

Thorunn and I were to see each other occasionally at opportune moments for the next four years, before things came to a crunch around Christmas '89, when I rang and asked if she was ready to start a new life with me. By this time there had been some press speculation that I had a new girlfriend. Thorunn was living with David and said she needed to get Christmas over with first – as you can see, my timing was impeccable as usual – but we both knew we were ready for fresh starts.

On New Year's Day, Vicki and I took out a small ad in the *Times* confirming our separation. Looking back now it seems like a rather pompous thing to do but the aim was to deal with any media interest. It read: 'David Gower and Vicki Stewart would like to put themselves and their friends out of their misery and confirm that sadly they have decided to separate as amicably as possible and go their own ways. As the matter has already been the subject of speculation by some members of the press, they hope that this brief announcement will obviate the need for further comment. (Fat . . . chance).'

It was an awkward and unpleasant time and matters were not helped by my escapade in St Moritz with the car in the lake, which only encouraged reporters to descend on the house in Leicester in search of a comment. Vicki's attitude, quite reasonably, was that whatever scrape I'd got into this time had nothing to do with her. We were still working through the separation at that point but in the end I made sure she had money, a car and somewhere to live.

Meanwhile, I felt that if I was going to revive my cricket I needed a change of scene. Leicestershire were a good club who had treated me very well ever since I'd started as a feckless teenager. I had many loyal friends there, and although there had been some issues with the likes of Charles Palmer during my benefit season, Mike Turner had never been anything but very supportive. It was certainly not a reflection on the club. Initially I told them that I wished to step down from the captaincy because I needed to concentrate on my batting and getting back my England place, but Mike knew earlier than some that I was considering leaving altogether. I think I tested his patience while I made up my mind but the split with Vicki made the separation from the club almost inevitable. Thorunn's friends were mainly in the south and she had no particular yearning to live in Leicester. My departure was announced in late January and Thorunn and I headed down to Esher where we stayed with Carrie Zetter, a school friend of Thorunn's and an avid dog lover. She had just rescued her latest, Dakota, a mostly Alsatian puppy, who was as mad as a March hare and kept bouncing off the walls of the dining room day and night. He also had a propensity for chewing anything he could reach, with a special liking for long woollen sleeves. Happily he turned out, after time, to be a great and thankfully very calm dog. From there we began looking for somewhere to live in Hampshire, somewhere that could become our home.

By this stage, too, I'd finally undergone surgery on my right shoulder, which for so long had hindered my throwing and made fielding a matter of occasional embarrassment. Having been dropped, and left with time on my hands, the autumn had seemed like as good a time as any to get the operation out of the way.

The choice of new county came down to Hampshire or Kent with one or two other counties showing interest too. Kent was the county of my birth and schooling, and they were led by my best mate, Chris Cowdrey. Chris had floated the idea of me joining them a couple of years earlier when he sensed that a fresh start might have been good for me, but perhaps heading for Canterbury was just a little too obvious a move. One of their senior committee men, whose blushes I might just spare, was deputed to come and discuss the possibilities and he took us to the Ritz Club for dinner. Very nice it was too. We chatted over the sort of offer Kent might be prepared to make and how keen they were that I return to my spiritual home. The only thing he struggled with was Thorunn's name. He was not the first to do so and many since have called her Lauren or Karen or something similar. In line with most of her friends I have always called her 'TH' but as a clue to the uninitiated

213

we normally recommend thinking of 'Foreign' and changing the F to a Th. True Icelandics would shudder at that but then they cannot understand why we cannot pronounce Eyjafjallajokull when one of their volcanoes goes into meltdown! Anyway, our man kept calling her 'Thingy', which was a pretty poor effort and although she did not take offence, indeed we found it suitably amusing, it might not have helped Kent's case. If I was going to spend the next few years of my career there, having my wife referred to as Thingy might have been tricky!

Our anonymous committee man need not worry that it was his fault I went elsewhere. Many other factors were involved in my decision. For some years I had thought about Hampshire as a very pleasant part of the country and we both preferred the thought of living there. Besides Hampshire, the club, had a lot of very good people – Robin Smith, Paul Terry and Malcolm Marshall for instance – who I knew I'd love to play alongside, especially Marshall. I liked the idea of being on the same side as a 'nasty' West Indian fast bowler. I'd done it briefly at Leicestershire with Andy Roberts, who'd joined us for a few seasons in the early Eighties, and was drawn to it happening again. I'd long admired 'Macko', of course. Mark Nicholas, the captain, was keen for me to head for Southampton and played his part too. In fact, I lodged with Mark for the first few weeks of the 1990 season.

I actually first met up with my new colleagues in Bridgetown, where Hampshire headed for a pre-season tour. I was already out there, doing some work covering the England tour as columnist for the *Times* and summariser for BBC radio's *Test Match Special*. This led to an unexpected call-up when injuries left the England squad short of manpower, Gooch himself being sidelined with a broken hand. I was asked to play against Barbados and decided to accept. My shoulder had recovered well enough and I was naturally keen to get back in with England if I could, even if this was an earlier opportunity than anticipated. I didn't bat very fluently, and only scored four, but was taken on to Antigua as part of the squad for the final Test match. I was excited by the thought of playing but knew it would have been very tough; in fact I had a poor net the day before the Test and, even though that had for me seldom been a great guide as to what sort of form I was in, this time I can say that they correctly took the view that I wasn't ready. But at least this suggested that despite the change of regime I was still in their thoughts. After years of poundings at the hands of West Indies, England had put up a good fight, probably meriting the 2–2 draw that would have been theirs but for West Indian time-wasting in the rapidly fading light in Trinidad, but the side was not particularly settled. From my point of view, there was hope of places soon becoming available.

In fact, they did – but unfortunately not for me, at least not in the Test side. I was recalled to the one-day team for the early season Texaco Trophy matches against New Zealand but was twice out cheaply to Richard Hadlee, once bowled behind my legs – always an irritating way to get out. But when it came to the Tests the selectors made changes without being persuaded by my score against Sussex of 145 on championship debut for Hampshire. To be fair, batsmen across the country were piling up runs in what proved a golden summer for run scoring and there were recalls instead for two Lancastrians, Michael Atherton and Neil Fairbrother – who as the left-hander in the middle order took the place that might have been mine.

Helpfully for me though, Fairbrother missed out during the New Zealand Tests and just as the final game of that series was going on I struck a timely unbeaten hundred in Hampshire's match with the Indians, who were that season's second visitors. I think I've mentioned how I found it difficult to get up much enthusiasm for county versus tourist fixtures but this was one occasion when I was really keen for runs, and with Mark Nicholas also making a century we made impressively light work of chasing down a target of 300-plus at five an over.

Conscious that I must be close to getting back into the Test side, I scored 50 and 25 in the two one-dayers with India that served as hors d'oeuvres to the Tests, but was incensed to miss out on the big innings that might have put a recall beyond doubt. To make matters worse, I stupidly ran myself out in the second game at Trent Bridge in a fashion that could only be put down to arrogance on my part. We had run one and, thinking of a second, I had ventured half way down the pitch from the non-striker's end. Kiran More, the keeper, was scrambling around trying to gather the off-target throw from the deep but had spotted that I was a long way out of my ground. When I realised that he was actually going to throw the ball at the stumps at my end – the cheek of it! – I was still a long way adrift. It was a smart piece of fielding but utterly foolish on my part, and a terrible waste because I'd felt in wonderful nick.

Worse was to follow. Hot-footing it to the south coast for a championship match the next day, I again started well against a spicy Derbyshire pace attack of Ian Bishop and Devon Malcolm on a typically quick Portsmouth wicket. Helped by gaps in the field created by a decent sprinkling of slips and gullies, I raced to 48 before running myself out again, this time attempting to take two to wide third man. If I was annoyed the previous day, I was doubly furious now and did not calm down until I'd turned the air in the dressing room a darker shade of blue. Happily, England still picked me – along with an uncapped Derbyshire batsman by the name of John Morris.

As I say, it was a run-drenched season but while Gooch, Atherton, Smith and Lamb filled their boots it took me until the third and final Test with India to get in on the act. I've already mentioned how things clicked for me in the second innings of that game at the Oval when we were following on, and the unbeaten 157 I scored to save the game and secure myself a place on the Australia tour. One additional memory of that performance is one of the Indian players Dilip Vengsarkar coming up to me as we walked off at the end of the game and saying, 'You don't fit into this team.' It was a slightly odd thing to say, though meant respectfully and sympathetically, but it was not long before he was proved to be pretty much spot-on.

As I've also described in the opening chapter, it was on that tour of Australia when my fundamental differences with Gooch and Stewart first surfaced. Gooch had just had a fantastic summer, scoring more than 1,000 runs in the home Tests, so perhaps he was feeling vindicated in his methods in a way he had not done before. I can understand too why he was of the view that the stringent training and preparation that worked so well for him should be de rigueur for everyone else. Now, I'd played under Gatting and Stewart and had learned to accept that others did things differently, so my reservations now were more than just a former captain bridling at the ways of a new man. The new management partnership no doubt thought they were correcting the wrongs of an earlier, more flamboyant era. But to my mind, they were merely pragmatic, unimaginative and dour. It was a regime built on pure hard work, training drills, and Gooch-like batting discipline – that admittedly laudable ambition to make not just hundreds but, as they are now called by him in his role as England's batting coach, 'daddy hundreds' The basic desire of trying to claw your way out of the mire by hard graft obviously has merit but I was equally sure that the way I had succeeded at this same level for the last 12 years was the way that worked best for me and that I was not going to change now.

With Gatting there was a mutual respect that helped us work together after he became captain. With Gooch it was a different feeling. He thought we needed a uniform discipline to get the results he wanted. I didn't appreciate the communist style; whereas, for instance, my team talks had been deliberately inclusive as I believed that to encourage players to speak up and be part of the planning process gave them a greater and more positive involvement, under Graham we got not much more than an announcement of the XII for the match and a few basic instructions. That was it. It was very one-dimensional and didn't cater for a team being made up of different personalities and characters. Deep down I resented this assumption and, thought, simply, 'This cannot be right.'

There were times in Australia during that 1990–91 tour when I began to wonder what I was doing this for. Why did I want to be part of a world that seemed so alien? The thought started to cross my mind as to what else in life I might do. Could I in fact do anything else but play cricket? One day I did in fact ask Peter Baxter, then the producer of *Test Match Special*, whether he reckoned I might be capable of working in radio. It was no more than a casual enquiry but it indicated the state of my mind, and how debilitating I found that tour.

At other times I tried to be more pro-active. In Sydney during the one-day series – much of which I missed with a cracked thumb – I spoke in confidence to some of the other players (Eddie Hemmings was one, I remember) to see whether they shared my doubts about the way the team was going about things. It turned out I wasn't alone. There was a feeling that the management was indeed missing things. Suitably encouraged, I summoned the courage to tell Mickey that I had something I'd like to raise during a team meeting, and duly did so, only to find no one prepared to speak up in support! It's a pity I had not done more on Machiavelli in my history studies and made sure I had backing. I said that I was not entirely happy with the way the team was run, I thought more people should be included in decisions, and that I knew a few others felt the same. Then I looked around the room . . . and no one said a word. My intention was not to be a revolutionary – I was hoping that this might be seen as constructive. It was a heart-felt principle of my captaincy that the whole group should feel involved, and be involved. All that happened, though, was that I ended up feeling isolated for my honesty.

This was the backdrop to my subsequent outburst on the third morning of the Sydney Test when Gooch spoke so negatively about our chances, and the management's heavy-handed handling (in my view) of my taking to the skies in company with Morris in Queensland. That Gooch, Stewart and Peter Lush, the tour manager, felt in all seriousness that Morris and I should be sent home tells you all you need to know about their po-faced approach to life, the universe and everything, to paraphrase Douglas Adams. Now there is a man who, having written so amusingly about intergalactic travel, would surely have approved a mere 30-minute diversion in a Tiger Moth! And, yes, I do have a personally signed copy of the *Hitchhiker's Guide to the Galaxy*.

The unravelling of my game from there was a shock all the greater for how well I had been playing up to that point. Those hundreds I scored in the Melbourne and Sydney Tests were among the best I ever made but in the remainder of the series and throughout much of the 1991 season I found that the harder I tried the worse things got. It was frightening to go from such sublimely good touch to more or less forgetting how to bat. What had felt beautifully natural had become totally unnatural, and it was genuinely depressing that I could not fix the problem. In the past I had tended to bat my way out of a bad trot by playing my shots – that's what I'd done with that one-day hundred at Lord's in 1985 – but this time that approach stubbornly refused to work. I'd end up holing out almost immediately at mid off, or something equally feckless. Hence the humiliating, painstaking work in the nets with Mark Nicholas giving me gentle throw-downs at Southampton as we attempted to rebuild my game from the bottom up. That I did not play for England during the 1991 season or tour with them in the winter was completely unsurprising: I'd done nothing to deserve to.

Why didn't I just quit then? It crossed my mind. But, strange though it may sound, I still felt I could score Test match runs. Only nine months earlier I'd been scoring Ashes hundreds and feeling brilliant, and I was still able to look forward to the next English season. By the end of the summer of '91, thanks in part to the help I was receiving on the psychological side from Brian Mason, I'd put enough of the pieces back in the jigsaw to want to get back to the game and finish the job. Spending an enjoyable winter in Australia and New Zealand commentating for Channel 9 on the World Cup, and not having to pick up a bat, can have only helped the healing process.

In many ways, I was in a much happier place than I had been for a long time but the situation with Gooch's England was one I was to continue to struggle with for the rest of my playing career.

Looking back on that period still grates but I know that the fault was not all theirs. The England team needed modernising. Everyone, to coin a phrase that I never thought I'd use, needs a bit of Gooch in them and practice is a necessary ingredient in any successful sportsman. The problem was that Gooch and myself were poles apart in the way we liked to do things but if we had both moved towards the centre we could have had a perfectly good relationship. That's an error I need to look back on, but then so does he. For my part I could have shown more understanding of his situation and been more accommodating.

I let myself down in the training disciplines but then I was unable to enjoy that side of things. It was just the way I was made. I'm like a puppy. Someone has to throw a ball for me to want to run around. Give me a game of squash or tennis, but not a running machine. In a team environment that is an attitude that does you few favours. If you set yourself at odds with the system you place yourself at risk – and must play better simply so that no one has an excuse to complain about how you do things.

Some people have suggested that Gooch kept me out of the side so that he could claim the England run-scoring record for himself, which he did during the final Test of the 1993 season, but I don't believe that for a moment. Rightly or wrongly – I would say wrongly – he harboured doubts about whether I fitted his blueprint of a 1990s England cricketer.

Even though I was recalled for the third Test of the 1992 series with Pakistan – Atherton and myself came in for Lamb and Botham, neither of whom played Test cricket again – he probably still had reservations about whether I was the right man. I made a fair comeback in that series but perhaps giving away my wicket after scoring 70-odd in Manchester, and giving the impression during that infamous taxi ride of not being sure how to get the best out of myself, only confirmed his suspicions. Maybe he had a point, but I would say that many of the doubts had been put there by him. That I held the England run-scoring record surely suggested that I must have done something right somewhere, but even so I was left wondering whether I belonged.

In the next match at Headingley I got a couple of not outs in a low-scoring game which we won to level the series. After Gooch's century put us in a strong position, Wasim Akram and Waqar Younis caused a collapse which I could only watch in dismay and amazement from the other end, and when I went in again there was a bit of work to be done getting us to our target. Mark Ramprakash helped finish the job but he was relatively inexperienced and needed encouragement, and I got as much satisfaction from helping him through that innings as I did from being at the crease when the victory came.

Nothing went right in the final Test at the Oval. We lost heavily and I was out twice in ways I'd rather forget, cutting a ball from Aqib Javed into my stumps and bowled off stump by Waqar, who, I have to say, was all over me that day. In the same over I must have played and missed at four or five deliveries that swung away from me so that the one that then just held its line and clipped the top of off stump as I shouldered arms was perfectly good enough. After such indignity, the thought did fleetingly occur, 'Can I still do this?' but when I reflected more calmly on my series as a whole I felt that I'd had two reasonable games out of three against what was a pretty special bowling attack.

I still felt reasonably optimistic about the future but, little though I knew it at the time, the door was actually about to be shut on me for good.

First I got a call from Gooch telling me that they'd decided to leave me out of the squad for three remaining Texaco Trophy matches – in an odd experiment that was not repeated, a five-match ODI series was played either side of the Tests, two before and three after – but that I shouldn't worry because I would be going on the winter tour of India. This sounded fine to me, as I was quite happy to acknowledge my shortcomings in one-day cricket and hadn't played in the first two games earlier in the season, both of which England had won. Allan Lamb, whose name was mentioned by Gooch as the man they preferred to go with, may have been dropped from the Test side but he remained a fine one-day player.

There followed a ridiculous sequence of events. About three or four weeks later, I attended the Cricket Writers' Club annual dinner, at which I received the inaugural Peter Smith Memorial Award, set up in memory of the late *Daily Mail* correspondent who was, as I've said, such a wise and kindly counsellor to me and many other players. He was someone respected in press boxes and dressing rooms alike. The award recognised the presentation of cricket to the public and I was hugely flattered to be the first recipient of a beautiful replica of the Ashes urn in a glass dome.

While I was at the dinner, though, I was stunned when Peter Hayter of the *Mail on Sunday* sidled up and said, 'You do know you're not going to India, don't you?' I knew the selectors had been meeting and were due to announce the squad in the next few days but I'd heard nothing and had been working on the not unreasonable assumption that what Gooch had told me on the phone meant my spot was assured. When I replied that no one had spoken to me and I'd no reason to believe I wasn't going, he said, 'I can tell you, you're not going.' Part of my confidence was based on the knowledge that since the days of Mike Brearley it had been standard practice for anyone being left out to be the first person to hear. I had got it wrong once with Chris Broad when we left him out of the previous India tour of 1984–85 but that was only because he'd gone away for a few days and we couldn't track him down. That was embarrassing and when I saw him I had to explain why we'd not spoken. A couple of days later, I saw Hayter again at a charity match I was playing in at Rowlands Castle near Portsmouth and he reiterated that, from what he'd heard, I wasn't going. 'Well,' I said. 'I can tell you still, no one's phoned me.'

Hampshire were without a game so I had a few days off. The next morning, I was at home and thinking that Hayter must have got it wrong because the squad was due to be announced on the radio in ten minutes and I had still heard nothing. Then the phone went. It was Gooch, calling from his car on the way to Derby where he was playing in a match for Essex. He said, 'Lubo, I've got to tell you you're not going to India . . .' I was furious and exploded at him, giving him full vent. Typically, the connection dropped out and he had to ring back. He pleaded with me to understand but I said there was nothing to understand other than that he'd said one thing and done another, given me his word and then broken it. He

223

could have phoned me any time over the last few days yet he'd put it off until absolutely the last moment. Why leave it until now? It was thoughtless, disrespectful or, if you like, just f***ing rude.

The excuse he gave, and it was one backed by Keith Fletcher, who had taken over from Mickey Stewart as team manager, was that they didn't want too many people over the age of 35. Mike Gatting was like me 35, Gooch himself was 39 and John Emburey was 40; it seemed curious to say that they could all go but I couldn't. The reason was a sham. In reality, Gooch would have cast his mind back to Australia and said to himself, 'I don't want the hassle of captaining him. I'll take Gatting instead. He'll do as he's told.' I thought I'd done enough in the summer to put the troubles of the past behind us, but apparently not. To make matters worse, the forgiveness that was not afforded me was extended to Gatting and Emburey, who had recently been on a rebel tour of South Africa and were now welcomed back because apartheid had finally, and thankfully, collapsed and South Africa were back in the sporting fold. My offence of being 'difficult' – if that is what I was – was deemed more serious than turning your back on the team altogether. You could agree or disagree with the decision but I would maintain that the way it was handled was just appalling management on Gooch's part.

I was not the only one outraged. Two MCC members, Dennis Oliver, a Kent businessman, and Donald Trelford, former editor of the *Observer*, rallied support for a vote of no-confidence among the club's membership in the England selectors. My treatment topped the bill but they were unhappy at the handling of other players such as Jack Russell and Ian Salisbury, also left out of the tour. It was kind of them to make such a rumpus on my behalf but also embarrassing. I could hardly publicly back the campaign – that was not going to improve my chances of getting back into the side – but nor was I going to disown it when my sentiments were essentially those of my supporters.

I also had rather more pressing and infinitely more pleasant matters on my mind. When Jon Holmes was first contacted by Donald Trelford, it was the weekend that Thorunn and I were getting married at Winchester Cathedral, which we followed with a Kenyan safari for our honeymoon. A fabulous itinerary, which took us from Nairobi to Mount Kenya, to Ol Pejeta, to the Masai Mara and the Nguruman Hills, near the border with my former home country of Tanzania, was all that was needed to put cricket and cricketing politics well in their places, a long way to the back of my mind.

Luckily I was also busy, with no time or need to mope, back in Australia with Channel 9, this time for the series against the West Indies and thus in the perfect place to watch and admire a young Brain Lara display all his genius in making a double hundred at the SCG. Thorunn and I were en route from Adelaide to Calcutta when the result of the MCC EGM came through. A vote at the meeting in Westminster Hall had been in favour of a vote of no confidence in the England selectors but the postal ballot turned the final vote against the motion.

So, picking up the mic now for Sky TV in India, I had to be as dispassionate as I could about the events of the next few weeks. England got off to a shocker in Calcutta, fell foul of some dodgy prawns in Madras and India romped home 3–0 in Mumbai, which is where, having concluded my primary obligations to Sky, I then turned the air blue on the *Today* show with Gary Richardson. You will understand that I had mixed emotions. I could be smug that I was not part of this debacle but had to be honest with myself that, even if I had been playing as I thought I should, I might not have been able to make any difference. I could just as easily have been part of this same shambles and I felt for those in the team who had been friends and colleagues for many years.

I suppose the main effect of the MCC vote from my point of view was that it encouraged me to keep going in the belief that I was not alone in thinking I had more to offer the England team.

One of the problems for Gooch, I'd concede, was my attitude towards one-day cricket. While I remained keen to play Test cricket I was indifferent about the shorter formats, and as this was a time when the same group of players would play Tests and one-dayers on tour this was more of a problem then than it would be today when specific squads are flown out for Tests, ODIs and Twenty2os. If they picked me for a Test series overseas, they had in effect got me for the one-dayers as well and if they didn't pick me for those I'd be left on the sidelines where I'd doubtless (in their eyes) foment unrest.

This new-found apathy for the games that Allan Border once described as 'hit and giggle matches' meant that I was finding it especially hard to get the bit between my teeth for Sunday league matches with Hampshire. I'd have done anything to get out of these games but I'd signed a contract with Hampshire that obliged me to turn out and the county weren't going to let me get away with anything less. Would it be worth becoming a Seventh-day Adventist, I mused? Even when my form was dire they would not drop me. My approach particularly annoyed Mark Nicholas, my captain, and I can understand 100 per cent that he must have thought me a complete prat at this stage. I pitched up only just in the nick of time for one home match in which I was due to open the batting and another time, at Portsmouth, I arrived late to find the rest of the team about to start their warm-ups so I joined them in my civvies. It wasn't a clever thing to do and I'm not proud of it. In fact, I behaved like a complete arsehole and Mark was quite rightly livid. They had every right to expect me to play and I was wrongly disgruntled.

It does beg the question, how would I have responded to the opportunities available today to play Twenty2o cricket for so much money? If the IPL had been invented in 1982, as an example, I would have been at my peak in both Test and one-day cricket and I would happily guess that the chance to make a quick $1 million would have been much too good to ignore. Let's assume also that central contracts were also in play. I can guarantee that I would have been agitating, as Kevin Pietersen has been, to be allowed to make the most of such an opportunity and like KP I would no doubt have done everything I could to talk up the positive elements.

What if the IPL had been conceived in, say, 1991? At that stage I would have been in mid-dispute with Gooch and England but out of form and maybe at less than my optimum market value. By then my loyalty to England would have been stretched, as you can imagine, and I would have been vulnerable to any approach and therefore would most likely have done anything I could to convince the world that T20 cricket was absolutely my thing. Hypocritical? Oh yes. Self-serving? Why not? It is why I would not rush to condemn any English player considering the attractions of the IPL currently. But one word of caution. England players now are very well provided for, with central contracts, good salaries, big bonuses and a lot of support from the system around them. I can understand them wanting parity with the Australians, who at this stage are better remunerated, and I can understand the professional ambition to share some of the spoils available in India. But in the same way that I took a decision not to risk a rebel tour to South Africa on the lure of extra cash, I would like to think that I would now be loyal to a Test side that is capable of great things and that to be part of the success of the last few years, the regaining of the Ashes, and the ascent to No. 1, would have been reward enough, with the odd couple of weeks of mercenary time a useful extra.

Whatever my antipathy to 40-over Sundays, Hampshire had some great cup runs during my time in the longer one-day formats and they were a very different thing altogether. These knockout matches produced great drama and a great atmosphere at the county's old Northlands Road ground in Southampton. They were hugely important to everyone at the club and definitely got my juices flowing. I vividly recall a NatWest Trophy semi-final in 1990 lost in agonising fashion to Northamptonshire by one run where sadly I didn't quite see the job through. We were chasing a big total of 280-odd and I scored 86 before I was caught trying to hit off-spinner Richard Williams over extra cover. I just got hold of the shot a little too straight. David Capel made such a song and dance about taking the catch I could happily have whacked him over the head as I trudged off. We were always up against it in the chase but somehow always managed a boundary at the right time to keep our hopes going. One more hit and we would have got home.

I remember the match as much for the aftermath as the game itself, as the beaten Hampshire players barely uttered a word in the dressing room and then congregated for a drink afterwards in the squash club bar. It was truly horrible. The county had lost at the same stage the previous year by just three runs so this was a doubly bitter blow. Raj Maru was almost suicidal and Malcolm Marshall, who had been such a great servant of the club and had missed out on the Benson & Hedges Cup win in '88 because he was touring with West Indies, was inconsolable. I was particularly struck by how anguished Macko was. He had achieved a great deal in the game but loved Hampshire as much as Barbados or West Indies and was desperate to get to a Lord's final with them.

I was reasonably sanguine, having played well enough to get some consolation out of the day, but then Macko had had a good game himself, keeping the chase going with an innings of 77, and yet he was so distraught he had hit the brandy. Maybe I should have felt more the same but not getting over-emotional was a kind of self-protective device I used; while I'd be disappointed about losing or personally not doing well, I found it helpful to hide it as best I could. Some people interpreted this as me not caring, but it was just a mechanism really. If the mechanism broke I was in trouble.

In the same vein, if you can believe there will always be another day, that too helps you retain perspective on the subject of defeat. The problem is that for many players such days do not necessarily come round again and for the chance to play in a Lord's final to slip away maybe forever is a tough break. At least for us at Hampshire we only had to wait a year and in 1991 we made it to Lord's, winning our semi-final at Edgbaston with ease and lifting the trophy after beating Surrey in a tight game by four wickets. I didn't contribute many runs to the campaign (1991 was, after all, my annus horribilis) but I did get to be the one to raise the trophy on the pavilion balcony, having been drafted in the day before the game as stand-in captain after Mark Nicholas had his hand broken by Waqar Younis in the championship match against the same opposition in the days leading up to the final.

It was a slightly nervy experience to start with. Although I had enough captaincy experience, it had been a while and I was fully aware of the responsibility that now lay on my shoulders. Under Mark, who had been captain since 1985, Hampshire had a good record in finals and there was the disappointment of that previous year's semi-final defeat to assuage. Winning the toss and bowling first was not the advantage it sometimes was in September finals, as the pitch was dry and the day started in bright sunshine. Robin Smith and Jon Ayling were the heroes at the end of the day, carving the winning runs in near darkness. That hands-on-trophy moment is always special and I was mighty glad it had worked out for the team. As I lifted it to salute the Hampshire faithful on the field below I sensed movement beside me and a split second later the club captain had his hands on the trophy too. Well, it was his team!

Sadly, Marshall missed out once more as he was again touring with West Indies but this was put right in 1992 when we won the Benson & Hedges Cup with him very much to the fore. I had a good tournament too, scoring an unbeaten 118 against Northants in the group stage. It seems that I could still play one-day cricket when the mood took me.

The decision to retire in the autumn of 1993 was tricky. I wasn't sure about it, took a lot of soundings and needed weeks to reflect. Those who know me well will recognise this indecision. Part of me was waiting for my appetite for the game, if it was still there, to kick in and prompt me to keep going. Some of those I spoke to thought I should have carried on. When Ray Illingworth became England team manager the following year he said that I shouldn't have quit because he'd have got me back into the Test side, but that's an easy thing to say when the moment has passed, not so straightforward a thing to make happen at the time. I was 36 when I announced my retirement from all cricket. That's a perfectly decent age to stop and – given the way I was thinking – it was enough.

A few might-have-beens muddied the picture. Even though England had performed disastrously on the subcontinent during the winter, I was not called on for the start of the 1993 Ashes, but on the day the series opened at Old Trafford (where Shane Warne would bowl his wonder-ball to Mike Gatting the next day) I scored 150-odd for Hampshire at Trent Bridge, putting Chris Cairns into the stands a few times, and thought I'd given myself a chance should fresh batsmen be needed at any stage. Then fate intervened: diving for a catch off Shaun Udal at slip, I fell on the ball and cracked a rib, and was out of action for almost three weeks. By the time I came back England were 2–0 down and contemplating wholesale changes. I had just one innings to make an impact. It came handily enough against the Australians at Southampton but I was out to a good low catch at gully, and when the squad was announced England went instead for the uncapped Graham Thorpe as their middle-order left-hander. Thorpe cemented his place with a hundred on debut and although another vacancy came up for the final Test at the Oval the selectors went for Mark Ramprakash.

Graham Gooch's resignation as captain midway through the series gave me hope that things might be different under Michael Atherton, but it seemed that I still had opponents on the selection panel, Atherton saying later that he felt the selectors were afraid to pick me for the Oval. I finished the season strongly with three hundreds in six championship matches but Mike said, quite under-standably, that he wanted to take to the West Indies a team for the future, one that he hoped might be able to compete with the best in five years' time. I had no issue with what he was saying but it pretty much ruled me out.

I was conscious that however good my end-of-season form was it wouldn't count for much on a tour not starting until several months later. West Indies too remained a strong side and even though I'd done okay in the Caribbean in the past, getting runs against them would still have been very hard. If I was even slightly off the pace mentally or physically it could have turned into a very long tour.

Once I'd calculated that my chances of getting back into the Test team were fairly slim the decision about my future became more straightforward. Some people encouraged me to play one more season regardless but I knew that while it might sound like a nice idea it could and probably would have been a disaster. The idea of going round the country waving goodbye to people is a wishy-washy one and if I'd learnt one thing during my career it was that if your heart is not in it, then it's an impossible game. My recent behaviour towards playing in the Sunday league was an indicator of fading enthusiasm that I could not ignore. When you start to regard the last five minutes in bed as the best part of the day then you should know you are in trouble.

Once I'd come to my decision I was immediately happy with it and very calm about the future. I told Thorunn that I was going to retire and she was fine about it. I then went to see Tony Baker, Hampshire's chief executive, and told him I'd made up my mind to finish. He said that the club would have been happy to have me back for another season but totally understood my decision.

I have never regretted the timing. I was later often asked to play in social games or benefit matches but rarely accepted as I had no great longing to get back into whites or strap on the pads again. I did accept an invitation to captain the Earl of Carnarvon's XI against the South African touring team at Highclere Castle in 1994 but then why would I not? The Queen attended the game and after I'd got out – for not many – I was asked to sit with her in one of the marquees, leading to a memorable photograph when she asked to try on a pair of my multi-coloured Bolle sunglasses!

My retirement was to a small extent influenced by other options Jon Holmes had shrewdly been lining up for me. Naturally I had told him what I was thinking and he had said that if I wanted to quit as a player he had been speaking to the BBC and to the *Sunday Express* about me working for them. I eventually told him I was 85 per cent of the way there and he said that was probably as close as I'd ever get. He hugely enjoyed the fact our final conversation on this subject was conducted at my house while I was wearing a pashmina of the type worn by Pathans in the tribal regions of Pakistan, and he asked to take a photograph so that he could show people how eccentric I really was!

Jon had in particular developed a good relationship with Brian Barwick, the then BBC's head of sport, and Brian was very enthusiastic about the idea of myself and Gary Lineker, also a client of Jon's and himself nearing the end of his football career, joining the BBC. I remember Fred Rumsey advising that offers to work in the media would not always be there if I chose to carry on playing, but Jon was pretty confident that they would not vanish overnight, so I didn't feel pressured into retiring when I did. Gary played his last

My time at Hampshire had some ups and downs. This is what they, and I, preferred to see.

I was suitably proud to emulate my father in receiving an OBE. Coincidentally, on the same day, Clive Lloyd, my opposing captain for the West Indies in 1984, and here with his wife, Waveney, was presented with his CBE. No prizes for guessing who won that series then!

There! I told you – it didn't always end up in second slip's hands.

What a fabulous day. On the steps of Winchester Cathedral with Thorunn, now officially Mrs Gower, flanked by the delighted groom and Chris Cowdrey, whose best man's speech later was a classic.

I eventually got past Geoff Boycott's record as the leading runscorer for England in Tests, making 73 at Old Trafford on my comeback in 1992 against Pakistan. It took a while but we tracked him down somewhere near the BBC box and I think he congratulated me!

Where does the time go? It only seems ten minutes since they were that size. It is long since that Samm
and Alex have graduated from the trampoline to the hockey fields and netball courts at Twyford
and Canford.

They Think It's All Over gave me eight years of pain and pleasure inextricably intermingled. Somewhere
in there are Gary Lineker, Rory McGrath, Nick Hancock, Jonathan Ross and me. But who's who?

The rose between two thorns. Some hours later, thanks to Lamb and Botham especially, I was distinctly the worse for wear. At this very early stage of my stag night, organised by Ian on Alderney, all was well.

I did not play much after retiring but did captain the Earl of Caernarvon's XI at Highclere Castle (pre-Downton Abbey!) against the South Africans in 1994. The Queen attended and took an inquisitive interest in my sunglasses.

David Shepherd is one of my favourite people. Inspirational as an artist and as a conservationist, the Wildlife Foundation named after him is my number one charity. Also in support at a dinner at the Natural History Museum in 1997 are Gary Lineker and Nick Hancock.

Wildlife is my passion and this is one of my favourites from my own collection, taken in 2010 at Leopard Hills in the Sabi Sands, South Africa, where luckily they do what it says in the name beautifully!

As Patron of the SAVE African Rhino Foundation, this was a photo op to highlight the appalling results that the poaching of these extraordinary animals has had on their numbers across Africa and elsewhere in the world.

This was the most gorgeous leopard cub, filmed at Leopard Hills, relaxing on a tree branch having feasted on an impala kill.

If in doubt, head for the cellar. Some of my favourite things, including a bottle of Lynch Bages, year uncertain but definitively delicious.

The finest commentary team in
cricket? No need to answer that!
Lord Gower, Athers, Straussie,
Beefy, Nass, Mikey and Bumble.
Sky's ensemble for 2013.

Surrounded by gorgeous girls.
Bliss! Alex, DG, Thorunn and
Sammi in the old town of
Funchal in Madeira, 2011.

England match in 1992 before spending a couple of years playing in Japan. The deal that took Gary and me to the BBC had been a long time in the making – Gary cut his teeth in radio, where they tried and failed to sort out his vowel sounds! – and if I'd played another year I don't think it would have changed much, though it is possible the *Sunday Express*, who took me on as their cricket correspondent, might have lost interest. I would maintain that my retirement was based on cricketing grounds first and foremost.

The job with the *Express* was probably a mistake as I was most inexperienced in newspapers and fulfilling the role of correspondent was a very different task than writing a column, which relied on opinion rather than reporting. Eve Pollard, as editor, was keen and Peter Watson, the sports editor, promised to steer me in the right direction, which he did and I learned straightaway that the structure of the history essays I had written so fluently at King's was completely irrelevant when it came to compiling a newspaper story. I know my appointment did not go down well with the man I replaced, the vastly experienced Pat Gibson, but all I can say is that it was a position I was offered rather than one I pursued. I saw him some weeks later at a Lord's Taverners dinner at the Park Lane Hilton. Classically we met in the gents and only he spoke, just the one word, which I feel should not be repeated here!

By this stage, I did have some experience of working for the BBC, though mainly in radio. I'd done some work for them on the West Indies tour of 1989–90 and appeared as an occasional summariser when they'd covered the later rounds of the Benson & Hedges Cup or NatWest Trophy if Hampshire weren't involved. I'd largely enjoyed the experience, with most of the team a delight to work with, although I did have a problem with Don Mosey who seemed unnecessarily gruff and forbidding. I'd come across Don during my playing days of course and he seemed to assume that I would not like him because he was from Yorkshire but on that narrow-minded assumption he was completely wrong. If I didn't like him it was only because he made it clear first that he did not care for me. Bizarrely, in his autobiography he described me as one of the most unwelcome guests of all time on *Test Match Special* on the basis that I once dared to correct the great Brian Johnston on a point of fact! It might seem a minor spat but it irked me that he should race to his assumption in the face of all the evidence; my mentor and major influence on my career had been Ray Illingworth, an archetypal Yorkshireman, I had always prided myself on being able to get on with all sorts of people, including Yorkshiremen, and I could recite the Monty Python 'Four Yorkshiremen' sketch almost word for word! If I came not to like him it was only because he lacked the charm that everyone else on the programme seemed to possess. With them, I sat in reverence.

My TV experience had come as much through Channel 9 in Australia, with whom I'd spent two winters, and Sky Television, who in those days covered England tours overseas, as with the BBC, for whom I had done only the odd Benson & Hedges or NatWest match. I was indebted as much to Channel 9 as anyone at this stage because they'd employed me in Australia when I was still pretty wet behind the ears. But John Gayleard, the producer, who would later move to Sky, was a great person to work for because he was happy to throw you in at the deep end and allow you to sink or swim – and if you sank he'd not condemn you too fiercely. As Mark Nicholas would be later, I was the Pom who lent some variety to an otherwise all-Aussie cast of commentators and I think I made a good enough impression for John to be well disposed to me in future, which as it turned out was ideal when Sky's role in TV coverage greatly increased.

Talking of sinking or swimming though, I must describe how I sank spectacularly during my first season with Channel 9. We were covering the World Cup in Australia when the games came along thick and fast. We were down in Hobart to cover a match between Australia and Zimbabwe and the night before the game I'd gone out for dinner on the waterfront with Tony Greig and a few of the other guys as usual. We'd had a perfectly pleasant and relatively sober evening and were about to leave the restaurant to head back to the hotel but, just as we were getting up, in walked my old mate from Leicestershire days, Brian Davison, who now lived in Tasmania. Of course, going off without having a drink with my old mucker wasn't an option so we sat down and got through far too many beers than were good for me. By the time I fell into bed it was two o'clock in the morning and I was in a horrendous state.

When my alarm call went off in the morning, I sat bolt upright in bed, thought 'Great. I'm not dead,' and then slumped back down again, groaning inwardly and thinking that actually death might hurt less. I lapsed into unconsciousness and was only woken by Greigy phoning from reception to tell me that the rest of them were heading off for the ground. I just about managed to reply that I would be along shortly, which turned out to be a slight exaggeration. Actually, it was a big exaggeration. I made it to the Bellerive Oval in time for the start, but only just. I brushed off Gayleard's enquiries by assuring him I was fine, donned a pair of dark glasses and joined Richie Benaud in front of the microphones. He asked me what I was wearing and when I told him a pair of Bollés, he muttered something about his fellow commentator 'wearing parabolics'. My powers of observation transpired to be seriously impaired and when Allan Border was stumped by about five yards he was halfway back to the pavilion before something in the depths of my brain suggested that I ought to say something about the dismissal.

To make matters worse, late in the day several of the other commentators left the game early to catch a flight to Adelaide so they would be in position for the start of the next day's game between India and South Africa, with the rest of us flying in the next morning to join them. Gayleard had little choice but to tell me that this left me in charge of the post-match presentation ceremony, something I'd never done before. And so, still feeling seriously ropey, I was handed the microphone at the end of the game and sent off to the podium. Even if I had not been nursing a hangover I'd have been anxious; as it was, the whole thing was doubly daunting. When Steve Waugh was invited up to answer a few questions as man of the match, I thought things were going rather well until it became clear no one could hear his replies because I was still holding the microphone in front of my mouth and not his, and I heard Gayleard barking in my hear, 'Point the microphone at him! . . . I said, Point the fucking microphone at him!' By the end I was sweating for two reasons. One was embarrassment, the other purely medical.

That night I did not go out with Davison and I got to Adelaide the next morning feeling a million times better, at least until Gayleard told me, 'Right mate, you can do the presentation again.' And, amazingly, second time round and sober, it was not so bad. I asked some of the right questions and used the microphone in the approved manner. And I thought: 'Maybe I *can* do this.' That was what was known as on-the-job training.

It was also excellent experience to slot into such an established and renowned team. You do not see or work with any better than Benaud, never flustered and masterful with the language as a commentator and presenter. I always enjoyed a conversation with Ian Chappell; you could guarantee he would be the one to have the last word but you would need to have your facts straight for any argument and he is one of those people with a phenomenal recall for conversations from years ago. Admitting you quite like Ian never goes down well with Botham! Greg Chappell was rather more urbane and I got on really well with him, never forgetting that dinner we had when I was in the early stages of my Test career.

One snapshot: I remember him one day at the MCG watching a leg-spinner operate out in the middle. We were up in the commentary box, which was both high up in the members stand and felt like miles from the centre of the ground. He was picking the leggies and googlies as he watched the hand from that great distance.

The other two members of that group were Bill Lawry and Tony Greig, who, as in the Billy Birmingham 'Twelfth Man' spoofs, would quite often start the day off together in the commentary box. Bill is simply one of the nicest men you will ever meet, devoted to his pigeons as per the spoof but likewise devoted to the game of cricket. He would always be in his seat, wired up and ready for the first ball of the day half an hour before the start of play. It was as if he just could not believe his good fortune at having the job and he did not want anyone to take that seat from him. That enthusiasm bubbles into every word he has ever uttered on TV – and there have been plenty.

Tony Greig became a good friend and ally. Of all of them he probably understood the principle of selling the game to the viewer the best. His whole motivation was never to be boring and he had a wicked but fun way of trying to wind everyone up when possible. We were on together one day when a batsman was celebrating a hundred and I saw the glint in his eye as he turned to me and asked, 'Which is more satisfying, good sex or a hundred in a Test match?' I had to hesitate briefly before, I think, muttering something about one being a more long lasting satisfaction. He knew how to have fun on the job too. Before you splutter into your gin and tonic or castigate me for such a banal follow-up to the previous tale, may I say I am, of course, referring to making the most of the opportunities that come from being part of a TV crew on tour. I'm not putting this much better yet, am I! The sort of thing I am talking about is what we got up to on a day off in the Caribbean on the 1993–94 tour. He was a major part of the Sky team in those early days and rather than lie round the pool at the Pegasus Hotel in Kingston he thought we could be much more enterprising. This meant commandeering a cameraman and a helicopter and taking myself and Ian Botham off around Jamaica to take some island shots that could be used as travelogues during breaks in the action. It was a police helicopter so we were accompanied by a senior officer as well. Forget the obvious tourist sights, the first 'place of interest' was a massive field of marijuana growing just below the Blue Mountains. 'What do we do with this?' we ask. 'You leave it where it is,' our man replied. Oh, okay. After that we flew up to Negril, checked out the 'beautiful people' on the beach there, then across to Montego Bay, where we had to touch down for one, yes one, hole of golf at Tryall. That had to be competitive too but Tony chose the hole with the most spectacular views and had of course brought a club or two with him for that very purpose. It was great fun to be around him and you could easily see why the players of his generation thought him one of the most charismatic leaders.

From these earlier forays, I realised that television was what I preferred. I would write various newspaper columns over the years, latterly and most regularly in a happy relationship with the *Sunday Times* lasting more than ten years, but from early on TV was the medium I felt most comfortable with. I found picking up a microphone and talking came more easily than tapping out my thoughts on a laptop. In either mode I like to think there is an enjoyment that comes from finding the right words – but no guarantee it's going to happen! There were to be some twists and turns along the way but, as I write, television has kept me very happily occupied for some 20 years already.

10

LIFE ON THE SMALL SCREEN

When I joined BBC Television's commentary team on a full-time basis in 1994, the job wasn't entirely new but there was a different feel to it knowing that this was now my career. There was hope on my part and expectation on the part of others. The idea, which was not just mine, was that I would develop a career which would involve me taking over from Tony Lewis as the main presenter. There was no timeframe on it, there was no rush and I was certainly not trying to push Tony out of the door, but I was made aware early on that that was what I was working towards.

I liked Tony a lot and learned a great deal simply from watching how he and others on the team such as Richie Benaud went about things. Tony was unflappable, a useful attribute to have when hosting a live programme which by its nature demanded that you be constantly prepared for the unexpected. You could not rely on a script because the script was forever changing, and thinking on your feet was absolutely a pre-requisite for the job. Tony was a hugely experienced broadcaster, having worked for the BBC on radio and television since the early 1970s when he was still playing and, briefly, captaining England. He had experience of broadcasting on plenty of topics besides cricket, which he had presented

239

since Peter West retired in the mid-1980s, and always abided by the first rule of the medium which was to engage brain before speaking. It may be the first rule, but I've seen it broken many times! Taking a moment to think is always the best policy. The results can be fascinating.

The BBC's cricket coverage ran like a well-oiled machine in those days. They had, after all, been covering England's home matches for as long as anyone could remember, and it was very easy to slot into the team run by Keith Mackenzie, the producer, and director Alan Griffiths. It was an interesting dynamic coming into such a team; whatever self-confidence I had acquired through becoming a successful international cricketer, below still lurked the shy youth, and I always like to take my time to assess a new environment before developing the assurance to just be myself. I have always tried to mask the shyness with what passes for some light humour, and the sort of banter you get from dressing rooms and commentary boxes makes that all the easier.

As for the job itself, I enjoyed the spontaneity of the whole thing; you can never be sure what's coming next and the ability to describe events without necessarily stating the bleeding obvious all the time and retaining a broadcastable sense of fun is the challenge. The mantra, as explained by John Gayleard in my days at Channel 9, was to be like a group of blokes in the pub having a natter about the game, batting back and forth the issues of the day and being seen and heard to be enjoying it all – but without the alcohol! I enjoyed not knowing what might be thrown at you. You could prepare for what was coming up, but only to a degree. Far more often, you simply had to assimilate events as fast as you could and make your judgements. It was a different kind of performance to playing, but it still generated a buzz of excitement. There wasn't the same personal threat as there was when batting against a Dennis Lillee or Jeff Thomson, or the risk of public vilification if you made a mistake, but there was a matter of pride at getting it right, saying the right things and, hopefully, keeping the viewers watching.

There were no commercial breaks with the BBC, of course, which wasn't a help when it rained and we needed a few moments to guess how long the break might be and for Tony to receive his instructions from Keith or Alan about how we should fill the time. In my current role at Sky, we can always use an ad break as a time to make a plan, but initially when the covers are pulled onto the ground and we head for the studio it is just a question of talking until someone says stop. The good news is that I think we get some of the best discussions out of those situations simply because time is not limited. For Tony a light rain shower was a bit of a nightmare, only because any communication with management was inevitably one-way traffic, much as it is for me now, with the big difference that during those ad breaks I can make notes about what we will be using to fill the time. Tony had a 'lazy', a mic which he could pick up and on which he could press the button which then muted his own mic and allowed him to speak to the truck without his voice going to air. When he did this it was normally a sign that the talking was about to stop and that footage from the archives was imminent. If it was Richie or myself in the studio alongside him, our job was just to keep talking to the camera until Tony was ready again to rejoin the fray. It was like being on BBC Radio 4's *Just a Minute* but without the same quality of humour!

On Saturdays we would be part of *Grandstand* and on occasion that show's presenter might pitch up at the Test ground and introduce it all from there. There was once occasion when Sue Barker presented the programme from Headingley and when play was interrupted by what proved to be a short shower I was deputed to stand under an umbrella alongside Sue at the Kirkstall Lane End. As I took my position I was under the impression that we had no plans for the fill and that I should give her as much time as possible

241

to receive instructions as and when they came through. Being young, enthusiastic and crucially not on talkback (so I could not hear what was being planned elsewhere), when she asked the first question about the state of play I just gave the longest answer I have ever given anyone in any conversation at any stage of my life. I thought I had surpassed myself in speaking for a good 13 minutes (may all of you who had to endure the ordeal without switching channels please forgive me) but in fact, unbeknown to me, they had got hold of Chris Old at the other end of the ground and were ready to interview him, if only I would shut up. But I didn't – at least not before the showers ceased – so the BBC's viewers never did get to hear from Chris that day.

The BBC also gave me a weekly radio programme to present as well as a magazine show on the telly, *Gower's Cricket Monthly*, which started life during the 1993 season even before I'd retired from playing. This too was all part of the long-term training. *Gower's Cricket Monthly* was a one-hour show for which at first we recorded all the links out on location, editing in the stories later, before progressing to a studio environment at Television Centre at White City, where we would record the show 'as live', thus able to fix any cock-ups in edit before broadcast. Eventually it was time to do a live show and my first was from Trent Bridge immediately after our coverage of the final day of the Test. It was the first time I had used autocue. Whereas reading a script off the screen in front of you sounds easy enough, the great tendency the first time is to focus so much on the words you are reading that it all looks a bit unnatural and it takes a little while to settle into the rhythm and to not stare blankly and immobile at the camera with your eyes obviously following the script like a five-year-old. Even now, 20 years on, I prefer to do things off the top of my head rather than use the autocue, which, as it happens, is just as well since everything we do live from the grounds is without it.

For a very early episode of the programme we went to New Road, Worcester, where the Australians were playing their first serious match of the 1993 tour. We climbed to the top of the Cathedral tower carrying with us a little replica Ashes urn borrowed from MCC with the strict instruction to take great care of it (they value their replicas every bit as much as the original urn housed at Lord's). The idea was that I would hold up the urn with the cricket ground in the background and say something like, 'For the next four months, this is what it is all about . . .' It was a nice idea but it almost immediately came to grief when the cork in the top of the urn fell out and disappeared under the duckboards. A frantic search ensued which fortunately led to us reclaiming the little stopper. We would have still had a link but the wrath of the MCC is not lightly incurred! At least it didn't happen to me while I was standing on the Oval balcony in 1985.

Working on the Test matches, it was a joy being able to learn from Benaud. As captain of Australia he had been the first player to understand the fact that the camera could be his ally and there is footage from that time of him looking straight down the barrel and addressing the nation as he would do for so many years as a broadcaster. He was wonderful to work with because he had such a wealth of knowledge and stories that he was never at a loss for something to say. But he also had that rare ability to say nothing when there was nothing to say, that 'let it breathe' moment that we are all as commentators asked to remember. If I wanted advice, although any of the team would be generous in giving it, he was the one I would go to first.

As for 'letting it breathe', he was the master. We did a Benson & Hedges Cup match at Derby once, where he and I were on together after tea. He had a trick where he would pick up the Benaud binoculars and slowly scan the ground, looking for God knows what and basically challenging you to speak if you thought it necessary. For a full ten minutes he said absolutely nothing and I dared to add only a couple of descriptive points while not much happened on the field. A wicket fell, at which point Richie picked up his mic and eloquently described the event. As the 'colour' man, I then began my assessment, only to hear in my ear that my mic was not switched on. That whole previous ten minutes had gone by without a word being heard from either of us, and no complaints either – which is a worry!

There were things to be learned from everyone on that team if you were prepared to listen. You learn to see people in a different light; Jack Bannister, who had been quite a harsh critic when I took on the England captaincy, questioning my ability to do the job, which he was of course perfectly entitled to do, turned out to have a wonderful but very dry sense of humour, a wealth of great stories from his playing days, could sometimes be a little dour but most of the time was great fun. He was very precise, very hard-working, and understood the game thoroughly.

I was the junior man in the team but had enough nous to trust my opinions. The thing you tend to do as a recently retired player is be kind to those who are still playing, partly because they are still your mates and partly because you're used to seeing the game from a player's perspective. That of course is what you are hired for, as one with the experience of playing for and probably captaining your country, and it is never a bad thing to retain memories of yourself as a player as it is all too easy to fall into the trap of criticising a shot, a dropped catch, a strange tactical decision without a thought as to how it used to feel when you were the one out on the field. One does need to be able to learn to comment harshly and to develop one's critical skills but for me the aim is to be purely and simply honest and fair to all.

The loudest voice in that box belonged to Geoffrey Boycott. Keeping Geoffrey quiet is not an easy task at the best of times but you had to be on your mettle at all times with him. He has opinions on everything, not just his specialist subject (cricket, if you were in any doubt) and is keen to express those opinions in fervent fashion all day and every day. As a co-commentator it kept you on your toes, knowing you would have something challenging to respond to at any given moment. I found that fun and it was certainly not difficult working alongside him because you could take issue with what he said and as far as the viewers were concerned it was always more interesting when two commentators were not in constant agreement. It is an easy trap to fall into to echo the words of what a colleague has just said but far more stimulating for us and the viewers if you can come up with an alternative view. That was rarely difficult when Geoffrey was sitting next to you.

Overall I got on well with Geoffrey, and still do. It is more mutual respect than empathy! There are plenty of well-worn stories about people saying that they took an instant dislike to Geoffrey. Why? Because it saved time. And there will be moments when he just annoys you. As a commentator, in those days on television and now more usually on BBC radio, it is easy to mock him by ticking off the Boycott-isms like a game of bingo. 'My grandmother could have played that with a stick of rhubarb . . .' Ching! 'Corridor of Uncertainty . . .' Ching! 'Techmeek . . .' Ching! But he knows the game thoroughly and is not afraid to speak out, and that usually makes for good listening. He'll be wrong sometimes, of course, even if not in his own mind.

He was not happy the day in 1992 when I took from him the England Test run-scoring record. Obviously I was out in the middle at Old Trafford at the time, but up in the BBC commentary box Keith Mackenzie, the producer, was keen for one of the cameramen to get a shot of Geoffrey at the moment I went past his 8,114 runs. But he was unwilling to play ball and somehow went missing.

Later in the afternoon, after I'd got out, Tony Lewis got us both together on the roof of the new media centre to share in a chat during the tea interval. One could sense that Geoffrey was not entirely happy to have lost his record but he was more miffed at Tony's suggestion that his had been a more selfish approach to the business of making runs and setting records and that I was the embodiment of a very different attitude to the game. I think we got Geoffrey to agree to 'self-centred'!

That did not worry me one little bit. I had known him for long enough and we'd had many a chat about attitude when we were both players. He was obviously proud that he had been England's leading run-scorer and I was just about as proud to have taken the title from him.

I could let his behaviour that day go more easily than his attitude towards my involvement in the Acfield Report some years later. This was the product of a committee chaired by David Acfield, the former Essex spinner, a Cambridge graduate and an Olympic fencer, with a rapier wit to boot and a shrewd mind on the subject of cricket. Not Geoffrey's cup of tea at all and the fact that Geoffrey had not been co-opted to the committee, whose remit was to look into the workings of the England team, seemed to rankle. We, the committee, came up with some sensible stuff about the England team needing to be more at the forefront of the English game, a view soon to be echoed by Lord MacLaurin when he came in as the first head of the newly formed England and Wales Cricket Board and began to change the emphasis away from the counties and more towards the national team.

When the report was published we were covering a Test in Leeds and during one of the intervals we discussed the findings of the report. There were three of us involved and Geoffrey sat on the end of the line in a sulk all the way through. 'Well, it's rubbish . . . ,' he said, refusing to engage or acknowledge that the report might have contained even one or two decent ideas. We all looked at him incredulously afterwards.

The following morning there was still an atmosphere. I have a feeling, unless I have elided two arguments into one, that we'd also had an opinionated discussion on another vital issue at the end of the previous day, regarding the over-zealous arrest of a carrot that had wandered, inebriated, onto the field after play. Fancy dress, Headingley and Tetley's all seem to go hand in hand but, although the carrot was certainly in the wrong place at the wrong time, I felt that the Leeds Rhino style tackle that felled it was heavy-handed. Geoffrey felt the carrot had got all it deserved. When we reconvened that morning, he was still on about it and muttering dark things about Acfield. It wound me up and I was seething when Geoffrey went off to tour the sponsors' boxes and Lewis and Benaud began the day's commentary. Then I noticed that he'd left behind one of his trademark panama hats hanging on a peg just behind me. I fetched it down, dropped it on the floor and began trampling it with both feet so noisily that Lewis and Benuad looked round in unison to see what was going on. Ah . . . it made me feel so much better! I picked up the hat, pushed it back into shape – they are great those panama hats, they easily recover from a pounding – and popped it back on its peg. Geoffrey never had any idea his hat was so badly abused. For me, it was a cathartic release.

A hugely enjoyable spin-off of my time with the BBC was joining *They Think It's All Over*, the sports quiz show with a difference that attracted a cult following for several years. Gary Lineker and myself were team captains and as former international sportsmen we lent the show a degree of respectability it scarcely warranted as it pedalled a heavy diet of irreverence, lewd language and good and bad humour. Our primary function seemed to be as the butt of jokes from comedians far better equipped to crack them than we were. We were essentially paid to smile and provide a few lines of our own, assuming, that is, we could get a word in edgeways – which was not often.

Before I go further, though, I feel I should explain something of my friendship with Gary, which began through us both living in Leicester and sharing the same agent. I'd seen quite a bit of Gary during my benefit year when he turned out several times for me in benefit matches at places like West Ilsley and Bray, where Michael Parkinson had helped arrange a game for me. At West Ilsley, Gary made a hundred, kept wicket, bowled and took a stunning catch at deep midwicket, proving himself to be a far better all-rounder than I ever was. If only he had finished off the day by downing a couple of magnums of Vega Sicilia, this would have been a truly Both-amesque feat. At Bray, where Parky as president obviously set them high ambitions, I opened the batting and realised very quickly that they were taking this game rather seriously. Nicking one, completely in character, to slip early on, I departed in low dudgeon and retreated unsociably to the dressing room. I therefore missed most of Gary's next hundred but recovered my good humour in time to applaud him to his landmark and was even persuaded to have another try with the bat myself towards the end of the innings.

There is no doubt Gary could have been a very fine cricketer; just how good it is hard to say. Although rumours that he could have played some games for Leicestershire are a slight exaggeration, he did acquit himself with ease when playing for MCC in order to qualify for playing membership. Once he'd done so, every time he came to Lord's when I was playing Test matches there, I would look up to the home balcony and see him waving the club tie at me to emphasise the fact that he was a member of MCC and I was not.

On that front, I did not become an MCC member until a couple of years after I had played for the club in the Bicentenary match of

1987. During that game, Lt-Col John Stephenson, then Secretary of the club, had offered all of us accelerated membership. At the time I didn't see the necessity and politely declined but some time later thought, 'Actually, why not?' and spoke to the Colonel who said he would get me the relevant application form.

This I filled in, sent it back to Lord's and waited for my red membership card to arrive. What I got was a letter from the membership committee suggesting that whereas I had most of the qualifications they were looking for as a potential playing member, could I give them half a dozen dates when I might represent the club in what they call 'out matches'. I replied that, much as I would love to do so, it seemed that I was 'a bit busy with Leicestershire that summer'. Could I, I proffered, possibly qualify on the real tennis court?

Let us not forget that by then I had played in MCC colours several times in matches such as MCC versus champion county and MCC versus various touring sides. The real tennis court quip was one of those harmless throwaway lines that always kept me amused, if no one else, but it turns out that when it was read out to the membership committee there was a degree of harrumphing. Despite ten years of Test cricket under my belt, I was apparently a tad too impertinent for their liking. Suffice to say it took time before my red card did arrive, though I only paid the subs for a short while before happily accepting the honorary membership that the club likes to bestow on those who have had lengthy England careers.

Peace broke out to the extent that when I was happily ensconced in the BBC commentary box alongside Tony Lewis, a long-time and dedicated servant to MCC, I thought I could finally contribute something more by joining the MCC committee. There are some very good and highly qualified gentlemen who have given great service to what is still a great and iconic club. I felt that on most matters I could sit quietly in committee and let them get on with it but where matters strayed into areas of my expertise, i.e. cricket and now television, I would have something more to offer. On the cricket committee that was fine. In general committee when the topic of the media came up, the then Secretary, Roger Knight, turned out to have something of a phobia about things like TV cameras and was very reluctant to accept that the club should start to think about seeing TV as an ally rather than an intrusion. It had always been the policy of the club, way before Roger, to defend the rights and the privacy of the members but I felt as though he was behaving like a headmaster, which of course he had been for much of his career outside cricket, and although in most respects you would say he was charming and urbane, I found his resistance to the media frustrating. Three years later, after my attendance at committee had declined markedly, I saw little point in continuing except for the privilege of being able to park in the ground.

Anyway, to return to my involvement of a less salubrious 'club', as panellist on *They Think* . . . as we soon came to know it, Gary and I stayed with the programme for almost eight years. The deal was the result of protracted talks between Jon Holmes and potential production companies. Eventually Talkback went ahead with it in 1995. The show had actually started life on BBC Radio 5 with Des Lynam as host and Rory McGrath and Rory Bremner as the regulars. I made an early guest appearance and did an impression of John Arlott which just about passed muster. The devisers of that programme wanted it transferred to television but for various reasons it took time to happen. Lynam was asked to host the TV show but ruled himself out, believing it would not work in that medium. Bremner also declined. I even flew back from the Caribbean to audition for the role.

Eventually a pilot went out with Nick Hancock in the chair and after that the show took off very quickly. The concept worked and people embraced it. Indeed, it became so successful that after a couple of series the BBC moved the show from the independent studios on the South Bank where it began life and put more of their own resources behind it. None of us wanted to miss an episode and if the schedule allowed I would fly back from commentating overseas to take part. If I couldn't make it Steve Davis (the snooker player, not the umpire) usually stood in as captain.

It worked so well in large part thanks to Nick, Rory McGrath and Lee Hurst. Rory was on Gary's team and Lee on mine, with Lee giving way to Jonathan Ross after three years. Lee was very funny and Rory very erudite as well as very funny. Behind Rory's rather shabby exterior was someone who loved accumulating knowledge. I later did some travel programmes with him and he was forever churning out fascinating snippets of information about the places we went.

We did one week in California for the *Holiday* programme, driving down Highway 1 from San Francisco. In Carmel, the town where Clint Eastwood was once mayor, we found ourselves in earnest conversation with some of the locals at our hotel after the day's filming and Rory mischievously told them, 'David is a close friend of the Queen, you know.' 'Oh really? Do you spend much time at the Palace?' Gullibility is a wonderful thing! Our next trip took us to Queensland (is there a tenuous link here somewhere?) where we had to take a campervan from Brisbane to Noosa via Fraser Island, again for *Holiday*. The classic scene was at the campground just outside Noosa. We arrived in the late afternoon, filmed the mundane chores of hooking up the camper to the water and electricity and then shot the breakfast scene. By then a thunderstorm had reached us so we had to move the camper under the only shelter, the awning of the camp office, to overcome the problem of the noise of rain on the roof of the van. 'Brilliant sunshine' was provided by a massive studio light positioned outside the window and we played the scene out with me rising 'sleepily' from the bunk above the driver's seat and taking a shower, singing 'Waltzing Matilda', while Rory cooked a massive fry-up on the gas stove. Apart from a fire – the result of a little over-exuberance with the bacon – all went well, though Rory by the time he had finished looked like he had just run a marathon in 40 degrees heat. With the scene wrapped we drove the van to the Sheraton, checked in, and headed off for dinner at one of Noosa's finest seaside restaurants. That's how to make a travel show!

Next we spent a week in Mumbai as butlers at the famous and fabulous Taj Mahal Hotel. For the purposes of the 'story' we had to work our way up from Bellboy to VIP butler and were set all sorts of tasks to prove our worth. On the first morning I was on the front doors opening them for everyone who was about to enter the hotel. Whilst most guests would sweep through into the lobby, every now and again someone would do a double-take, come back and ask, 'Are you who I think you are?' 'Times are hard,' I would say. 'Have a good day at the Taj.'

We mastered room service on day two. Our mentors on the hotel staff explained that the target time for delivery of a request for a pot of tea was five minutes from phone call to the knock on the guest's door. Christ, I thought, things have changed since I was first here. In 1980, when we had been there for the Jubilee Test, a cup of tea from room service was a half-day affair. If at the same time you put in a request to the hotel operator for a call to the UK, it was touch and go which might arrive first. Nowadays it is all completely different. Tea takes five minutes and an international call is instantaneous.

The climax was a gathering in honour of Indian authoress Shobhaa De, who was launching a new book with a drinks party in her suite on the sixth floor. There was a team of butlers, and Rory and I, ready to serve canapés and drinks to the glitterati of Mumbai. The champagne was almost chilled in time and as the guests arrived we would welcome them as deferentially as possible. With cricket the religion that it is in India, once again I was recognised time and again. When Sunil Gavaskar arrived he definitely could not believe what he was seeing. Sledging is not allowed as a butler, so all I could say was, 'Good evening, Mr Gavaskar. What can I get you to drink?' As the party loosened up I found myself pretending to take champagne around the room for the official guests, who would then say, 'We cannot have you doing this for us. Get your friend to bring us some more.' So while I got stuck into the Krug, Rory was once again sweating his b******s off as he raced around, professionally explaining exactly what all the snacks consisted of. The lovely Shobhaa was heard to say, 'It seems that David has turned into a guest.'

Our final project together was a lesson in how not to make a television show. We were approached by an independent production company, or, to be more accurate, a wee Scotsman who had mortgaged his house and persuaded half a dozen naïve investors to put up the money, to film a series set in the winelands of France. Over the next six weeks we headed first to the Loire, on to Champagne, Beaujolais, Beaune and Bordeaux. We had a great time, covered a lot of ground and drank some beautiful wine. We even had an E-Type Jag, sourced by one of the investors, who had to maintain the beast and repair it when I drove over too lumpy speed bumps or down the odd rough vineyard track. He soon became nicknamed, 'The Mechanic.' If you want an image of the show it was almost exactly the same as the series that did make it to the screens a few years later, which saw James May and Oz Clarke having a lovely time in the winelands of France with an E-Type Jag. Our film was never seen.

Our 'producer' had gambled on food and wine being the flavour of the month for television at the time. He had sold the idea to the investors but not to anyone else and he had to blag our way into all sorts of places on the promise of a show that did not exist. Optimistically he hoped that he would sell it to the BBC, Channel 4, someone, anyone, and then make some more money on the spin-off book etc. Week by week we were not sure if we would be paid. At one stage couriers were despatched with cheques to ensure that Rory and I would continue.

It was a classic cock-up. The director was a man used to *The Bill* and *Coronation Street*, a lovely man but with zero experience of documentaries. The main cameraman at least knew the ropes on that score and ended up directing much of the shoot. Unfortunately he had a major bust-up with his gay lover, who had also been his number two, in about the second week in Lyon and was largely inconsolable thereafter. His very heterosexual brother came out as replacement but we had the odd problem with him too. Shooting in Beaune, we had to wait one morning until he got a cab back from oversleeping with his latest conquest in Dijon.

We were, I have to say, warmly welcomed and very well entertained everywhere we went. We had dinner at one chateau in Muscadet where the owner had declared his estate to be independent of France. He was president of his own republic, his wife prime minister and the other members of the family all held 'cabinet' posts. As the local landowner he was welcomed in the town as an old-style aristocrat and it seems that the authorities just let him get on with it.

We somehow made it through to Bordeaux and finished the shoot. On the final evening there was drama everywhere as the tensions of the previous six weeks exploded over dinner. Rory and I looked on bemused but we thought peace might just have broken out by the end of it and we went to the Irish Bar (the obvious choice in one of the world's great wine regions!) just up the road for a final farewell drink. When our still maudlin cameraman threw his pint of Stella Artois, reassuringly expensive but still bloody wet, all over me, and not by accident, I made my excuses and left. The next morning I was on the plane back home clutching a case of Bordeaux's finest and that was that.

Unfortunately, great though a lot of the footage was, there was no coherent strand and what was meant to be six half-hour shows got edited down to one one-hour show, and despite Rory's efforts to get it moulded into something sellable, nobody bought it. I felt so sorry for the investors whose money therefore evaporated into thin air and it must have been even more galling for them to see that May–Clarke show on the air later, the same concept but delivered by a genuine and properly organised production company. A cautionary tale if ever there was one.

Nick Hancock was brilliant as the host of *They Think . . .* The radio show version had been much more warm and cuddly in its essence with Lynam as suave, genial and dry witted as you would expect. Nick gave the TV version a decided edge, which was all down to the somewhat acid quips and put-downs that Gary and I suffered in the name of team spirit and comedy. The truth is it was all for show and the real Nick is a very different animal. He is an absolute sports fan, despite being a Stoke City supporter from birth, and someone who seemed to know far more about cricket lore than I did. It's always a worry when someone knows more about your own career than you do and it seemed almost weird that at the end of a show he would come across and start a conversation on the 1984–85 tour of India. Sadly he could remember who was in the touring party while I, who after all had only captained the team, struggled to name the squad in full! Nick would also apologise now and again in the Green Room for having to take the piss out of Gary and I because, although it was one of the basic premises of the show that the comedians mock the accomplishments of the international sportsmen, owing to that love of sport he found himself in something of a dilemma. It seems that he was able to deal with his dilemma rather professionally as the put-downs just kept on coming, show after show!

Jonathan Ross was very quick at assimilating jokes and elaborating on them. He came armed with good material and was razor-sharp at using it. On his first appearance on the show he was like a tornado on speed, and came out with a whole raft of stuff that was at best lewd and for the most part jaw-droppingly crude. I sat there next to him completely bewildered and without a clue as to how to deal with it. The audience was aghast. It was extraordinary stuff. I actually spoke to Harry Thompson, the producer, before the next show and told him that if Jonathan was going to continue like that I was not sure I could carry on! Jonathan duly came in the following week, charm personified, full of apologies and explaining that he'd got a bit carried away. But his style was to keep pushing things to the limit, and often beyond, safe in the knowledge that a lot of what he said would be edited out before the programme was aired.

As I got to know him better, I was able to sit back and enjoy the comedy and admire the way his mind worked – in a word, frenetically. I even wore one of his suits one week. Every week he would bring in a couple of the most lurid things his tailor could devise and I got to try a surprisingly fetching snakeprint two-piece suit – a first and last for me!

It was intimidating trying to compete with them all – well, in fact, you didn't compete, because it was pointless trying. Before each programme we would all meet up in the afternoon, each team with its own team of three or four writers who had spent the week preparing lines which they thought might work, although Gary and I were aware that they wouldn't necessarily sound funny coming out of our mouths. I might have been able to time a cricket ball . . . but a joke was a different matter altogether. Jonathan had a scriptwriter allocated only to him and they would have been firing stuff backwards and forwards to each other for several days, so that by the time the show came around he was ready to unleash it come hell or high water. With that famous slight speech impediment it meant we were treated to gems on the lines of, 'Now tell me, Nick – where exactly is Woger Fedewer in the world wankings nowadays?'

We therefore sat in the studio with ammunition written on a pad in front of us ready for possible use, although finding the right moment was not always easy. It was a great moment when you plucked up the courage to compete on your own without recourse to the notes. I once cut Lee dead after he had embarked on some fabulous fairytale story lasting several minutes; he was as bald as a coot but made some reference to having long flowing hair. 'Until that, I believed every word . . .' Oh the joy that gave! But most of the time you were required to shoe-horn in some kind of quip about Manchester United that you did not really mean. At other times you would make a half decent remark that ended up being edited out or, worse still, nicked by another panellist. Once we came up with yet another joke about the size of Gary's ears (this was a common theme). How does Gary carry his golf clubs? Behind his ears. I actually came up with that one as far as I remember – yes, I know it was not exactly joke of the year – and was waiting for the perfect moment to unleash it. I must have waited too long – because just as I was about to deliver the line . . . Sam Torrance nicked it! Ah, well. It was a team game. I still got paid. Basically we recycled six gags for eight years. It was great fun, if a little embarrassing at times.

Not everyone who came on as a guest necessarily grasped the concept of famous sportsmen being religiously mocked in the name of comedy. One can only assume that they had not seen the show before, thought it was just *A Question of Sport* by another name and that it would be an easy gig. Chris Eubank was one of those. He arrived for his first appearance in typical Eubank style sporting the trademarks of monocle, jodhpurs and cane. In the afternoon I learned a lot about Chris; among other things that he had been brought up in the Bronx and had the importance of politeness and manners drummed into him at an early age, and they were things he remained very particular about. We got a taste of what he was like during the pre-programme meeting when he'd tell someone off if they didn't let him finish what he was saying. He'd say, with that gentle lisp that he had, 'Don't interrupt, it's so rude.' He obviously had no idea what he was letting himself in for.

On the show itself he kept going off on tangents and at one point said, 'I want to tell you about the history of the cane . . .' Oh, really. And off he went. Of course we did not dare interrupt and in the end we all pretended to be asleep in our chairs, but this only made him more aggrieved at how rude we all were. Normally a programme was edited down from 60 minutes to around 25–30 but this time we had almost 90 minutes because of Chris's mono-logues. They decided to keep some of them in but he left looking a bit bemused.

That experience did not stop him coming on again. The first time he was on my team but this time he switched to Gary's. Ditching the English Gentleman character he went instead for the ethnic look, which involved a kaftan and some sort of multi-coloured beanie hat. Jonathan, in his customary position next to me, had turned up this time in a lime-green suit. It was customary for someone, almost always Jonathan, to interrupt Nick's intro-duction with some quip or other but this time it was arranged that I should jump in and say, 'Nick, before you start, can I just say how nice it is that both teams now have a badly dressed twat with a speech impediment.' Jonathan knew I was going to say this and was perfectly okay about it but Chris looked at Nick with a star-tled expression and said: 'Is he allowed to say that?' 'Er, yes.' 'Well,

I think it's incredibly rude.' And he kept looking across at me as if to say, 'Why did you say that?'

After the show we all headed down to the Green Room where he was still in his full gear, and he came straight across and asked again, 'Why did you say that?' So I had to explain: 'Look, it's a joke, it was given to me. I have a piece of paper here with it written down by that scriptwriter over there, Jim Pullin. He gave it to me. It's my job to say these lines.' He still wasn't appeased and I started to get a little worried. After all, he was an ex-boxer. Maybe he'd resort to using his fists? That could be nasty. I encouraged him to have a drink and reminded him of Jim Pullin's whereabouts. It was no time to be a hero.

As chance would have it, I bumped into him again a few weeks later at a charity function on the *Queen Mary* 2 out of Southampton. Two thousand people came along for supper and a night on the ship while we gently steamed around the Isle of Wight before returning in the morning. It seemed like there were a couple of hundred celebrities on board too to give the evening a bit of sparkle. And whom should I meet but Chris and his then wife? Of course, the first thing she said to me was, 'Why were you so rude to my husband?' Once more, for the record, Chris, it was nothing personal!!

They Think It's All Over played a big part in the creation of the 'Lord Gower' persona which is with me to this day. This partly arose out of the idea that somehow I had a posh voice. Perhaps I did compared to some of my colleagues on the show – Gary with his earthy Midlands tones was never going to be mistaken for landed gentry – but I suspect someone like the Duke of Westminster would have regarded my accent as rather unremarkable. Anyway, the Duke wasn't on the programme and Lee Hurst was and he made great play of the Lord Gower persona. Gary and Rory would also go to any lengths to win while I like to think I rose above such grubbiness. Lee came up with the idea that I had servants, or at least a Filipino house boy under the desk (I told you it could be lewd), and this became a running gag that was expanded upon as the show went on. When we went to Silverstone to do some go-karting for one of the Christmas videos, for example, they had me arriving in something that passed for a Rolls Royce, while Rory was delivered to the course in the back of an ambulance attended by a couple of buxom nurses and Gary, as a footballer, of course came in by helicopter.

It was funny and it worked, so much so that when I found myself going into the Sky studios one Christmas I almost slipped into character, talking about having to leave the estate in Hampshire to come to work. Nasser Hussain then gave it more legs after I failed to arrive for the start of a Test series in the Caribbean because heavy snow prevented me leaving home for the airport. Nasser latched on to this with glee. 'How big is your driveway?' he demanded to know. 'How long does your driveway have to be that you can't get out of it because of snow?'

Of course, there's no escape now. 'Lord Gower' has been picked up by others including Giles Smith, who writes a brilliant 'Sport on TV' column in the *Times*. When I hosted the 2007 World Cup from luxury beachfront accommodation in Barbados that Sky had turned into a temporary studio, while the rest of the commentary team schlepped around the Caribbean, he played it for all it was worth. I feel like I've been one of his favourite targets, though subject would probably be a more apposite way of putting it. Either way, I love how he puts it together and almost want to be that character for real. Athers would come in chortling merrily every time Giles did a column on us and if any of us is slightly miffed by it, it tends to be Beefy, whose occasional ennui Giles has also accurately latched on to. I don't expect Giles or any of you to have much sympathy for my plight but that was actually quite a tough gig in the Caribbean; sitting in the hot sun with some extra hot studio lights in front of you, sadly required to compensate for the bright light all around us, made for very steamy work. The lights must have put up the temperature by ten degrees and there was also the danger of being hit by the odd falling manchineel apple from the tree above the set. Bloody solid those little fruits – and we have a slow motion VT of one landing right on my head to prove it. Anyway, who am I trying to kid? That was the most spoilt we have been in 20 years of covering cricket for TV and it was brilliant.

Charles Colville and I shared the presenters' duties and we had two production crews, so that one crew would work for, say, four days on and then take a break while the other took over. For them it was mighty hard work making sure there was a VT ready and waiting for the discussions at the start of the day, at lunchtime, and then for the 'fill' after the game, which could last quite some time on those days when a match finished disappointingly early. And when that four-day shift ended, boy did they party! The Crocodile's Den and Harbour Lights did not know what had hit them!

As for 'Lord Gower', I hope it reflects the persona rather than the real person. I find it amusing and it works within the dynamic of a commentary team of six or seven people. It is entirely affectionate as far as I can tell. And if it's not, I can take it!

ΙΙ

WHAT COULD POSSIBLY GO WRONG?

In my early days working at the BBC, I was still able to commentate for Sky during the winter. The two broadcasters had distinct strategies in those days and there was no real conflict of interest. The BBC held the rights to all England's home matches, as well as the county one-day competitions. Sky had got a foothold in the cricket market by signing up to cover England's overseas tours but was happy to leave it at that while it built up an identity, and subscribers. As long as that was the case, neither party minded commentators such as me working for both – in fact it would have been unrealistic to expect us not to work for other companies at other times of the year.

By the mid to late 1990s though, Sky began to increase its stake. It bought the rights to England's home one-day internationals and the Benson & Hedges Cup, and decided it wanted to assemble its own team of commentators. From then on, commentators like myself basically had to choose between Sky and BBC.

I had no hesitation in staying at the BBC. At the time it was the obvious thing to do. BBC was the free-to-air terrestrial channel. Sky's viewers had the unwelcome novelty in those days of paying to watch. Probably like most other people, Jon Holmes and I thought the BBC would be the home of cricket for the rest of anyone's lifetime. Logically it was the only horse to back.

We soon found out how much we knew, or rather how little. When it came to the next round of bidding for England's home games, we and the BBC got a horrible shock. In what must have been a decision that came out of the blue for everyone except the England and Wales Cricket Board and the two broadcasters involved, the deal was awarded to Channel 4 and Sky, with Channel 4 getting six of the seven home Tests every year and Sky pretty much everything else. The BBC got nothing – and I was effectively out of a job.

The BBC had of course submitted a bid. I'd been involved in it. A cameraman was sent down to my house to film me in the garden – sorry, on the estate! – presenting a prepared script outlining the reasons why the BBC should retain the rights for another four years. Looking back on it now, it was a very low-key 'pitch', but that was precisely because the corporation had failed to detect the threat. It thought the bid was a formality. I explained some of the things the BBC stood for, the experience it possessed at covering big events, and its love of the game. Why would these arguments not win the day? They had in the past. But the BBC's argument that it had been doing the job for years was actually a negative factor. The other bids must have looked fresher and more appealing. Apparently Channel 4's presentation was an all-singing, all-dancing affair.

When the BBC was told it had lost the rights neither the long-established cricket production team could believe it, and nor could we. I thought, 'Christ, how did that happen?' and was on the phone to Holmes pretty sharply. 'What do we do now?' 'Er, I don't know, but leave it with me.' Our well-thought plan had gone awry.

Fortunately the hiatus did not last long. Mark Nicholas, who retired as a player at Hampshire a couple of years after me, had already developed a busy media career as a newspaper columnist and television commentator. He had done a fair bit of work for

Sky. He joined their team in South Africa one winter, when he was perhaps juggling a few too many balls in the air for John Gayleard's liking (Mark kept flitting off to interview people for a documentary he was making, much to John's irritation). He definitely had qualities, loved the camera as much as it loved him, and with Sky's profile expanding it was keen for a former player to present its international matches while Charles Colville, an excellent all-round broadcaster and presenter, fronted domestic games. So Mark became Sky's main presenter in the mid-1990s.

But Channel 4's arrival had changed the landscape completely, not only for viewers but commentators. As newcomers to the market, Channel 4 needed to recruit a set of commentators from scratch and Mark was the man it went for to lead the team. He was also to be involved in production so he had a big role to play, one he would do very well, but from my point of view his departure created a convenient gap at Sky that needed filling. The original ambition had been that I would one day be the BBC's front man but by a roundabout means that job ended up being mine at Sky.

Of course, at the time it was not as obvious as it looks now that Sky was the place to be. Back then, it always seemed likely that England's home matches would be the preserve of a terrestrial broadcaster, whether BBC or Channel 4. In fact, Sky would win the rights to those games in 2006 as well as overseas Tests and World Cups, which only grew in popularity. As a career move, the switch to Sky was a bit of a fluke but it turned out to be absolutely the right one as Sky outstripped Channel 4 for longevity. Apart from anything else, what I've done with Sky has been enormous fun and professionally very satisfying.

I joined Sky in time to host and present its coverage of the 1999 World Cup in England. This was a huge enterprise for all of us, with games coming along thick and fast all over the country for six weeks, and once again it was a case of learning on the hoof. By now John Gayleard, my one-time producer from Channel 9, was the producer at Sky, so I knew what to expect. He had not got time to mollycoddle you. He was brash, forceful and demanding, but also understanding enough to brush aside your concerns if you had a dodgy ten minutes. He could shout at people big time but ten minutes later say, 'Mate, don't worry.' He just wanted everyone to be aware that there was a standard to be met. Sky had its own way of doing things, but this was where all the stuff I'd done at the BBC became so valuable. Even if I'd rarely been the front man there, I felt I had some experience to fall back on.

There were a few early glitches. On the second day of the tournament I stood on the balcony at Hove following an India–South Africa match and said to the viewers, 'Let's just have a look at the card from today's game . . .' And I looked down at the monitor and nothing appeared. I looked up at the camera, back down at the monitor, and still nothing. After what felt like an hour, the card finally appeared. But you soon learn that such problems are not really the disaster you might think they are, and that they are going to occur every so often. It's in the nature of live TV. Half the trick is to not turn them into a crisis or a drama, but have confidence in your ability to talk your way through the difficulty.

There will be times – and many of them – as either a presenter or a commentator when the words just don't come out quite right and all you can do is live with it. I find a smile helps ease the pain both for me and the viewer, a tacit acknowledgement that a phrase, word or the mere pronunciation thereof could have been better, though there is always the dilemma whether or not to admit to having mangled the language or having botched the odd word.

Richie Benaud, whose advice I had always valued supremely at the BBC, had a simple theory, 'Let the viewer at the other end worry about it.' He was not one prone to error so, bearing in mind his brilliance as a wordsmith and broadcaster, any example of a

Benaud balls-up is a rarity. I did see him once at the SCG in Channel 9's studio make a gentle error over the bowling figures and, thinking that he was recording a highlights link, ask the producer if he could do it again. 'No, Rich, you're live,' was the response and the great man continued as if nothing had happened.

At a NatWest Trophy semi-final at Chelmsford he once referred to Essex's Paul Grayson as Adrian (his first name as listed in the *Playfair* annual) but, no sooner had we nudged him and pointed out the error, Richie without missing a beat merely added, 'or Paul, as he is known round here.' The classic was when he was at the end of his spell with Channel 4 and, when they cut to Richie in the commentary box in the build-up to play on his final day for a poignant farewell, the moment was only very slightly marred by the fact that Richie picked up his pen and spoke into that rather than the microphone.

Nowadays, in the ever-competitive atmosphere of the Sky box, any mispronunciation is likely to be pounced upon by one's fellow commentators so any chance of 'letting the viewers worry about it' tends to disappear in a nanosecond.

There are times one just cannot cover up the error. I was in the studio at Lord's with Michael Atherton one lunchtime a summer or two ago and we had a feature on Charlotte Edwards, the very talented and successful captain of the England women's team. It was a great piece, reflecting well on Charlotte, who had just become the most capped female player for England. I had introduced the piece with all the words in the right order but my attempt to 'back announce' it as it finished went awry and I described Charlotte as the most 'fapped' player (some sort of elision of female and capped). Luckily 'fapped' remains a non-word and utterly meaningless. The trouble is that it does, I admit, sound possibly rude and Athers was chortling loudly no sooner had the word left my mouth. No chance to recover from that one then!

When we had to cover England's 2012–13 tour of India from our studio in Isleworth because the Indian board threw in an eleventh-hour demand for a hefty 'facilitation' fee for Sky's commentators to access the stadiums, I am sorry to admit that I lost concentration just for a moment. I went from pretending to be fascinated by one of the latest factoids to come from Benedict Bermange, Sky's invaluable and near-celebrity statistician, to looking up at the monitor where a wicket appeared to be falling caught behind. Out came the words in a suitably excited manner, 'That's a remarkably similar dismissal to one earlier . . .' – which, of course, it was, as all that was on the screen was a replay – called for by the Indian director some 4,000-odd miles away, I might add – of an earlier wicket, that of the left-handed Alastair Cook. In my defence, shaky as it is, at least there was a left-hander at the crease in Eoin Morgan. I did try and cover up with the words, 'As indeed it was', but I could only have got away with it if I had not been so enthusiastic with the first reaction. Nick Knight was on with me at the time and he certainly was not going to let it pass, nor were the others who I had woken from their slumbers on the sofa in the adjoining room.

Covering that tour in the way we had to highlighted the difficulty of using another broadcaster's pictures. While we in the studio might have wanted to discuss one aspect of play, the host broadcaster would show several replays of another incident – replays we were powerless to stop and hard for us to ignore in commentary, even though there might be precious little left to say about the delivery they were still constantly replaying. To make matters worse, you didn't even know how many times they might show something. After two replays you'd be hoping that would be all and could move on . . . and then another one would come along. It is great that today's coverage incorporates so many more cameras, and better and more animated graphics, but we like to think that these are designed to help illustrate what the commentators are saying and you need to be in control of them!

I soon found that I loved presenting. It's a job with its own set of challenges and if you aren't switched on each and every day then that day can go horribly wrong. And while you need to be switched on, mobile phones need to be switched off. At Lord's a couple of summers ago now, we were wrapping the day and minutes from going off air at the end of what had felt like a long day, not helped by the long night the previous evening. It was not the smoothest of finishes – just as I was hoping for a piece of VT to come up on screen to illustrate a point I was discussing with Michael Holding, I could feel the dreaded vibrations in my jacket pocket, the precursor to Coldplay ('Charlie Brown' is my ring tone – and why not?!) about to come through loud and clear on my lapel mic immediately adjacent. Oh shit! 'Keep going', I said to Mikey, as I lobbed my iPhone towards the cameraman immediately in front of me. He, to his credit, kept one eye on the job as he caught the phone. At the end of the show, as I was apologising all round for mucking up those last few minutes, up came a slow-mo action replay from another of the studio cameras, in which you could see this phone cart-wheeling across shot!

Despite moments like that, for me there is the same sense of pride in performance that came with playing so, okay then, no surprises that there might be the odd lapse of concentration. There's an ethos, as you would expect, which expects us to be professional in our approach to broadcasting but also allows us to have some fun with it all, so a degree of levity and dressing room humour is not just tolerated but encouraged – until it goes just that bit too far.

There are constraints with TV commentary – Rule One is watch the monitor and react and add to what is on it, which denies us the absolute freedom you might have on radio to wander off on a tangent. Diversions are allowed and the major difference between the BBC and Sky, the obvious one of ad breaks, means discipline when it comes to stopping talking just before one of those breaks. And on those days when the action might be drifting and we err towards the garrulous, there are reminders from producers not to ramble without due care and attention as there is some poor bloke back at base trying to compile highlights from that live coverage – and his job is all the harder if we are rabbiting on over all the pictures.

Ironically one of the most enjoyable parts of the job is the opportunity that those otherwise hated rain breaks give us to discuss matters at greater length, something which is not always possible in the course of our normal build-ups, during which there always seem to be more than enough issues to deal with and which are more defined by a pre-formed running order. At times like that I am absolutely reliant on the professionalism and enthusiasm of those in the studio with me and one really appreciates that they both know their stuff and like talking about it at length.

Apart from the standard day's work, elucidating, explaining, entertaining, enlivening, evading ennui, extrapolating and anything else beginning with 'e', the real key is in dealing with the major issues. One of the biggest challenges was presented by the ball-tampering row at the Oval in 2006 when the Pakistanis refused to come out again at the tea interval. With no play to commentate on, and no indication as to when – or even if – play might resume, we had unlimited time to talk but very little information to go on, as officially very little, or indeed nothing at all, was revealed either to the unfortunate spectators in the ground or to us as broadcasters. As open-ended discussions go, that was more open-ended than any. We did the obvious thing in getting all our experts to have their say on the matter over the course of the rest of the day's non-action, and I remember the issue within the bigger issue was that we could find precious little evidence of anything untoward being done to the ball on any of our tapes.

I would say though that in these matters you have to back the umpires, who in this 'modern game' have the unenviable task of having to keep an eye on the state of the ball as well as everything else that is in their job description. Darrell Hair obviously took the lead while Billy Doctrove acquiesced to his senior partner. Darrell could be blunt to a fault but I had many a chat with him over the years, including a few dinners here and there, and I would not expect him to be anything except fair. Strict yes, but fair. As such I felt that he was very poorly treated by his bosses at the ICC, who seemed to fear falling foul of Asian politics more than they were prepared to abide by the principles that (a) the umpire is in sole charge of policing a game of cricket, and (b) that you should back your employee where possible unless or until he has been proven to be in error.

The spot-fixing scandal in 2010, which also involved Pakistan, was another big challenge. Claims that three players had been involved in the deliberate bowling of no-balls during the Lord's Test broke late on the third night and we came in early the next day to prepare what we should say before play re-started, if indeed it would re-start, as there was some doubt as to whether the Pakistanis would continue after they failed to warm up that Sunday morning. Intellectually, that was an interesting topic to get right in 30 minutes and you had to be on your mettle.

It required first of all that our VT department make sure we had all the right footage, not just the pictures of bowlers overstepping but other angles which for instance showed Salman Butt, the captain, at midoff, looking at his bowler rather than at the batsman as one of the now infamous no-balls was delivered. At times like this my job is to make sure that all sides of the story are introduced into a discussion, at the same time as allowing our pundits to be as strong in their opinions as they wish to be but within legal limits. We are all aware of the things that can and do happen like this, and to be honest there have been many times when the more cynical of my colleagues have – at least off air – suggested there might be something questionable afoot. Obviously on air one has to be infinitely more considered and one of the major concerns on that morning for our producer, Paul King, was that no one went too far and landed either themselves or Sky in legal hot water.

What was interesting, as we looked at the footage, was the difference between the no-balls bowled by 'the kid', Mohammad Amir, and those delivered by Mohammad Asif. The latter would appear to have been more skilful in just edging over the line whereas Amir was so far down the pitch that even at the time Michael Holding, always a shrewd observer on these matters, just said, 'Wow!' in those mellifluous bass tones that are his trademark. I thought we dealt with the matter that morning with suitable skill, after which it was time to continue calling the match as before but with eyes wide open in case of further, albeit now unlikely, skulduggery.

Another test was the Ian Bell run out at Trent Bridge in 2011. Bell was given run out after strolling off the field in the mistaken belief that the ball had just gone for four; in fact it was kept inside the rope by a fielder and the Indians perfectly justifiably appealed for a run out. As the incident happened on the stroke of tea there was no chance to rehearse our responses to a confusing situation. India were entitled to claim the wicket, as Nasser Hussain rightly made clear in our discussion, but maybe Bell had been acting under a misapprehension and there was a possible 'spirit of cricket' issue. I had some minor empathy with Bell as I was once run out in a similar way in an island match against Barbados, when the umpire had walked off towards square leg at the end of an over and I, thinking that 'over' had been called, strolled down the pitch for a spot of light gardening thinking the ball was dead. The Barbados fielder saw his chance, I was given 'run out' by an umpire who was by now almost in position for the start of the next over and oblivious to my protestations. 'Sod it', I thought, 'I'll save my runs for the Test match' and off I went. The salient difference between that little incident and Bell's was that he, having thought that he might

271

as well head off towards the pavilion for his cup of tea, had a moment's hesitation when he seemed to realise that he might have misjudged the situation. Whereas I was convinced the ball was dead, he could not be quite so sure. Of course, while we were talking on air, the Indians talked over the matter in the dressing room and to their immense credit decided to withdraw their appeal and allow Bell to continue batting.

Over the years, Sky's coverage has expanded into a sizeable operation with a huge number of matches covered at international and domestic level. The team is big enough that the work is shared around in a way that is good for us as commentators and for the viewers who must appreciate the variety.

When I started, my old mucker Ian Botham was already an established member of the team, as were Bob Willis, Paul Allott and Michael Holding. Botham and Willis I'd played with through most of my Test career, Allott I had known since the Young England tour to the West Indies in 1976 and Mikey I'd had a career against. Since then we've welcomed on board David 'Bumble' Lloyd, who joined not long after me, and two recent former captains Nasser Hussain and Michael Atherton. All have their virtues, if vividly contrasting ones.

Beefy is your jingoistic punter's pundit with an instinct for the game which will pass others by. He's not one for undue or unnecessary preparation. Whereas Atherton will take time over an issue before he publicly talks about it, Beefy goes, well, yeah, I know the answer. And out it comes, on the hoof.

He also has a natural and overriding sympathy for the player, as we saw when he spoke up in support of Andrew Flintoff after the infamous 'pedalo' incident at the 2007 World Cup. I was in our beachside studio in Barbados talking to Athers in St Lucia with Beefy alongside him. Beefy had just got out of bed and been confronted with the issue, and details of what had gone on the

night before were in any case still emerging. There were sugges-
tions that some supporters had 'shopped' Flintoff to the papers,
and Beefy said: 'Well, what I want to know is, what were those
supporters doing up at 3am?'

'Er, but Ian, they're not playing for England . . . it doesn't really
matter what *they* were doing up at that time of night.'

'Well, yes . . . I suppose . . .'

That's Beefy. His friendship with Flintoff came through first
before his critical faculties fully clicked in. But he harrumphs and
moves on. Something like that would not bother him and he
certainly won't waste time later on unnecessary self-analysis.

One of Ian's outstanding qualities is his loyalty to his friends, of
whom there are plenty, and whom he will defend at all costs. Of
those numerous friends it would be hard to know who he counts
as number one but one man, Viv, will always be right up there. Sir
Vivian Richards was his best mate when the two of them first
shared accommodation in Taunton and nothing has changed since.
For the two men to have been knighted is extraordinary – in a
good sense, I might add – and it was typical of Ian to celebrate
with Viv at yet another Beefy barbecue in North Yorkshire. You
don't see Ian succumb to undue emotion often – unless another
spread-bet has gone awry – but to see the two of them so genuinely pleased in each other's recognition was actually quite moving.
And then they recovered to drink the place dry again!

You do get some interesting conversations out of the two of
them. Over a curry in Birmingham the chat moved onto the royal
family. Beefy is, as you might expect, an ardent royalist, whereas
Viv is more arm's length when it comes to our head of state. 'I did
not even get knighted by Queen Elizabeth and I am not sure about
Charles.' Ian, ever loyal, replied: 'You know there is 80 per cent
support for Charles as our future king?' DG. 'We don't vote for
who wears the crown in a game show, you know.'

As we left that night, I shared a cab back to the Hotel du Vin with Ian, who then launched into another of his favourite topics, what he would do as Prime Minister, and by now the red wine had convinced him that he would indeed be a bloody good PM. With the right backing he was adamant he could make it to Downing Street – as a true blue Conservative.

'What about your past?' I teased him. 'What about all those stories?' Once again that unshakeable self-confidence came through. 'They're all out in the open. I can deal with them!'

'Look, if you feel we need a different hand on the controls, why not support Boris?' – meaning, of course, Boris Johnson.

'I know Boris well. Maybe that's a good idea.'

He and 'Bumble' were also hilarious with that India series we covered from home. We got on to a discussion about the Decision Review System and India's reluctance to use technology that to most others seems natural and advantageous. And they both came up with the idea that if India didn't want DRS they didn't have to have it, but why should that stop England using it? Now I know that strange hours – we were on air from 3 or 3.30 in the morning through that series – and sleep deprivation can do strange things to a man's power of reason, but I could scarcely believe what I was hearing.

I looked at Beefy, who was in the studio alongside me and I looked at Bumble, who was up in the 'commentary box' three floors above us and thus visible on my studio monitor only. 'Are you two serious?! Are you genuinely saying that in the same match one side should use DRS and one side not?'

'Aye.'

'. . . Well, I think you're both bonkers.'

For genuine humour and all-round entertainment purveyed in those friendly, bucolic Lancashire tones that have become so recognisable from ING adverts and other forays into the TV world, who else would you turn to but David Lloyd? Behind the eccentric humour lies . . . an eccentric mind. But for all that, Bumble has an absolute passion for the game, how it should be played and in turn how everyone should conduct themselves on the field, in the commentary box or in the world at large. He has excellent credentials as a former England player, Lancashire captain, umpire, and county and international coach. He has seen the game from all angles and commands respect as the only man in our team to have qualified for – and used – his free bus pass!

I did actually play with him in an England side, despite the age difference, in a one-day international against West Indies at Old Trafford in 1980 when his pain threshold was sorely tested by a blow to the elbow from Malcolm Marshall. His talent as a pain magnet had been well established on that brutal tour of Australia in 1974–75 when all of England's batsmen endured Lillee and Thomson in their pomp. I recall seeing Keith Fletcher heading one off the George and the Dragon badge on his England touring cap and the ball bouncing back towards extra cover but it was Bumble who had the most wince inducing and therefore the best tale, the story of the 'pink Litesome'.

The item in question, as some of you of a certain age will no doubt recall, was pretty much the only gentleman's protector available in that era and as a protector of the crown jewels for every batsman against even medium-paced bowling it left much to be desired. Against Jeff Thomson it proved to be wholly inadequate. On the fastest pitch of the series at the WACA in Perth, Bumble was struck amidships. The impact instantaneously split the pink Litesome along the seam that went vertically down the box. As Bumble crumpled to the ground, the seam opened and immediately closed, trapping just enough of those precious parts to add not just insult but considerable extra pain to injury. Bernard Thomas, the physio, sprinted out to offer the usual assistance under the circumstances, which basically amounts to standing next to the victim trying not to giggle, the default reaction of all cricketers to seeing any of their colleagues struck in the balls. Bumble, as ever, was not short of a line and when he could finally find his voice said to Bernard, 'Please can you take away the pain – but leave the swelling!'

It is but one of many, many stories that he has used as part of his after-dinner routines, another area where he has made a considerable and deserved reputation for himself. If there's a quiet passage of play towards the end of the day and things need livening up a bit, the cry goes up, 'Send for Bumble!' No one in the box can go off piste quite so superbly as him. That's his role really, to keep us and everyone else entertained. The way he's embraced Twenty20 cricket despite being the oldest member of our team is particularly impressive, to the point where he is now the acknowledged Twenty20 specialist, and not just for the mascot race. He's not only capable of engaging with the man in the street, he *does* engage with the man in the street, actively seeking him out. When others of us might think that a good restaurant is the place to be after a day at the cricket, he is more likely than not to seek out a seedy pub and see who he can find to talk to there. He's a man of the people and that's a great asset to have when the job is communicating with the public.

He loves his comedy sketch shows and is always on YouTube looking at his favourites. He will draw our attention to something like the Harry Enfield and Paul Whitehouse '40–45 Years' sketch, in which they play two senior city types, Charles and Sheridan, lamenting the loss of a colleague, Bunny, who was 'only 85'. How long had he and his widowed wife been married? '40 to 45 years'. The phrase is repeated and repeated and becomes insidiously funny. As they continue, Charles says, 'There comes a time in all our lives when we have to take account of our age and one has to say goodbye to the Matterhorn and hello to the Peak District.'

'Climb down from the Montrachet to the Pinot Grigio, as it were', offers Sheridan.

'Ooh, I wouldn't go that far!'

A sentiment that I share entirely. Those lines crept into commentary all bloody summer.

'Bumble' is mischievous but never malicious. During the summer of 2012, before the spoof '@KPGenius' Twitter account had been exposed as a thorn in the side of the England superstar, 'Bumble' had already spotted that there might be space for a new fake account in the Twitter-sphere. In conjunction with Mark Lynch, the man in our ears as the leading director of Sky's international cricket coverage and a man with a sense of humour every bit as impish as Bumble's, they created a Lord Gower account and began tweeting.

The first I realised what was going on was at the Lord's Test when I had a phone call from Jon Holmes saying, 'Lineker wants to know if it's really you.'

'Really me what?'

'Tweeting.'

'F*** off! What have I said then?'

Apparently it all began with a tweet along the lines of, 'It's not me doing this – it's my butler'.

To be honest, I am quite fond of my fake Lord status, though as yet have not plucked up the courage to ring any of London's finest restaurants and try and book a table as Lord Gower. The characterisation as developed by Lloyd and Lynch was brilliant. With Lord's and the members in full view, champagne (Bollinger please) got an early mention and when we headed for Cardiff and the first of the ODIs that followed the Tests, my alter ego was accused of having a spot of bother at the toll booth for the Severn bridge – not carrying cash of course! Bumble even got his words in a horrible twist with one tweet advising the world that while in Wales I had been invited to drinks with the 'Principal Principle of the Principality.'

On that day at Lord's, no sooner had I learned about this new existence than Beefy was heading down the corridor to the studio

277

and asking me, 'What is your secret nickname that only Gary Lineker knows?'

Lineker – or 'Linebacker' as I call him – as an avid Twitter user had, after consultation with me, drafted a trick question for the fakers to try and expose them as frauds. Only he and I would know the answer and if they could not respond correctly that would be that. However, in seconds I duly told Beefy – he would have beaten it out of me anyway! – that the nickname was 'Dregsy' (sadly one I acquired many years ago when I stayed with Gary at his house in Abbey Road, and had an alleged habit of polishing off other people's brandy at the end of the evening). With the right code-word sent for 'Linebacker' to see, the illusion continued unabated and grew and grew, Lord Gower attracting a suitably impressive following. Unlike KP I was all in favour. My comedic stock was rising by the minute and I had to do nothing! Eventually Sky management decided that enough was enough and a quiet word in the ear of the scriptwriters meant that the account was no more.

There comes a time when every team, whether on a sports field or off it, needs new blood. It's never great fun being the one who has to make way to accommodate that new blood but at least in this business Sky have always done their best to make sure that good men are not just put out to pasture. Tough though it would have been for Bob Willis and Paul Allott to be moved sideways out of the Test match commentary team when Mike Atherton and Nasser Hussain joined, Bob has made a great niche for his trenchant comments on our live highlights shows and Paul has found his own spot hosting the Sunday morning show *Cricket Writers on TV*, while both have continued to be stalwarts of our coverage of domestic cricket.

With Nasser's Test career coming to a close, he was an obvious candidate to join us, and indeed no sooner had he announced his retirement than Vic Wakeling, the head of Sky Sports, was confirming Hussain as part of our commentary team. It was fascinating watching

Nass at the start of this new career. He had precious little experience of broadcasting but proved himself to be a quick learner. He has a natural passion for the game, indeed a greater passion than most, and the steely determination that we'd all seen in evidence on the field as player and captain meant that he was not going to be intimidated by joining a well-established team. Nor was he cowed by Ian Botham's undisguised animosity. Beefy, as he made plain, was not a fan of Nasser's but both in the commentary box and on those rare occasions when we could prize Nass out of his hotel room and into a restaurant, where of course he always runs the risk that he might be asked to contribute to the bill, he always held his own under heavy fire.

There was one explosive night at a very fine restaurant in Hobart – which I promise is not a contradiction of terms – where the two of them entered into a bellicose discussion on the merits or otherwise of Duncan Fletcher. In a nutshell, Nass, having worked very closely with Duncan, defended the England coach to the hilt whereas Beefy, fuelled by some rather fine Aussie red, had come to the conclusion that Duncan, after the Ashes whitewash, had obviously lost the plot. Without being disloyal to my mate of 30 years, Nasser's sober, steadfast and reasoned defence won the debate as he rebuffed every assault from an impassioned Botham. The two of them, though in many ways poles apart in the way they see the world, now have a firm mutual respect for each other.

In terms of learning the business, I remember Nasser being asked to do his first player interview with Matthew Hoggard in Port Elizabeth. Nass basically didn't have a clue and asked anyone and everyone how he should do it. Truth is, you only learn by doing these things and, as it was recorded rather than live, he could always start again if necessary. In the event he got through it fine until the closing words when he could not quite think how to finish it and simply said, 'Thank you, Hoggard.' Matthew said, 'Pleasure, Hussain,' and we all had a good giggle.

It was a very minor error, though Nass was annoyed that having got through most of the interview the final words might have let him down. It matters not a jot; things like this are all too easily shrugged off and Nass in many an interview since has proved himself to be an intelligent and fearless inquisitor. I also find him a fulsome and energetic contributor to our studio discussions where that passion for the game and his understanding of the way cricketers work shines through.

Our next recruit was Athers, who joined us from Channel 4. It was ironic but their last live series was one of the most entertaining and well watched of all time, the 2005 Ashes. However, prior to that summer they had already decided that the sums did not add up commercially and with Sky now the sole rights holders for English cricket it was an obvious move to make sure that Athers, as the most cerebral of Channel 4's commentary team, would come on board.

He is the one who thinks most deeply about what he wants to say on air. There is an element of that same dour spirit that Jim Laker used to bring to BBC's commentary when I was a player but with enough dry humour and the sort of sagacity that one would hope for from a Cambridge history graduate all thrown into the mix.

From my point of view as the presenter of our coverage, I am acutely aware that I have to be on my mettle when Athers is in the studio, simply because he is as likely to fire back an incisive question in my direction as I am to feed him an ordinary one to get the discussion started. To be honest, I enjoy the intellectual challenge. It is part of what makes a team like ours work that everyone has something different to offer. He can also be incredibly stubborn and that is where we try and score our points against him but he has the great gift of mostly being right!

He has also managed to become an outstanding journalist, deservedly taking the title Sports Journalist of the Year a couple of years after taking over at the *Times* from the legendary and estimable

Christopher Martin-Jenkins. He loves his words; whereas Hussain can be thrown if I introduce a word such as 'lexicon' into a studio chat, Atherton is a keen student of language and always on the look-out for a phrase or word with which to bamboozle the rest of us. Hussain and Atherton, of course, are great mates from way back and have been taking the mickey out of each other religiously since they were teenagers. Many is the time that Hussain will come into the commentary box of a morning to tell Atherton either that his article in the *Times* that morning was rubbish or that it was excellent as far as he could tell but that he couldn't understand most of the words used.

I remember Athers on one tour in Christchurch, New Zealand checking with me whether I knew what the expression 'Janus-faced' meant. Before I had a chance to bluff my way into some sort of answer he explained that it meant 'two-faced', after the Roman god who was always portrayed as having two faces, as he looked both to the future and the past. He was suitably proud of this term which he was plainly planning to use in his next article. As this was a Saturday he had a sudden panic that I might nick it for the *Sunday Times* in the piece I was due to write that afternoon. Realising this he made me swear on *Wisden* – metaphorically that is, we didn't actually have to get a copy out of Benedict's briefcase – that I would not steal his new favourite word.

As I say, he is bright enough to win most verbal battles but I did wrong-foot him during our coverage of the India–England series in 2012–13. While the rest of us were languishing in the early hours of the morning at Sky's Isleworth studios, battling the effects of sleep deprivation, he was our man in India. Because of the restrictions imposed by the BCCI, every time we wanted to speak to Mike he had to leg it to a neutral location outside the various stadia. There he would be wired for sound and positioned in front of a camera, probably on a piece of waste ground or in a car park, and as soon as he got his breath back I would be asking his opinions on the issues of the day.

By the time we got to the fourth Test in Nagpur, we had seen some extraordinary stuff as England fought their way back into the series, evoking all sorts of memories of my tour there in 1984–85. That final Test promised much, especially, we thought, an early finish. Everyone felt the Indians would produce a raging turner as the best chance of a win to square the series and early sightings of the pitch supported that theory. As it turned out, it remained the flattest of decks throughout five full days and the turgid match that resulted was fine for England and their ambitions to take the series but for me in London it was becoming tougher and tougher to find a pithy question for our man in the tropics. Just before the start of one of these two-way discussions we had seen Mike yawning. He jokingly blamed this on my trite questioning so I quickly threw him a completely irrelevant question, namely, 'Who was the first prime minister of England?' I thought the Cambridge historian might at least dredge something up from the back of his mind but it had the desired effect and threw him to the extent that he demurred and opted to go back to the cricket instead. (I was hoping he might say Robert Walpole who, although generally recognised as the first de facto prime minister, never actually used that specific title, as Walpole and several successors were technically, 'First Lords of the Treasury.' The first time the words 'prime minister' were used was in 1905 when the man in office was Sir Henry Campbell-Bannerman – here endeth the history lesson.)

As for Michael Holding . . . how lovely it is to be on the same team as him for once. That voice! It is the voice for which the words deep and mellifluous were invented, in the same way as that nickname from his playing days, Whispering Death, could not have been more succinct.

To face him in the mid-1980s was the ultimate test of nerve and skill so to sit and listen to him is an absolute relaxation in comparison. He is one of those men who are ever mindful of the courtesies of life and of the correct and polite way to do things. But do not let that fool anyone for one moment that he is any way a pushover. He is as sharp as any when it comes to analysing the game, will stand on principle almost to a fault and finds it hard to forgive those who fail to live up to his standards, especially those West Indians he feels have let the region and its cricket down, be they players or administrators – and the latter category is a veritable mine of discontent!

He judges modern batsmen by and large on the basis of whether or not they would have got runs against him and I would have to say that is not a bad way of looking at it. On Alastair Cook he formed an early opinion – 'Can't bat.' Even Mikey, not one for turning, might have to reconsider that verdict now but it was based on those early days of Alastair's where work on his technique was indeed needed, work which has been done and which has paid off in outstanding style.

Things like ball-tampering and spot-fixing bring him quickly to the boil. Mention Allen Stanford and you will get that exaggerated Caribbean style, audible pursing of the lips, which means an eruption of Krakatoan proportions is imminent. On all these things he is well-informed and supremely opinionated – and very good value.

He also knows a thing or two about horses – a lot actually. When I was at the BBC, Benaud would always set up his little desk in the box so that when he was not at the microphone he could check up on the horses on his laptop. Fear not, he always had one eye and ear on the cricket and somehow never missed anything even when it seemed to all that his attention was firmly on the 2.30 at wherever. He knew his horses.

Mikey is the man for advice on nags now. He is well connected to a host of trainers, basing himself for the English summer near Newmarket. Top of that list would be Sir Michael Stoute but Mikey knows them all and they all know him. If you want a tip on a horse go to Mikey first, though Botham and Atherton both feel they know a bit too.

A few summers ago we ran a syndicate in the box, supposedly to be administered and run by Mikey. The plan was if we stuck to his tips and backed 'certainties' every couple of weeks we should not go far wrong. Of course it came unstuck and the simple reason was 'Bumble'. Team discipline unravelled all too quickly and once Mikey had reluctantly revealed his account details for the bookies 'Bumble' was placing daft bets every 20 minutes and the game was soon up. The pot ran out quicker than Beefy's first bottle of Chardonnay at the end of a day's commentary.

We also have one more absolute legend with us on a part-time basis, when he can fit us in between poker tournaments and everything else that keeps him immensely busy. When Shane Warne first arrived in our box, we immediately noticed a change. He was yet another breath of fresh air, more Botham than Atherton certainly, but you could see why so many people from his former colleagues in the Australian team to Rod Bransgrove and the management team at Hampshire, where Shane had played, held him in great regard. He is an absolute natural in all he does, instinctively open and entertaining, while knowing the game inside out. Other things had changed too; those teeth seemed awfully white and the waistline had been notably reduced – apparently with the help of some vile protein shake that he was by now consuming in preference to his previous favourite snack, French fries and ketchup.

Anyone who is a friend of Liz Hurley, let alone engaged to her, is a friend of a commentary box full of rampant ex-cricketers, who would like to kid themselves they have still got what it takes. She is, of course, ever so welcome when Shane brings her to the cricket and it is quite touching to listen to him explaining the game to 'EH' and her son, Damian. When the Rose Bowl hosted its first Test match in June 2011 I felt that I should entertain my colleagues and production crew at home, so a barbecue was arranged and all including Shane and EH invited. The moment

Shane confirmed that Elizabeth was coming, my eldest daughter, Alex, said she would be coming back from school at Canford that night and would be more than happy to help serve the food, along with friends Katie and David, all of whom were desperate to be in the same room as Elizabeth (and, of course, Shane).

We had a damned good night. In return for all the wine we had drunk at Beefy's over the years of barbecues at his home when matches had been up in Leeds and Durham, I gave him too much of my Lynch Bages (I should have slipped him onto the ageing Talbot much earlier in the evening) and left him to it at the kitchen table. Some of my local friends (Henry Thornton, you know who you are!) spotted the fact that Beefy seemed to have the best wine to himself and carefully positioned themselves by him for the rest of the night. When Elizabeth's Range Rover pulled into the drive it was as if Liz Taylor had pitched up and then, as the two of them had been apart for a little while, she and Shane spent the next part of the party nestled on the sofa in the conservatory.

It took my sister-in-law, Kris, to prize them apart and bring them to join the rest of the fray, which they did very successfully, not before a slight misunderstanding of her opening line to Shane. He had been trying to get a signal on his mobile phone, not easy in our part of rural Hampshire, and she had asked, politely enough, 'Are you on Orange?' 'Am I what?!' When Shane realised that she was not referring to his healthy tan, they got on a lot better!

When asked for his verdict on the do the following day, Athers said it was on a par with Beefy's extravagant barbies 'but with staff', said with a Mancunian short 'a'. In my defence, although the local butchers sent a couple of men down to make sure the lamb was cooked to perfection, the only 'staff' were daughter and friends trying not to say anything stupid to Liz while pretending to clear the plates.

Whatever the 'talent' that you see on screen, there are a lot of people you never see doing their absolute best to make us look and sound good. If playing international cricket was ever about team-work then putting on an outside broadcast is more so. The chain of command begins with the producer, who has to be in constant touch with director, VT department (still known as 'tapes' though modern technology means that everything is now on some sort of hard drive), and pretty much everyone else. The director (Mark Lynch is the best in our game but the next in line, Will 'Five Names' Sawrey-Cookson and James 'Lawse' Lawson, do a fantastic job too) is in command of every picture from the moment we go on air until the final credits. He is in constant touch with every cameraman, with VT to make sure the right replays come in as required – and never stops talking. That is not a complaint, just the nature of the job. Somehow, between picking which angle to take from the bank of video screens in front of him in the truck, 'Coming to 5, take 5. Coming to 2, take 2, roll blue, super the computer . . .' and so on through the day, he also comes up with a stream of witty asides sparked by what is on the screen or what we might be saying about it. The traps to avoid are being heard to laugh at his jokes on air or repeating something you have just heard in your ear on air – unless it is too good a line not to use!

As far as I am concerned as the presenter, the one man I need to be on the ball, apart from me, is the producer. I have been very lucky to have had very good men in that role. John Gayleard, who I have already talked about, was very good at taking me through the first stages and was always supportive. When he moved on, the job went to Barney Francis, whose father, Tony, I had known as a sports journalist from my playing days. Barney played for Hampstead (exactly how well is always a matter of good natured conjecture) and was very well versed in the game. He was very bright and rela-tively young when he took on the job but very authoritative. That latter quality is exactly what is needed at, say, the end of a day's play, when a course has to be plotted to get us through the remaining time before going off air – how much studio chat would there be, how much of a VT package would there be, how many player interviews were we doing. Once the calculations are done, all I want is for that to be communicated clearly so I know where I am going. I had complete faith in Barney's judgement.

His talents were fully recognised when he was lined up to take over from Vic Wakeling as the managing director of Sky Sports. The man chosen to take over as executive producer in cricket was Paul King, who was promoted from within the department. A Derby County fan and a contemporary music expert (he and 'Bumble' know all the less than mainstream bands going), he picked up seamlessly from where Barney left off. His is a somewhat different style, mainly more relaxed, but that same decisiveness and clarity of purpose is there. There will be the odd day when we go into what he calls 'Free Form', where we forget about a tightly structured running order and just wing it. That is when you realise just how good the team is. The pundits always find something to say, VT always finds some pictures, and a half hour just seems to take care of itself. It's either talent or magic!

The good news is that there always seems to be something to talk about. The game does change, as we have seen all too obviously with the emergence of Twenty20 cricket, which has both excited and confused the cricketing world. The excitement is obvious, especially when Chris Gayle is crashing a century off just 30 balls in the Indian Premier League. The confusion is equally obvious; what to do about the other forms of the game and how to retain Test cricket as the pinnacle?

Any solution to that riddle is unlikely to come easily while the BCCI retains its influence over the ICC, a body which, despite its recent attempt through the Woolf Committee to steer itself towards greater independence from the stronger boards, remains powerless when it comes to the major issues. Everyone, for instance, except the BCCI, thinks that DRS is a good idea. The statistical evidence is overwhelming that it helps an already excellent group of umpires get more decisions right, yet the BCCI remain unhappy that the technology is not 100 per cent accurate.

The IPL is enormously successful and Indian cricket is enormously rich. Why would they want that to change in India? Why would they care that England's players are largely excluded when the IPL season conflicts so badly with the start of the English county season? The IPL is of course an Indian domestic competition so there is no obligation to worry about the concerns of other nations when it comes to scheduling, though it does seem strange that it is played at pretty much the hottest time of the year and that an earlier window might appeal even to the home players involved. But, again, who cares? Everyone is making extraordinary money so the physical demands – criss-crossing India is not an easy gig when you are doing it every other day for six weeks – are largely ignored. There are concerns in some quarters about the effect all this is having on India's most talented players.

With other nations doing their best to join in with their own leagues, it is self-evident that Twenty20 is squeezing out other forms of the game. Increasingly, one wonders how 50-overs cricket will survive. The last World Cup was deemed by the ICC in a big PR shove to have saved 50-overs cricket, and it could not have been more pleased that it was India who came out winners. It was a fantastic atmosphere in the stadium in Mumbai and on the streets afterwards when India beat Sri Lanka in the final, yet the truth is that the World Cup is too long for even the most ardent fans. Not even football tries to milk its major global event to the tune of seven weeks.

I would love to see the ICC and the national boards arrange the three elements of international cricket in a workable co-existence. But I doubt that I will still be commentating if and when such a thing happens. I fear the vested interests and financial power of one nation will continue to block meaningful change.

In English cricket over the last few years we have seen some magnificent stuff. We have seen a very fine captain in Andrew Strauss, working in unison with an excellent coach, Andy Flower. There is an opening batsman, Alastair Cook, who has already broken a stack of individual records and will surely become the highest run-scorer for England by some distance. His strength of mind and purpose, both God and Gooch given, is extraordinary. There is an attack, led by James Anderson and Graeme Swann, which was given the accolade of being England's best ever by common consent in our commentary box on their performances a couple of years ago. It is a formidable array of talent and the success in reaching No. 1 in all three forms of the game was well deserved, even if the trick of staying there proved harder. And yet, despite all this, there is one man we talk about most.

In the opening chapter of this book, I talked about my run-ins with the England management during a tour of Australia, and what I saw as their heavy-handed response to the Tiger Moth affair. I find myself coming back to this now as I reflect on the divisive issue of Kevin Pietersen.

There are salient differences in our cases but also some interesting parallels. We would both say that we had issues with the management and Kevin might have questioned, as I did, whether it was really necessary for him to be cast out in the way that he was.

Before going further with this, it might be worth first backtracking to Pietersen's sacking as captain in 2009 – yes, he was an ex-captain, just as I was on that 1990–91 tour – which may have been relevant to what happened later. I say sacking, although I think officially it went down as a resignation, but to all intents and purposes a sacking is what it was.

I always thought it was botched horribly. It was, of course, still too soon to be definitive as to whether Kevin would have made a good captain in the longer term, although I suspect that captaincy was never really his destiny. We'd had that Test at the Oval in 2008 where he patted everyone on the bum three times a minute, an extraordinary love-in which I wouldn't recommend, but he was there for his men and you can understand what he was trying to do. There was something positive in there. Then England had lost in Chennai, where I'd defend him up to a point, because if Sachin Tendulkar and Virender Sehwag play well in India you've got a problem, but it was nevertheless a shock to lose a game after setting the opposition nearly 400 to win. But then I've had a few shockers myself. My suspicion is that Kevin would not have been a great long-term captain, because there are too many personal issues in his life, but there's no real proof either way.

In terms of his relationship with the then coach, Peter Moores, I would tend to take the captain's side. If you are captain of England and don't see eye-to-eye with the team director or coach, or whatever you call him, then you have an issue, as I proved with Mickey Stewart during the '89 Ashes, although whatever my differences then – and they were never that major – I have to say that at no stage did I even consider going to Ted Dexter and saying anything along the lines of, 'I cannot work with this man.' But I think you have got to respect Kevin for being so bold as to say, 'Look, I'm not sure this is right. I'm not sure this is the right guy to be doing this job.' As a top-quality player understanding what top-quality players needed, he was entitled to speak up and say that Moores was not providing what was required beyond a few fielding drills. And to make his points as he did, to higher management and the board, was right. He did it behind closed doors and in confidence. There's nothing wrong with that either. Whether his judgement on Moores was right or wrong is, in a sense, irrelevant because if as an England captain who wants to get the best out of himself and his team thinks he can do that with someone else as coach then he's 100 per cent entitled to say so. His own longevity as captain depended entirely on whether his team won or lost.

Nor can I condemn him for being on safari in South Africa at the time the story came out. For a start, and as you will know by now, I am passionate about wildlife so I can only approve of the way he chose to spend his down-time. More importantly, he was not to know the story was going to leak in the way that it did. It's simply unfortunate from his point of view that when the issue did become public he happened to be in the wrong place at the wrong time.

My initial thought was that the situation was unsustainable but that if someone was to go it had to be the coach. For both coach and captain to go was novel and perhaps suggested someone knew something that we didn't. But to me it smacked a bit of the Establishment deciding, 'In fact, on reflection, we don't like this bloke as captain. His face doesn't fit. Let's get rid of him.' All of a sudden he became a little less English and a little more South African. On all that, I'll defend him wholeheartedly.

His response to that episode was interesting. Well over a year later, he did an interview at Lord's during the Pakistan series and frankly admitted that he was feeling down. It showed a human element and certainly didn't sound prepared, unlike many of Kevin's public utterances, which sound over-prepared and sadly mis-prepared. Like a lot of top players, Kevin tries to portray himself as invulnerable but it's not true, just as it wasn't entirely true with Beefy. I think if you've lost the captaincy you're allowed to feel sorry for a short while but the quicker you get out of that state the better. To bleat about being sacked much after that suggests you have not got a grip of yourself as you should have done. You have to be strong and tell yourself, 'I'm a pro cricketer, I'm a batsman. Get runs and be happy.'

291

What effect all this had on Pietersen's longer-term relationship with the new management is hard to say but perhaps there was a lingering sense of grievance. The trouble that surfaced in 2012 came after months of him winding up the management. He'd been bigging up the Indian Premier League, with which he had a highly lucrative contract, and doing his best to clear a full window for himself to play in it. In this respect his case was very different from mine. Although my fading interest in one-day internationals did mirror his, I had no such agenda to push.

Where we were similar was in both of us bridling at the management wanting to treat everyone in the team the same. Pietersen was pleading a special case as someone armed with a big IPL contract, not an easy thing to do but he did in this case have the nous to promote the obvious plus points of IPL as a learning ground for new techniques and a place to mix with the world's best players and learn from them. I felt with the Gooch–Stewart regime that they wanted to apply a one-size-fits-all template that made no allowances for people being different. As captain I made allowances for the likes of Botham and Edmonds, and when Gatting and Stewart were together they realised too that some of us were going to operate differently. Graham's issues were with training and fielding practice, and as I've said I could have done better on that front, but I came up with more runs than most on that Australia tour, at least until the Tiger Moth incident. It seemed they would have liked nothing more than to send me home so that they could all get on with a decent fielding session.

That would have been an even crasser over-reaction than the fine they did impose, and fortunately the regulations did not allow for it. In Pietersen's case, dropping him from the team for several weeks was an option available to the ECB and the team management, and they duly took it.

What I would say is that there is a big difference in character between KP and me; he is far more professional in his approach to the game and in his preparation than I ever was and I can only praise and respect him for that. I have no idea how he does or does not get on with his team-mates but I suspect that I had more empathy and involvement and fun with mine than he does with his. At least that is the way it looked when he was complaining, 'it is not easy being me in this dressing room' and making it very plain that he did not see anything remotely amusing in the fake Twitter account, with Graeme Swann at that stage less than flavour of the month as far as he was concerned. If I'd been playing today, I would have got on with some-one like Graeme Swann, no problem. And if someone had set up a fake Twitter account, as mentioned earlier, I would have been cool with that. I liked feeling different, I like being different, and I'm not going to complain if someone suggests as much.

The texts were a different matter and I cannot for one second fathom what induced him to send messages to the South Africans in this way. What was in them I guess we will never know for sure and further speculation now is futile. Realistically, the problem is one of loyalty. Every team nowadays has enough of its own research to go on and a few short texts will hardly add anything to their plans that they would not already know. For the South Africans it could not have worked out better. It did not matter to them what was actually in the texts, the fact that they could reveal that they had been sent was enough to act as the final straw for Andy Flower and the England management. A summer's prodding from Pietersen had pushed them too far. Dissent, when constructive and well presented, is allowable in my book but if you have issues with the way things are being done, there are acceptable ways of putting one's own view forward, though it takes skill to do it in a way that does not antagonise. Sending texts to the opposition is a very different thing from grumbling about your captain or the system. Having a moan is pretty standard stuff.

I'm damn sure that my team grumbled about me at times and that tour of the West Indies in 1986 would have been very much a case in point. Indeed the grumbling was both audible enough and visible enough, especially on the matter of how I was allowing my great mate and acknowledged superstar of the team, Ian Botham, what was regarded as too much free rein in the way he was allowed to prepare for the Tests. In hindsight I would accept they had a point but I would still happily treat Beefy differently compared to less gifted players who had not achieved anything like his success on the field. It took an angry (on my part sadly) team meeting to attempt to bring matters back in line and to be honest I don't suppose it worked. My guess is that the damage was done and the muttering went underground.

KP complaining about his treatment from the rest of the camp was one of my lowest moments as a broadcaster. The timing could not have been worse. At the very time when the Olympics were going on, and we were hearing one British hero after another say how proud they were of their success, we had the sublime pleasure of watching Pietersen smash Dale Steyn and Morne Morkel to all parts of Headingley, only for him to have to spoil it all with what he said afterwards. We stayed on air specially to hear what he had to say, hoping and expecting something like 'That was absolutely fantastic.' But all he came out with was, 'That was the hardest thing I've ever done.' I was screaming at the screen. He'd just played like God and had every right to be savouring his success and yet instead all we got was a whinge. I really had to bite my tongue on air. I simply couldn't understand that. Then, later he said: 'It's hard being me in this dressing room.'

Now I may believe that you need to give some leeway to talent but how much do you actually give? How much rein do you give genius? If I'd been Pietersen's captain, would I have dropped him? Despite the impression I might have given during our coverage of the issue at the time and even at the end of the season when we

were discussing the possibilities for the winter that I was still finding it hard to believe that the rift could be healed between Pietersen
and Flower, I think I would have attempted a heart-to-heart chat.
The message would have been a stern one along the lines of, 'Okay,
we know you're different but just grow up and play. You're a cricketing genius, but be a human being as well, for goodness sake. And
for Christ's sake stop being so bloody thin-skinned about a Twitter
account.' But by then it seems the management had had enough.

As for Pietersen's appearance on YouTube, that was a horrible
mistake. It was staged and false. If you want to negotiate, do it
quietly and honestly. The fact that the management said subsequently that they'd have rested him from some games anyway
suggests that not much communication took place.

For a period, it was difficult to see how Pietersen was going to
play again. Then Andrew Strauss stepped down as captain, and
player, and it became easier for the new man, Alastair Cook to say
that Kevin was a world-class player whom he wanted in his team
for India. I'd said the same thing about Phil Edmonds ahead of the
India tour of 1984–85 when Peter May and the selectors were
wondering if I wanted to have to 'deal with' Philippe on that tour.
I was adamant that 'dealing' with him was not an issue for me and
that I wanted the best left-arm spinner in the country to be with
me in India. He came and we had a lovely time together for four
months. Similarly, if I'd been captaining Pietersen, I'd like to think
I could have dealt with him without having to drop him.

This was, incidentally, a case where Atherton – as mentioned he
does have the knack of being right, damn him! – was indeed suitably prescient. At the very time that many including myself
wondered if the rift between Pietersen and the England management had become so unbridgeable that he might never play again,
Athers quietly stated that we would see Pietersen in action in the
Tests in India. And so it proved.

When KP then played one of the genuinely great innings to help win the Mumbai Test, his rehabilitation appeared to be complete and Cook was no doubt delighted that both his star player and his team were back on a steady course, at least for the time being.

While the escapades of a Pietersen keep us all fascinated – and players of his ilk will always keep us watching and keep us talking – it is the eternal variety among cricketers that keeps us truly interested. There is room for all, from the complete professional through to the ardent amateur and the maverick. The game will be redefined but I hope not completely reinvented. The basic skills will remain the same but new ones will always emerge. I had no idea when I finished my playing days that as a commentator I would be required to describe either the Dilshan scoop or the incredible Pietersen switch-hit.

Whatever the game holds in store for us all in the years to come, I am just grateful that I have been part of it for so long. While my enthusiasm for the game and its people remains boyishly buoyant, enough to subdue any incipient cynicism on the subject, I shall look forward to each and every issue the game throws at us for many years yet. It is only on the odd bad day, or when the rain has obliterated another, that I even begin to sympathise with Lord Mancroft, who once said, 'Cricket is a game which the British, not being a spiritual people, had to invent in order to have some idea of eternity.'

I 2

LOOKING FORWARD

That things can change rapidly was proven emphatically over a winter that saw England go from a highly respected side to a bunch of apparent no-hopers in the space of a few weeks. The fact the tour lasted three months and at no stage seemed to get any better was probably a reflection of several things that taken together I can only describe as a perfect storm. It is worth remembering that when England left home, almost everyone – including me – thought they would win the Test series. Even the Australians suspected they might lose, although with the benefit of hindsight Michael Clarke might tell you different.

While the Australians suddenly found inspiration, dedication and an absolute unity of purpose, it was Mitchell Johnson's pace that was the key factor in England's consistent demoralisation. Time and again, he demonstrated how that extra yard of pace can make all the difference. Brisbane was a revelation. At the time, I thought it was a shock from which a good side like England might recover, but by the time the second Test was decidedly done and dusted in Adelaide it was clear that the balance of power had shifted more dramatically than we'd first thought. How different might things have been had England finished off Australia when they had them 132 for six on the opening day of the series, or if just one or two batsmen could have made a score in England's first innings in either of those first two Tests?

If Johnson was Australia's star, Brad Haddin was not far behind, batting as consistently well or better than at any stage in his career to date and regularly getting his side from positions of weakness or semi-strength to ones of absolute strength, and making sure that England had little hope of getting back into the series. Nor were England out-bowled only by Johnson; all of Australia's attack were exemplary. Rather like with England themselves in the 2005 Ashes, something clicked into place for all the bowlers, who gained strength from knowing they were fulfilling their appointed roles to perfection. It was one of those self-perpetuating situations that we have seen before on modern tours where one side (usually the home one) is hard to shift after taking the upper hand. With the schedules the way they are, with few games outside the Tests in which to regroup, momentum has become something very hard to arrest. As I say, the perfect storm.

For all Australia's brilliance, that so many England's stars did nothing to confirm their reputations was unusual to say the least. Even in a bad series, one or two batsmen usually get runs and keep their side vaguely in contention, but when your top five do so little you aren't going to win anything. Startling, again, to think that beforehand it was believed that several of England's top order would actually quite enjoy Australian conditions, as they had in 2010–11. Yet only Ben Stokes – playing in his first series – was able to score a hundred, which served only to emphasise just how poor was the established batting. Alastair Cook was completely out of sorts, hitting one of those patches every good player suffers at some stage where things just don't work, however talented, professional or determined they are. Ian Bell found odd ways to get out and Kevin Pietersen just seemed to believe it would happen for him because he was Kevin Pietersen.

England's preparations were palpably inadequate. The blueprint from three years before, Strauss's triumphant tour, would have been seemingly still very fresh and the extra minor percentages that the legions of back-room staff add to the equation should have meant that England arrived suitably well briefed. Having won the key moments in the summer, maybe everyone just assumed that they would do so again. I cannot believe that anyone from Andy Flower downwards was complacent going into this series, simply because it had been one of the standard questions asked by all sorts in the media for the last few seasons, whether or not any complacency had set in, from the day that England had reached that No. 1 Test ranking after the India series in 2011.

Perhaps it was as simple as assuming that the same things would work and that Australia wouldn't do anything different. But how Johnson bowled shouldn't have been a complete surprise. He'd looked superb in the one-day series in England, during which it seemed he had already gone some way towards undermining Jonathan Trott. You can look back and think, why didn't Trott play at Southampton in the final ODI? Was it a back spasm as stated, or was it in fact the first sign of the problems that came to a head in Brisbane?

While sympathising deeply with Jonathan's predicament (and for that matter applauding the way he was intent on making his way back into the Test side, as he proclaimed in the build-up to the 2014 season), for England to have admitted after he had boarded the plane home in distress that they had known about his condition for some months, and yet had still been prepared to gamble on him in the cauldron of an Ashes series Down Under, looked crass.

Nor would anyone seriously have predicted that Matt Prior would end up being dropped after three Tests, even if he had had a tough summer at home. He is one of the good guys in the England team, a genuinely pivotal character, one you back under virtually all circumstances. Yet he too became part of that perfect storm. You can see in the way he bats that, because he relies so much on a good eye and on the point of contact being spot on, everything has to be working properly or there is a danger that it doesn't function at all. I can assure you, having lived the same way for the best part of 20 years in first-class cricket, that it is not a long way from the centre of the bat to the outside edge. For me then and him now, it was and is all about making the right point of contact and until the start of last summer that point of contact was pretty near the middle of his bat. You could sense in Adelaide his determination to battle through and make it work, but over-riding your instinct until everything is working properly is a hard trick to pull off.

And then there was the decline of Graeme Swann, which was perhaps most striking of all. All it took was just that minor diminution of his powers, against people who decided they could take the attack to him on good pitches, and the balance of power tilted dramatically. What was really frustrating was watching Nathan Lyon, Australia's spinner, bowl so well at our guys on the very same pitches, but then the match situations were usually very different – except of course for the first day at Brisbane, where Swann was but one member of an attack unable to break the Haddin–Johnson stand that turned the match and, ultimately, the series.

I did have some sympathy for England. There is an issue with playing back-to-back series against any country, let alone Australia, and while it can be argued that it is the same for both sides, it clearly isn't when the prize is as big as the Ashes and the team that wins the first series is asked to scale their Everest again straight after. No sooner do they congratulate themselves on winning the Ashes than they must steel themselves for a repeat. The side that has come second, on the other hand, is eager for the opportunity to put things right and certainly not wanting for motivation. The fact they were at home would only have encouraged Australia further.

However, having said that, it was just extraordinary that at no stage could England summon the kind of intensity that had served them so well at home, when every time it had needed someone to do that 'step up to the plate' thing (one of Bumble's favourite clichés!) and grasp control of the game, then Bell or Broad or whoever had done exactly that.

Of course, the major focus in the aftermath of the tour fell on the departures of Kevin Pietersen and Andy Flower. Before the decision on Pietersen was taken, I thought England should try to keep him in the side. When a team wants to get back on track, you can either start afresh, rebuilding a team and that nebulous, ephemeral thing known as team spirit, or you can just try to win some matches to see if that does the trick.

England's next assignments, a World Twenty20 and series against Sri Lanka and India, would have been right up his street. If you want someone to blast a match-changing hundred against those two sides, who better qualified than Kevin? All you have to do is cast your mind back not so far to his innings at Colombo and Mumbai in 2012 to see what I mean. The immediate corollary is that one just does not know quite how bad things were in the dressing-room, though one assumes that it must have been pretty bad for the verdict among the key management figures to be unanimous.

It seems there was not one major transgression, simply the strong feeling that enough was enough, that Kevin had been Kevin for too long. I have a lot of respect for Flower and for what he achieved as team director and it seemed to me that he had obviously, despite his public denials, had just about as much as one can take of Kevin. Maybe, if he had remained at his post and his captain had been keen to keep the problematic superstar in the fold, he would have been persuaded to keep managing the 'problem'. But for Cook, as captain, to go from being desperate for Pietersen to be in his side in India 18 months earlier to condoning his removal is the most damning evidence of all. If the captain is not on your side, then you've got a problem.

Everyone one talked to in the aftermath of that sacking wanted to know what the inside story was. Someone like me, believe it or not, is reliant on second-hand evidence and may be privileged to hear a better class of rumour than most, but that is all that it is. As bits of the story emerged and the likes of Prior and Swann, accepted 'team' men, added their own comments, it became clearer that KP was an expendable luxury.

One of those who asked all those same questions was my next door neighbour, best remembered as the former Southampton manager Lawrie McMenemy. Lawrie was and still is a master of man-management, one of those who seems to know instinctively whether an arm round the shoulder or a kick up the backside is needed. He asked if Kevin was rascal or villain? Under Lawrie at Southampton in a great era of that club's history, he had to manage several rascals, players who could be cheeky, maybe tricky but who were very much on side in a team sense, and the odd villain, a different sort of animal, disruptive and unwanted. The villain was seldom tolerated. In the end, as far as England's senior figures were concerned, it seems that Kevin was more villain than rascal.

The other key figure in the decision was Paul Downton, the new managing director of England cricket. I knew Paul well as a colleague on England youth tours and in the full Test side, and we once shared a long partnership together that saved a Test match in Jamaica. He's a very good man and I would trust his judgement. But what a way to enter a new job – picking up the debris strewn everywhere from the aforementioned perfect storm and deciding the best way forward. It would have been far easier for him to say, 'Let's not go too far.'

It would be interesting to know how Darren Lehmann might have handled Pietersen in this situation. In his role as Australia's head coach, Lehmann is living proof that rebuilding team spirit can be a prelude to winning again. I know I can be sceptical about the whole concept of 'team spirit' and have more than once queried whether it comes before success on the field or after it, the chicken and egg of sports psychology, but it does seem that Lehmann found a way of engendering it beautifully for an Australian team that was failing to pull its weight, had lost confidence, and had forgotten what it was to enjoy a game of cricket.

The Australians did not 'get' Mickey Arthur but identified readily with Lehmann and the results were startling, firstly for England and then for the next team in the Johnson firing line, South Africa. I have no idea whether Lehmann would have got rid of KP, but I suspect he might well have found a way to keep the famous ego in check, to allow Pietersen nonetheless to retain his pride and to keep him going. To my mind, it's all about having the character to deal with a big character, and Lehmann certainly has that.

As for Flower, I think that all coaches have a shelf life and if you keep on ramming home the same messages then eventually those messages are going to weaken. He had been in the job five years and history suggests that is about as long as any head coach manages, if not rather more. Even before he resigned, I was thinking he was going to have to reinvent himself a little, and find new ways of doing things, if he was going to survive. If he could do that, he might still be able to provide something useful. It's not that what he was saying before was wrong, but as situations change so a coach needs to alter the message and the mood. After Australia, England clearly faced a period of redevelopment with a very different set of players from those that done so well for them over several years.

It is also worth remembering that coaches can only achieve so much. In this respect, I thought the most perceptive line to come out of all the fall-out from the tour was Matt Prior's reported comment in the players' meeting after the defeat in Melbourne for which he got unfairly vilified. 'Fuck the management,' he had apparently told his team-mates. This did not mean that he had no time for Flower and the rest of his back-room staff, only that the players had to take responsibility for their games and not look for excuses by blaming management.

Well said. As Ian Botham has never tired (himself) from saying: coaches should only ever be there to help, to add a little bit; the real nub of whether you play well rests with you the player. My ambition as captain was to give people responsibility. The job of coaches is to get players to make decisions for themselves, not to tell them what to do. Andy Flower, Graham Gooch and David Saker are armed with knowledge that the players should tap into, but ultimately the players have to go to bed thinking, 'Tomorrow is my day.' If all the ideas come from the dressing-room or a computer, that's wrong. If you're going to be good as an individual and a team it must come from within, whether it's devising a method for scoring runs against Mitchell Johnson or bowling to a field against David Warner.

It is a long time since England have been in such a big rebuilding phase. You'd expect Cook and Bell to be hell-bent on restoring their reputations and quickly among the runs again, but the rest of the top five looks very fluid. I'm assuming Stokes, fitness permitting, will be a fixture at No. 6 for the foreseeable future. Joe Root clearly has things to sort out, but like Stokes he is exceptionally promising, with a good temperament suited to the cut and thrust of Test cricket. He's got to take another step forward and that step is to put the pressure back on the bowler more, because against Australia he was just soaking it up rather than putting it back, and that only encourages the bowler in his work. Pietersen's fault, of course, was that he went to the other extreme in his desire to dominate. Somewhere in between is where Root wants to be. He's never going to be a Pietersen, no one is, but he needs to develop his game so that he can productively alter the balance of power out in the middle. Then we've got the likes of Gary Ballance, James Taylor, Eoin Morgan and Jonny Bairstow also in the mix for places. Personally, I'd prefer Morgan in the side because I'd back his flair and talent – mercurial though it may be – to win more games than the steadier accumulation of, say, a Taylor. In the post-Pietersen era, he's a gamble worth taking.

The bowlers, too, need to get their confidence back and the attack is going to face some stiff challenges now that Swann has retired. England will arguably miss him every bit as much as Pietersen, if not more. Monty Panesar may have to play because there is no one else as far as I can tell. That said, there's evidence to suggest he's not bowling as well as he once did and that he is in need of more moral support, too. How much patience England are willing to extend to him remains to be seen.

While there's clearly a case for investing in the future in the shape of the young leg-spinner Scott Borthwick, I didn't see anything in Sydney that suggested that he is quite ready to be given a run. Maybe that's harsh and others who have seen more of him have more faith than I. All I'd say is that if you are selecting a Test team, a leg-spinner is a high-risk option. If you've got a Shane Warne or an Abdul Qadir at your disposal, then great, but if not then you have to ask yourself whether you're likely to have enough runs to play with to allow your leggie to take one for 70 off ten overs, or three for 100 off 18.

The biggest challenge of all, though, faces Cook as captain, who needs to learn as much as he can about the job in a short space of time. With the team he now has at his disposal, the temptation is going to be to attempt to win games through attrition and control because England don't have the flair to do it any other way. Lose control and you lose the game, that's going to be the fear (hence Panesar rather than Borthwick perhaps, because at least you know what you're going to get). Whenever you lose, your captaincy comes under scrutiny, but believe me – as someone who knows a thing or two about losing 5–0 – when you are whitewashed in a major series your every mistake becomes catastrophic, and your every minor misjudgement a melodrama.

I also understand that when your team is up against it and you yourself are not scoring runs, it's perfectly human not to think at lightning speed and be just that little slower coming to your conclusions. When your confidence is high, and the adrenalin is pumping, you trust your instincts and everything flows. It's easier to pull off clever moves when you are on top. When you're being blasted all over the field, you don't have that many options. That said, Cook's captaincy in Australia did raise some questions.

There were times when we were sitting in the commentary box and wondering, why? And, before you ask, the game hasn't changed that much since the 1980s. There are times when you can put extra slips in. There are times when you have to seize the moment. Bouncing Brad Haddin might work now and again, but generally speaking you get him out the same way you get everyone else out, by denying him runs, putting the pressure on with an extra slip and short leg, and bowling to a plan. If Haddin walks in and sees deep square leg going out, and only two slips and a gully, he's not overly fussed about the length ball on off stump. Mind you, the captain's not the only one to blame in such situations; as already mentioned, the players must take ownership of their own games and take their share of responsibility.

For Alastair, the summer of 2014 may well be one that turns

him into a good leader – or sees him sent back to the ranks to concentrate on making another umpteen thousand Test runs.

Hot on the heels of England's problems came major changes at the ICC with the way the world game was to be administered. Essentially, England, India and Australia were taking control of the levers of power and with it a greater share of revenues – revenues they maintained they did most to generate – and managed to sell the deal to their colleagues around the ICC table on the basis that the new arrangement would provide more money for everyone under future broadcasting deals. After initial doubts in some quarters, it seems everyone, or at least a good working majority, has now got onboard and given the proposals their support. The take-it or-leave-it nature of what was widely termed a 'power-grab' was what stuck in the craw of many.

Part of me would like to say that it's all wrong because it flies in the face of the independent governance of the game that Lord Woolf called for in his recent review. And of course it would be lovely if the game could be run in the way he envisaged. But in reality who is in a position to do that? Who could be a truly independent director and leader, while combining the three vital elements required to do the job well; a knowledge of the game, of big business and of the politics? In truth, when the big broadcasting deals are struck, the broadcasters want to sit round a table with representatives from India, England and any others who are in a position to deliver guarantees as to which major events they are willing to stage, and when. It's hardly a secret, either, that some national boards have hardly been able to run cricket in their own countries – for a variety of reasons, not all of their own making – let alone across the world. And let's be honest, too: the previous system wasn't working.

It seems to me that there is a lot of sense in what was put

forward. Indian business might operate in a slightly different way to its British equivalent, but it gets things done; and even though the Indian economy is not what it was 12 months ago, you can't deny the commercial clout at the Indian cricket board's disposal. Such is the demand for their presence overseas – where a visit from India can bank-roll the game for years rather than months – that India themselves do not play at home anything like as much as they would like. Some of India's demands are hardly unreasonable. As for Giles Clarke, the chairman of the England and Wales Cricket Board, he has done well to get England back to the centre of things after a rocky period following the Allen Stanford debacle in which it seemed we would never get on with India again. He's fought England's corner and found a way back to the top table. He's displayed a worldly understanding of what's needed to stay at the forefront – and a little bit of national pride means I don't actually mind England being there.

I'm in two minds though about the better associate nations such as Ireland and Afghanistan being given the opportunity to join Test cricket. I don't mind them wanting to raise their game, I just don't know how they are going to do it to the requisite standard, and fear that they will struggle to achieve, and then maintain, the necessary standards. Do they, in short, possess enough good players? Will they ever possess enough (even if, in the case of the Irish, the exodus that brought the likes of Morgan and Boyd Rankin to England is halted)? I know there are weak links today, with Zimbabwe and Bangladesh hardly good enough to give the better nations a game, but I resist any move that would further erode standards.

The attraction, I suppose, is that with a couple more teams we could create a two-division system of Test cricket, with a second tier containing Bangladesh, Zimbabwe, Ireland and Afghanistan that could work well – although in that case I'd question whether anything but the first division really constituted Test cricket.

Perhaps this would be a price worth paying if it kept the flag flying for the five-day format.

Personally, I'm delighted that the proposed world Test championship is not happening. I just don't see how grounds would sell out for matches involving two neutral teams. Even Australia v South Africa in a cosmopolitan city such as London would struggle, I believe, and as for staging that fixture in Mumbai … well, all I can say is, good luck. The present system of ranking points and a mace for the leading team is about as much as you can do to make each Test match and series relevant. I guess you could have a show-piece game every 12 or 24 months between the top two teams, rather like the seasonal play-offs in rugby, but with any play-off match in cricket there is always the problem as to what happens if it ends in a draw. This was one of the chief stumbling blocks that put paid to the world championship idea. Marketing a world Test championship final, as with a play-off, is also fraught with difficulty when you don't know until the last minute who is going to be taking part. I'd rather have a Champions Trophy, and so too would the administrators, it seems. From the point of view of the broader audience, the last two or three Champions Trophies have worked really well and in many ways work better than the World Cup itself, which is a much more drawn-out affair.

Forget gimmicks such as world Test championships. Test cricket will be kept alive through stars such as Mitchell Johnson captivating audiences in the stadiums and on television around the world with his electric fast bowling. Johnson will inspire a generation of young fast bowlers in Australia and probably elsewhere too, and what he did in the Ashes was 1,000 times more important than him bowling well in the ODIs in England. Similarly Brendon McCullum scoring New Zealand's first Test match triple-century against India will do every bit as much, if not more, to stir interest in his own country than him scoring a blistering hundred to launch the Indian Premier League back in 2008. Which innings will he be more proud of when he looks back in retirement? The 300 I suspect, and rightly so. Sachin Tendulkar's extraordinary career too did a lot to reinforce the primacy of Test cricket, with the Indian nation rearranging the world so that he could finish his career in front of his own adoring public in a Test match.

While I would never seek to block the development of any part of the game that brings in new devotees and helps to spread the word further and wider, there are for ever going to be aspects that I would regard as sacrosanct. As Giles Clarke said after the ICC deal was done, it is more important to focus on those parts of the world that already have a love and a desire for cricket rather than seeking to introduce such an arcane activity into China on the off-chance of it taking off there. One of the great cricketing success stories in the last few years has been the extraordinary and entirely laudable rise of Afghanistan cricket and that is the sort of progress the ICC should be fostering, so, while I do have those misgivings about them and the Irish being viable Test nations, then at least I am happy to offer them the structure to encourage them to try.

But for me Test cricket was and is so special that while I am still in any sort of position to defend and promote it, that I will surely do. Just don't ask me to accept that it should be played into the night. Other things are sacrosanct too, and they include a proper, sociable dinner after a stunning day's play at Lord's, a time to talk about this great game and debate the issues that will always be part of it. Breakfast just would not cut it!

ACKNOWLEDGEMENTS

There have been many people who have been on my side during the life described in these pages and I am indebted to them all. My parents, Richard and Sylvia, have to be at the top of that list for the simple reason they put me on the right path in life right from the start. I was delighted that my mother could see at least some of my Test career and to see the pride in her face gave me as much satisfaction as anything I ever achieved on the cricket field. The tragedy is that my father was never to see me play Test cricket.

There are many of my colleagues, past and present, who are and always will be great friends. Of the 'non-combatants', the non players, the man who has done most to guide me through thick and thin is Jon Holmes. He once told me to beware if your agent pitches up in a helicopter, and he is yet to do that, but his judgement and advice have been invaluable to me over the years, and if he does live in a sizeable property of his own, with a flat in London, and holds sway over the Garrick Club, he deserves it!

My wife, Thorunn, while I hope enjoying the fruits of my labours, has had to endure the long absences that are part and parcel of being both an international cricketer and a commentator. There again the odd Christmas in Australia or South Africa does make a nice change. She has given me unswerving support through-out and I love her dearly for it.

Although my life has been dominated by cricket, my girls have made sure that netball and hockey have featured heavily over the last decade and a half. Alex and Sammi might not have taken cricket exactly to their hearts, but at both Twyford and Canford schools they have played their sport with suitable pride, tenacity and no little skill, to make their father very proud.

At Twyford, the netball teams consistently punched above their weight and it was a joy to watch both in the national finals year after year. At Canford, they take their hockey very seriously and I have been there on the touchline for more national finals with both of them, trying and failing to maintain the composure that I like to feel is the hallmark of my work for Sky!

During my playing days, fatherhood was always a distant possi-bility. Now that the two of them are either through or nearly through their childhood, I, like so many fathers, wonder where the time went. They are my pride and joy, and my dearest desire is to see them happy and prosperous in whatever it is that they find a passion.

As I write, Alex is bound for a Biology degree at Bristol and Sammi has another year at Canford, after which she seems to headed for something very similar. Where they got their scientist's genes from is anybody's guess – indeed, even a geneticist might struggle on this one because there are precious few BSc holders in either of our backgrounds.

I have no doubt they will continue to inspire me and test me in equal measure!

DAVID GOWER'S CAREER RECORD

Statistics compiled by Ian Marshall (to 1 April 2014)

FACTFILE

David Ivon Gower, born Tunbridge Wells, Kent, 1 April 1957

Education: Marlborough House; King's School, Canterbury; London University

Height: 6'0"

Counties: Leicestershire 1975–89; cap 1977; captain 1984–86 and 1988–89; benefit 1987 and Hampshire 1990–93; cap 1990

Other teams: MCC 1977–87; D.H.Robins' XI 1977–78 to 1978; Young England 1978

Honours: Cricket Writers' Club Young Cricketer of the Year 1978; *Wisden* Cricketer of the Year 1978; OBE 1992

Test debut: England v Pakistan, 1–5 June 1978, at Birmingham, scoring 58

One-day international debut: England v Pakistan, 24–5 May 1978, at Manchester, scoring 33

First-class debut: Leicestershire v Lancashire, 30 July–1 August 1975, at Blackpool, scoring 32

Limited-overs debut: Leicestershire v Surrey. 13 July 1975, at Leicester, scoring 11

Trophies won: Leicestershire – County Championship 1975; John Player League 1977; Benson & Hedges Cup 1985; Hampshire – NatWest Trophy 1991; Benson & Hedges Cup 1992

DAVID GOWER'S MATCH-BY-MATCH TEST RECORD

Test	Opponent	Venue	Date Started	1st Inns Score	2nd Inns Score	Result	Captain
1	Pakistan	Birmingham	1-Jun-78	58	–	Won I/57	
2	Pakistan	Lord's	15-Jun-78	56	–	Won I/120	
3	Pakistan	Leeds	29-Jun-78	39	–	Drawn	
4	New Zealand	The Oval	27-Jul-78	111	11	Won 7w	
5	New Zealand	Nottingham	10-Aug-78	46	–	Won I/119	
6	New Zealand	Lord's	24-Aug-78	71	46	Won 7w	
7	Australia	Brisbane	1-Dec-78	44	48*	Won 7w	
8	Australia	Perth	15-Dec-78	102	12	Won 166	
9	Australia	Melbourne	29-Dec-78	29	49	Lost 103	
10	Australia	Sydney	6-Jan-79	7	34	Won 93	
11	Australia	Adelaide	27-Jan-79	9	21	Won 205	
12	Australia	Sydney	10-Feb-79	65	–	Won 9w	
13	India	Birmingham	12-Jul-79	200*	–	Won I/83	
14	India	Lord's	2-Aug-79	82	–	Drawn	
15	India	Leeds	16-Aug-79	0	–	Drawn	
16	India	The Oval	30-Aug-79	0	7	Drawn	
17	Australia	Perth	14-Dec-79	17	23	Lost 138	
18	Australia	Sydney	4-Jan-80	3	98*	Lost 6w	
19	Australia	Melbourne	1-Feb-80	0	11	Lost 8w	
20	India	Bombay	15-Feb-80	16	–	Won 10w	
21	West Indies	Nottingham	5-Jun-80	20	1	Lost 2w	
22	Australia	Lord's	28-Aug-80	45	35	Drawn	
23	West Indies	Port of Spain	13-Feb-81	48	27	Lost I/79	
24	West Indies	Bridgetown	13-Mar-81	17	54	Lost 298	
25	West Indies	St John's	27-Mar-81	32	22	Drawn	
26	West Indies	Kingston	10-Apr-81	22	154*	Drawn	
27	Australia	Nottingham	18-Jun-81	26	28	Lost 4w	
28	Australia	Lord's	2-Jul-81	27	89	Drawn	
29	Australia	Leeds	16-Jul-81	24	9	Won 18	
30	Australia	Birmingham	30-Jul-81	0	23	Won 29	
31	Australia	Manchester	13-Aug-81	23	1	Won 103	
32	India	Bombay	27-Nov-81	5	20	Lost 138	
33	India	Bangalore	9-Dec-81	82	34*	Drawn	
34	India	Delhi	23-Dec-81	0	–	Drawn	
35	India	Calcutta	1-Jan-82	11	74	Drawn	
36	India	Madras	13-Jan-82	64	–	Drawn	
37	India	Kanpur	30-Jan-82	85	–	Drawn	
38	Sri Lanka	Colombo, PSS	17-Feb-82	89	42*	Won 7w	
39	India	Lord's	10-Jun-82	37	14*	Won 7w	

Test	Opponent	Venue	Date Started	1st Inns Score	2nd Inns Score	Result	Captain
40	India	Manchester	24-Jun-82	9	–	Drawn	
41	India	The Oval	8-Jul-82	47	45	Drawn	
42	Pakistan	Birmingham	29-Jul-82	74	13	Won 113	
43	Pakistan	Lord's	12-Aug-82	29	0	Lost 10w	Cap
44	Pakistan	Leeds	26-Aug-82	74	7	Won 3w	
45	Australia	Perth	12-Nov-82	72	28	Drawn	
46	Australia	Brisbane	26-Nov-82	18	34	Lost 7w	
47	Australia	Adelaide	10-Dec-82	60	114	Lost 8w	
48	Australia	Melbourne	26-Dec-82	18	3	Won 3	
49	Australia	Sydney	2-Jan-83	70	24	Drawn	
50	New Zealand	The Oval	14-Jul-83	11	25	Won 189	
51	New Zealand	Leeds	28-Jul-83	9	112*	Lost 5w	
52	New Zealand	Lord's	11-Aug-83	108	34	Won 127	
53	New Zealand	Nottingham	25-Aug-83	72	33	Won 165	
54	New Zealand	Wellington	20-Jan-84	33	–	Drawn	
55	New Zealand	Christchurch	3-Feb-84	2	8	Lost I/132	
56	New Zealand	Auckland	10-Feb-84	26	–	Drawn	
57	Pakistan	Karachi	2-Mar-84	58	57	Lost 3w	
58	Pakistan	Faisalabad	12-Mar-84	152	–	Drawn	Cap
59	Pakistan	Lahore	19-Mar-84	9	173*	Drawn	Cap
60	West Indies	Birmingham	14-Jun-84	10	12	Lost I/180	Cap
61	West Indies	Lord's	28-Jun-84	3	21	Lost 9w	Cap
62	West Indies	Leeds	12-Jul-84	2	43	Lost 8w	Cap
63	West Indies	Manchester	26-Jul-84	4	57*	Lost I/64	Cap
64	West Indies	The Oval	9-Aug-84	12	7	Lost 172	Cap
65	Sri Lanka	Lord's	23-Aug-84	55	–	Drawn	Cap
66	India	Bombay	28-Nov-84	13	2	Lost 8w	Cap
67	India	Delhi	12-Dec-84	5	–	Won 8w	Cap
68	India	Calcutta	31-Dec-84	19	–	Drawn	Cap
69	India	Madras	13-Jan-85	18	–	Won 9w	Cap
70	India	Kanpur	31-Jan-85	78	32*	Drawn	Cap
71	Australia	Leeds	13-Jun-85	17	5	Won 5w	Cap
72	Australia	Lord's	27-Jun-85	86	22	Lost 4w	Cap
73	Australia	Nottingham	11-Jul-85	166	17	Drawn	Cap
74	Australia	Manchester	1-Aug-85	47		Drawn	Cap
75	Australia	Birmingham	15-Aug-85	215	–	Won I/118	Cap
76	Australia	The Oval	29-Aug-85	157	–	Won I/94	Cap
77	West Indies	Kingston	21-Feb-86	16	9	Lost 10w	Cap
78	West Indies	Port of Spain	7-Mar-86	66	47	Lost 7w	Cap
79	West Indies	Bridgetown	21-Mar-86	66	23	Lost I/30	Cap
80	West Indies	Port of Spain	3-Apr-86	10	22	Lost 10w	Cap
81	West Indies	St John's	11-Apr-86	90	21	Lost 240	Cap

Test	Opponent	Venue	Date Started	1st Inns Score	2nd Inns Score	Result	Captain
82	India	Lord's	5-Jun-86	18	8	Lost 5w	Cap
83	India	Birmingham	3-Jul-86	49	26	Drawn	
84	New Zealand	Lord's	24-Jul-86	62	3	Drawn	
85	New Zealand	Nottingham	7-Aug-86	71	26	Lost 8w	
86	New Zealand	The Oval	21-Aug-86	131	–	Drawn	
87	Australia	Brisbane	14-Nov-86	51	15*	Won 7w	
88	Australia	Perth	28-Nov-86	136	48	Drawn	
89	Australia	Adelaide	12-Dec-86	38	–	Drawn	
90	Australia	Melbourne	26-Dec-86	7	–	Won I/14	
91	Australia	Sydney	10-Jan-87	72	37	Lost 55	
92	Pakistan	Manchester	4-Jun-87	22	–	Drawn	
93	Pakistan	Lord's	18-Jun-87	8	–	Drawn	
94	Pakistan	Leeds	2-Jul-87	10	55	Lost I/18	
95	Pakistan	Birmingham	23-Jul-87	61	18	Drawn	
96	Pakistan	The Oval	6-Aug-87	28	34	Drawn	
97	West Indies	Nottingham	2-Jun-88	18	88*	Drawn	
98	West Indies	Lord's	16-Jun-88	46	1	Lost 134	
99	West Indies	Manchester	30-Jun-88	9	34	Lost I/156	
100	West Indies	Leeds	21-Jul-88	13	2	Lost 10w	
101	Australia	Leeds	8-Jun-89	26	34	Lost 210	Cap
102	Australia	Lord's	22-Jun-89	57	106	Lost 6w	Cap
103	Australia	Birmingham	6-Jul-89	8	–	Drawn	Cap
104	Australia	Manchester	27-Jul-89	35	15	Lost 9w	Cap
105	Australia	Nottingham	10-Aug-89	11	5	Lost I/180	Cap
106	Australia	The Oval	24-Aug-89	79	7	Drawn	Cap
107	India	Lord's	26-Jul-90	40	32*	Won 247	
108	India	Manchester	9-Aug-90	38	16	Drawn	
109	India	The Oval	23-Aug-90	8	157*	Drawn	
110	Australia	Brisbane	23-Nov-90	61	27	Lost 10w	
111	Australia	Melbourne	26-Dec-90	100	0	Lost 8w	
112	Australia	Sydney	4-Jan-91	123	36	Drawn	
113	Australia	Adelaide	25-Jan-91	11	16	Drawn	
114	Australia	Perth	1-Feb-91	28*	5	Lost 9w	
115	Pakistan	Manchester	2-Jul-92	73	–	Drawn	
116	Pakistan	Leeds	23-Jul-92	18*	31*	Won 6w	
117	Pakistan	The Oval	6-Aug-92	27	1	Lost 10w	

DAVID GOWER'S TEST MATCH AVERAGE BATTING AND FIELDING

	M	I	NO	HS	Runs	Avge	100	50	Ct
v Australia	42	77	4	215	3269	44.78	9	12	26
v India	24	37	6	200*	1391	44.87	2	6	13
v New Zealand	13	22	1	131	1051	50.04	4	4	11
v Pakistan	17	27	3	173*	1185	49.37	2	9	8
v Sri Lanka	2	3	1	89	186	93.00	-	2	5
v West Indies	19	38	3	154*	1149	32.82	1	6	11
Home	65	113	9	215	4454	42.82	10	19	40
Away	52	91	9	173*	3777	46.06	8	20	34
Overall	**117**	**204**	**18**	**215**	**8231**	**44.25**	**18**	**39**	**74**

DAVID GOWER'S TEST CENTURIES

Score	Balls Faced / Fours / Sixes	Opposition	Venue	Season
215	314/25/1	Australia	Birmingham	1985
200*	279/24/0	India	Birmingham	1979
173*	284/16/0	Pakistan	Lahore	1983-84
166	284/17/0	Australia	Nottingham	1985
157*	270/21/0	India	The Oval	1990
157	216/20/0	Australia	The Oval	1985
154*	403/16/1	West Indies	Kingston	1980-81
152	318/16/0	Pakistan	Faisalabad	1983-84
136	175/16/0	Australia	Perth	1986-87
131	202/14/0	New Zealand	The Oval	1986
123	236/15/0	Australia	Sydney	1990-91
114	259/16/0	Australia	Adelaide	1982-83
112*	196/14/0	New Zealand	Leeds	1983
111	253/14/0	New Zealand	The Oval	1978
108	200/16/0	New Zealand	Lord's	1983
106	198/16/0	Australia	Lord's	1989
102	221/9/0	Australia	Perth	1978-79
100	170/8/0	Australia	Melbourne	1990-91

MOST TEST CENTURIES FOR ENGLAND

100s	Innings	Player	Career
25	183	A.N.Cook	2006-
23	181	K.P.Pietersen	2005-2014
22	140	W.R.Hammond	1927-1947
22	188	M.C.Cowdrey	1954-1975
22	193	G.Boycott	1964-1982
21	178	A.J.Strauss	2004-2012
20	131	K.F.Barrington	1955-1968
20	170	I.R.Bell	2004-
20	215	G.A.Gooch	1975-1995
19	138	L.Hutton	1937-1955
18	147	M.P.Vaughan	1999-2008
18	**204**	**D.I.Gower**	**1978-1992**

MOST INNINGS OF 150 OR MORE FOR ENGLAND

150s	Innings	Player	Career
10	138	L.Hutton	1937-1955
10	140	W.R.Hammond	1927-1947
10	161	K.P.Pietersen	2005-2014
8	88	D.L.Amiss	1966-1977
8	**204**	**D.I.Gower**	**1978-1992**
8	215	G.A.Gooch	1975-1995
7	163	A.N.Cook	2006-
7	188	M.C.Cowdrey	1954-1975

7000 RUNS IN TESTS FOR ENGLAND

	M	I	NO	HS	Runs	Avge	100	50
G.A.Gooch	118	215	6	333	8900	42.58	20	46
A.J.Stewart	133	235	21	190	8463	39.54	15	45
D.I.Gower	**117**	**204**	**18**	**215**	**8231**	**44.25**	**18**	**39**
K.P.Pietersen	104	181	8	227	8181	47.28	23	35
G.Boycott	108	193	23	246*	8114	47.72	22	42
A.N.Cook	102	183	10	294	8047	46.51	25	35
M.A.Atherton	115	212	7	185*	7728	37.69	16	46
M.C.Cowdrey	114	188	15	182	7624	44.06	22	38
W.R.Hammond	85	140	16	336*	7249	58.45	22	24
A.J.Strauss	100	178	6	177	7037	40.91	21	27

3000 RUNS IN ASHES TESTS

	M	I	NO	HS	Runs	Avge	100	50
D.G.Bradman (A)	37	63	7	334	5028	89.78	19	12
J.B.Hobbs (E)	41	71	4	187	3636	54.26	12	15
A.R.Border (A)	47	82	19	200*	3548	56.31	8	21
D.I.Gower (E)	**42**	**77**	**4**	**215**	**3269**	**44.78**	**9**	**12**
S.R.Waugh (A)	46	73	18	177*	3200	58.18	10	14

MOST MATCHES AS CAPTAIN OF ENGLAND

Tests	Player	Career
54	M.A.Atherton	1993-2001
51	M.P.Vaughan	2003-2008
50	A.J.Strauss	2006-2012
45	N.Hussain	1999-2003
41	P.B.H.May	1955-1961
34	G.A.Gooch	1988-1993
32	**D.I.Gower**	**1982-1989**
31	R.Illingworth	1969-1973
31	J.M.Brearley	1977-1981
30	E.R.Dexter	1961-1964

DAVID GOWER'S ONE-DAY INTERNATIONAL AVERAGE BATTING AND FIELDING

	M	I	NO	HS	Runs	Avge	100	50	Ct
v Australia	32	31	3	102	794	28.35	2	3	10
v Canada	1	-	-	-	-	-	-	-	-
v India	16	15	-	81	469	31.26	-	4	6
v New Zealand	24	24	2	158	874	39.72	3	4	11
v Pakistan	15	15	2	114*	451	34.69	1	-	8
v Sri Lanka	4	4	1	130	179	59.33	1	-	3
v West Indies	22	22	-	59	404	18.36	-	1	6
Home	45	43	5	130	1387	36.50	3	6	15
Away	69	68	3	158	1783	27.43	4	6	29
Overall	**114**	**111**	**8**	**158**	**3170**	**30.77**	**7**	**12**	**44**

DAVID GOWER'S ONE-DAY INTERNATIONAL CENTURIES

Score	Balls Faced/Fours/Sixes	Opposition	Venue	Season
158	118/18/4	New Zealand	Brisbane	1982-83
130	120/12/5	Sri Lanka	Taunton	1983
122	134/8/0	New Zealand	Melbourne	1982-83
114*	122/6/0	Pakistan	The Oval	1978
109	85/12/1	New Zealand	Adelaide	1982-83
102	118/14/1	Australia	Lord's	1985
101*	100/9/0	Australia	Melbourne	1978-79

HIGHEST SCORES FOR ENGLAND IN ONE-DAY INTERNATIONALS

Score	Batsman	Opposition	Venue	Season
167*	R.A.Smith	Australia	Birmingham	1993
158	**D.I.Gower**	**New Zealand**	**Brisbane**	**1982-83**
158	A.J.Strauss	India	Bangalore	2010-11
154	A.J.Strauss	Bangladesh	Birmingham	2010
152	A J Strauss	Bangladesh	Nottingham	2005

3000 RUNS IN ONE-DAY INTERNATIONALS FOR ENGLAND

	M	I	NO	HS	Runs	Avge	100	50
P.D.Collingwood	197	181	37	120*	5092	35.36	5	26
A.J.Stewart	170	162	14	116	4677	31.60	4	28
I.R.Bell	140	136	11	126*	4635	37.08	3	29
K.P.Pietersen	134	123	16	130	4422	41.32	9	25
M.E.Trescothick	123	122	6	137	4335	37.37	12	21
G.A.Gooch	125	122	6	142	4290	36.98	8	23
A.J.Strauss	127	126	8	158	4205	35.63	6	27
A.J.Lamb	122	118	16	118	4010	39.31	4	26
G.A.Hick	120	118	15	126*	3846	37.33	5	27
N.V.Knight	100	100	10	125*	3637	40.41	5	25
A.Flintoff	138	119	16	123	3293	31.97	3	18
D.I.Gower	**114**	**111**	**8**	**158**	**3170**	**30.77**	**7**	**12**

DAVID GOWER'S FIRST-CLASS AVERAGE BATTING AND FIELDING

	M	I	NO	HS	Runs	Avge	100	50	Ct/St
1975	3	5	-	32	65	13.00	-	-	2
1976	7	13	4	102*	323	35.88	1	1	4
1977	25	34	2	144*	745	23.28	1	3	8
1977-78	2	2	-	59	76	38.00	-	1	-
1978	21	31	2	111	1098	37.86	2	5	6
1978-79	12	20	1	102	623	32.78	1	3	7
1979	17	27	4	200*	957	41.60	1	8	8
1979-80	9	15	2	98*	354	27.23	-	3	6
1980	24	36	1	138	1142	32.62	2	3	16
1980-81	8	14	1	187	726	55.84	2	2	4
1981	19	33	4	156*	1418	48.89	5	7	20
1981-82	13	18	3	94	755	50.33	-	7	7
1982	20	35	2	176*	1530	46.36	2	12	10
1982-83	10	19	1	114	821	45.61	2	6	9
1983	19	32	5	140	1253	46.40	5	5	18
1983-84	9	14	1	173*	746	57.38	2	4	7
1984	18	30	2	117*	999	35.67	2	6	17
1984-85	11	15	1	86	482	34.42	-	4	10
1985	21	29	2	215	1477	54.70	6	3	10
1985-86	8	16	-	90	447	27.93	-	3	4
1986	14	23	2	131	830	39.52	1	6	11/1
1986-87	9	16	2	136	508	36.28	1	2	4
1987	20	31	4	125	1197	44.33	2	6	5
1988	22	38	4	172	1317	38.73	2	5	16
1989	17	30	1	228	1102	38.00	3	4	13
1989-90	1	1	-	4	4	4.00	-	-	-
1990	20	32	5	157*	1263	46.77	3	3	17
1990-91	10	19	1	123	578	32.11	2	3	3
1991	23	38	5	80*	1142	34.60	-	8	13
1992	20	33	7	155	1225	47.11	1	8	14
1993	16	28	1	153	1136	42.07	4	5	11
Overall	**448**	**727**	**70**	**228**	**26339**	**40.08**	**53**	**136**	**280/1**

INDEX